THAT'S DANCING!

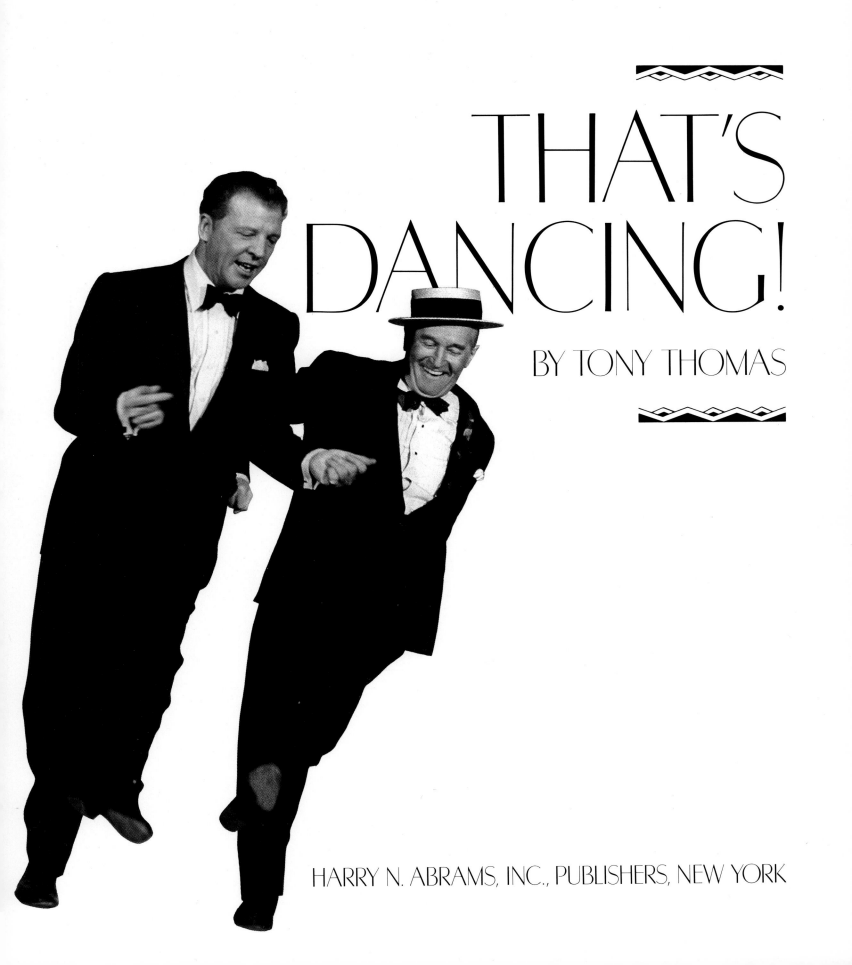

THAT'S DANCING!

BY TONY THOMAS

HARRY N. ABRAMS, INC., PUBLISHERS, NEW YORK

WLEDGMENTS

Books of this kind can be put together only with help from others. In terms of research I am grateful to Linda Mehr and her staff at the Margaret Herrick Library of the Academy of Motion Picture Arts and Sciences in Los Angeles, and to the highly knowledgeable and helpful Miles Kreuger, the founder-director of the Institute of the American Musical, Inc., Los Angeles. For helping me find the best possible illustrations for the book I had a formidable ally in Dory Freeman, the veteran head of the stills department at MGM. In locating other photos I was helped by Gunnard Nelson, Lisa Capps, Rudy Behlmer, Eddie Brandt, Bob Colman, and Collectors Bookstore of Hollywood. I also tip my hat to the co-producers of the film *That's Dancing!*, Jack Haley, Jr., and David Niven, Jr., who were always available for support. Finally, I thank my editor, Lory Frankel, for her considerable help and guidance with the manuscript, and the book's designer, Ray Hooper, for making it look so beautiful.

Tony Thomas

CONTENTS

DANCING—FRAME BY FRAME

FRED ASTAIRE

BUSBY BERKELEY

RAY BOLGER

CYD CHARISSE

RUBY KEELER

GENE KELLY

ANN MILLER

GENE NELSON

DONALD O'CONNOR

ELEANOR POWELL

INDEX

DANCING— FRAME BY FRAME

"A row of girls onstage has a definite theatrical effect. A row of girls on film is old-fashioned. I wanted to get a cinematic effect." So says Bob Fosse, the Oscar-winning director of *Cabaret* and the man who revealed a great deal about himself in the virtually autobiographical *All That Jazz*. Like most of the great choreographers, Fosse began his career as a dancer, and he admits, "You know, I think this whole thing started for me when I was a kid and would go to the neighborhood movie theater that showed quadruple features on Saturday. If they happened to show an Astaire movie, I'd stay over and come home late at night dancing over the fireplugs. If life had let me just dance down streets like Fred did, I don't think I would ever have gone into choreography or direction."

Fortunately for lovers of dancing, life caused Fosse to go beyond simply being a dancer and become one of the most inventive and exciting choreographers of either the stage or the films. He choreographed both the stage and the film versions of *The Pajama Game* and *Damn Yankees*, and no one has a clearer conception of the difference between the two forms. But no one, whether choreographer, dance director, or performer, can succeed in film without fully realizing that difference, without understanding it and taking advantage of the endless possibilities offered by the motion picture form.

Dancing for the movie cameras is rather like film music in the sense that it is very hard to describe. If a film score is not just right it can be very wrong. This is also true of film choreography. Dancing on the stage has the advantage of an immediacy with the audience that generates an emotional response; when the same dancing is filmed, it has to arrive at the emotions in another way. All film is fantasy, and dancing in the movies becomes a special kind of fantasy, requiring special kinds of talents. It took Hollywood several years to understand this.

When sound came to the motion picture in 1927 it gave birth to the only kind of movie that had never been made before: the musical. It was a gleeful birth, and producers rushed to take advantage of the fact that singers and dancers could now be heard. The producers assumed that all they had to do was to place a camera in front of singers and dancers and cry, "Action!" The novelty soon wore off. What might have been pleasing in the live theater became dull when photographed and projected. This was largely due to the limitations of the primitive recording equipment in those first few years. Microphones were stationary—and so was the action. The bright promise of the movie musical seemed to tarnish rather rapidly, until men of imagination came along to exploit and develop the potential of movement and editing that film allows.

The first movie musical that really impressed the public was MGM's *The Broadway Melody*, which had its première at Grauman's Chinese Theatre in Hollywood in February of 1929. It was advertised as being all-talking, all-singing, and all-dancing. It was a major step forward from the cumbersome musicals of the previous two years, mostly because it had a story to tell, albeit of the backstage brand that would virtually plague Hollywood in the years to follow. Charles King headed the cast, as a jaunty song-and-dance man who is loved by a pair of song-and-dance sisters, played by Anita Page and Bessie Love. Page was the one who got him.

The Broadway Melody (MGM, 1929). Dancing on the silver screen begins to take shape. Page 8: *Down to Earth* (Columbia, 1947). Marc Platt and Rita Hayworth.

The *Broadway Melody* was the first movie musical to commission an original musical score. Nacio Herb Brown wrote the music and Arthur Freed supplied the lyrics, and aside from the title song they had hits with "You Were Meant for Me" and "The Wedding of the Painted Doll," all of which cropped up in Metro musicals over the years. The film won an Oscar as best picture of 1929 — the first sound picture to be so honored — but the most important thing about it was that it began the Hollywood career of Arthur Freed, a career spent entirely at MGM. In his first ten years there he was a songwriter, but with *The Wizard of Oz* in 1939 he took on the role of producer, and became by far the most important, dedicated, and loving producer of musicals in the history of film. The forty musicals he produced between 1940 and 1960 represent much of the best in the genre. However, before Freed eventually came into his own, other men had to come along and develop the potential of the movie musical.

By 1933 recording equipment and film cameras had improved enormously. Now all that was needed were the ideas and the concepts and the imaginations to make musi-

cals come alive. Two films — *42nd Street* and *Flying Down to Rio* — showed the way. With the wild cinematic choreography of Busby Berkeley in *42nd Street* and the much more subtle artistry of Fred Astaire in *Flying Down to Rio*, the movie musical was launched. In the following twenty years — now known as the Golden Era — the dancers and the choreographers created every kind of magic in the movies.

Obviously, it was never easy. Any kind of dancing is hard, and inventing and performing complicated, extended, imaginative dances for the movies is very, very hard. Gene Kelly explains, "There seems to be a common misapprehension that dancing and the motion picture are well suited to each other — they are not. The dance is a three-dimensional art form, while the motion picture is two-dimensional. I would compare dancing basically to sculpture and the motion picture to painting. So the difficulties we have in transferring a dance onto film are simply those of putting a 3-D art form into a 2-D panel."

Gene Kelly is, of course, highly visible as one who has contributed — as director and choreographer as well as dancer — to the film musical. Not at all visible are the men

In Bob Fosse's *All That Jazz* (Fox, 1979), Roy Scheider, as a director very like Fosse, demonstrates a routine. Opposite: Director-choreographer Bob Fosse shows Shirley MacLaine the steps he has in mind for "There's Got to Be Something Better Than This" in *Sweet Charity* (Universal, 1969).

All That Jazz (Fox, 1979). Roy Scheider, as a Broadway director-choreographer, envisions chorus girls circling his hospital bed.

who have devised the choreography and directed the dances in the hundreds of pictures that have pleased millions throughout the years. These unsung heroes of the musical film rarely even see their names writ large in the credit titles of the films on which they worked. In any book about dancing in the movies, they deserve first mention. Just as an actor shines when given a good script and a singer excels with good songs, so dancers need people to invent the charming and exciting things they do.

If, for example, you think the ensemble dancing in *Carousel* was magnificent, the man to thank is Rod Alexander. If you were impressed with the dancing of Donald O'Connor and Vera-Ellen in *Call Me Madam*, tip your hat to Robert Alton. It was Dave Gould who devised the dances in *Born to Dance* and Bobby Connolly who did them for *Broadway Melody of 1940.* Jack Cole created the dances for *Gentlemen Prefer Blondes*, Seymour Felix did *The Great Ziegfeld*, Charles Walters did *Meet Me in St. Louis*, Eugene Loring guided the dancing in *Funny Face*, and LeRoy Prinz was the man behind *Yankee Doodle Dandy*. And no one need think beyond Jerome Robbins's choreography in *West Side Story*

to gain some understanding of what such a man can do with the marriage of dance and film.

These were the men who produced motion picture choreography in the years when the musical reigned supreme in Hollywood, with dozens of titles to their credit. Michael Kidd is another. He is perhaps easier to discuss for the simple reason that he has also appeared on screen as a dancer, most noticeably in *It's Always Fair Weather*. Seeing him dance provides a clue to his choreography, which reveals a clear understanding of the possibilities offered by the camera. Kidd has also excelled as a stage dance director, but whenever he has tackled film he has brought to it a completely different conception. On film he is best represented by *Where's Charley?*, *The Band Wagon*, *Seven Brides for Seven Brothers*, *Guys and Dolls*, *Li'l Abner*, and *Hello, Dolly!* All of them are characterized by excitement of movement, by kinetic force. With Kidd, dance and gymnastics are closely allied. In addition to his innate sense of photography, Kidd possesses the insight that dancing on film is most effective when it is an integral part of the film's character and story line.

In *Seven Brides for Seven Brothers* Kidd used the dances to define the character of the brothers — their restlessness and discontent without women, their high energy and their inability to express themselves in any manner other than physical, particularly in the celebrated "barn-raising" sequence, in which they compete with the townsmen to impress the girls. Before the film started shooting, Kidd discussed with producer Jack Cummings and director Stanley Donen the essential need for the dances to be a part of the storytelling.

On the subject of using the camera as a choreographic tool, Kidd explains, "I have found that the camera's ability to see more than the human eye allows an emphasis on close-ups at important moments and at the same time gives varying angles to the dance which stage audiences could not catch from their static position." In other words, Kidd, like all accomplished film choreographers, thinks as if the camera itself had an intelligent, inquisitive, mobile mind.

There is one Hollywood choreographer — Hermes Pan — who deserves particular mention, because his career extends from the ground-breaking *Flying Down to Rio* in 1933 to the present. Pan was an assistant to Fred Astaire on that film, and he soon became Astaire's co-choreographer. His association with the famed dancer lasted until *Finian's Rainbow* in 1968. When the Astaire-Rogers cycle at RKO came to an end in 1939, Pan broadened his movie work by devising dances for other dancers and sometimes appearing on screen himself. He was under contract to 20th Century-Fox during the years of World War II — the years when Fox had a long and successful run in the musical form — and he charted many of Betty Grable's routines. In *Sweet Rosie O'Grady* he danced "The Wishing Waltz" with her; however, dressed in a tuxedo he resembled Astaire, which limited his on-camera appearances. With the upsurge of movie musicals at MGM under Arthur Freed's leadership in the forties and fifties, Pan's talents were much in evidence, not only in his work with Astaire but with almost anyone who ever danced in front of a camera.

Working with Astaire, Hermes Pan strove for a smooth integration between the plot and the dialogue and the dances. "We spent a great deal of time trying to find out how to get into a musical number gracefully. Many songs would

Seven Brides for Seven Brothers (MGM, 1954). A fantastic leap in the barn-raising number, choreographed by Michael Kidd.

come out of the dialogue. We experimented with camera movements because we'd taken great pains to figure out the best camera angles and recording of the dances."

What Pan and Astaire sought was to preserve the fluidity of movement. To accomplish this they had to persuade producers and directors to avoid cutaway shots to other characters and locations, so that the dance could be shown in its entirety. Their success in this technique was a boon to Hollywood's other choreographers. "When I hear music, I can almost see the motions of the music. It paints a picture for me. A lot of dancers see and feel that. I know Fred does. But it's difficult to discuss abstract things like music and dance. Dancing is an emotional thing, an outburst of feeling that comes spontaneously." How to translate that feeling into film dancing was the challenge constantly met by Her-

mes Pan and the many other dedicated men behind the cameras. There is a great deal of evidence that they succeeded.

The clearest definition of the possibilities of film as a medium for dance came from the Russian-born master choreographer George Balanchine, whose work in film was unfortunately limited to *The Goldwyn Follies of 1937*, *On Your Toes* (1939), and *I Was an Adventuress* (1940). Balanchine had had great success with Diaghilev's Ballets Russes when he was hired to help form the American Ballet Company in 1934. In 1936 he was invited to create a ballet for the Rodgers and Hart stage musical *On Your Toes*, resulting in his brilliant "Slaughter on Tenth Avenue," which he restaged for the film version.

Balanchine, the first major choreographer to bring the art of the ballet to the American musical, felt that the movies

Michael Kidd, dancer, in *It's Always Fair Weather* (MGM, 1955). Opposite: Hermes Pan dancing "The Wishing Waltz" with Betty Grable in *Sweet Rosie O'Grady* (Fox, 1943).

should take dance more seriously. "Films should be a product of greater imagination and fantasy than the theater because of the larger scope which elements of space and time have in motion pictures. I also think the responsibility of anyone working in films is greater than in the theater because he is addressing people all over the world. This is why I think a serious, creative, inventive approach to the films is an absolute necessity."

Balanchine was far too successfully involved in the world of the ballet and the theater to have much time to put his idealistic concepts of film to work, but there was no film choreographer who went untouched by his views. "Creating dance for movies imposes completely new problems on the choreographer. It renders his task far more intricate and difficult, gives him new riddles to solve, and opens a wide range of possibilities for the exercise of his invention."

George Balanchine's concepts of the possibilities of fusing the art of dance with the craft of cinematography found a conspicuous champion in Gene Kelly. In fact, Kelly has been the only star dancer to invent film dances for all the dancers in the films he directed as well as for himself. Once involved in making movies, Kelly quickly realized the difference between dancing for a live audience and for the camera. He continually strove to compensate for the kinetic force of live dancing that is lost in filming, which led him to experiment with dancing with cartoons, dancing with himself in double exposed images, and dancing across imaginatively devised settings and locations.

Kelly credits Busby Berkeley with making him aware of this cinematic sense of movement and he adds, "You have to construct a dance so that it can be cut and edited, and do it in a way that won't disturb the viewer. You learn to use the camera as part of the choreography. It's possible that a lot of fine dancing has been ineffectual in the movies because it was never photographed imaginatively. Filming dancing will always be a problem because the eye of the camera is coldly realistic, demanding that everything look natural — and dancing is unrealistic. That's the challenge, and all art is a compromise between your ideas and whatever means you have at your disposal."

That's Dancing!, MGM-UA's 1984 compilation of sequences drawn from the entire history of sound films, was the brainchild of Jack Haley, Jr., who had produced, directed, and scripted the enormously successful *That's Entertainment* in 1974. Explaining his reasons for making *That's Dancing!* Haley says, "It isn't enough simply to enjoy this material for your own reasons — any producer of compilations has to guard against self-indulgence. What made me resolve to one day do it was the audience reaction to the original *That's Entertainment.* Wherever I went around the world with the film I noticed one thing in particular — that it was the dancing that really turned people on. This was especially true in England and Japan. Everyone loved the songs, they enjoyed hearing Judy Garland and the others sing, but when dancing appeared up there on the big screen there was a feeling that came with it, a response in the audience, a response to the beat and the rhythm and the movement of dancing. There's an infectious, kinetic quality to really good dancing, and I made up my mind then to create a film devoted entirely to it."

However, *That's Dancing!* took a long time to get into production. Says Haley, "Making movies in Hollywood has never been easy but it is extremely difficult today because of the great financial risk factor in production and exploitation, and the lack of any clear demographics on what audiences will pay to see. *That's Entertainment, Part II*, which was put together after I left the studio, had not been nearly as profitable as the first venture, and because of that there was an industry reaction against doing any more compilation films. Once a reaction like that sets in it is difficult to change people's minds."

Haley did find an enthusiastic ally in David Niven, Jr., with whom he had co-produced the feature film *Better Late Than Never.* Niven, after five years as head of European production for Paramount, first became an independent producer with *The Eagle Has Landed.* Since he shared Haley's sentiments about *That's Dancing!*, he joined forces to bring it into being. It turned out to be harder than either had imagined, but they eventually persuaded MGM-UA that a market existed for such a compilation film. Haley could cite his own success in television with such series as *That's Hollywood*, which ran for three years, and such specials as "Life

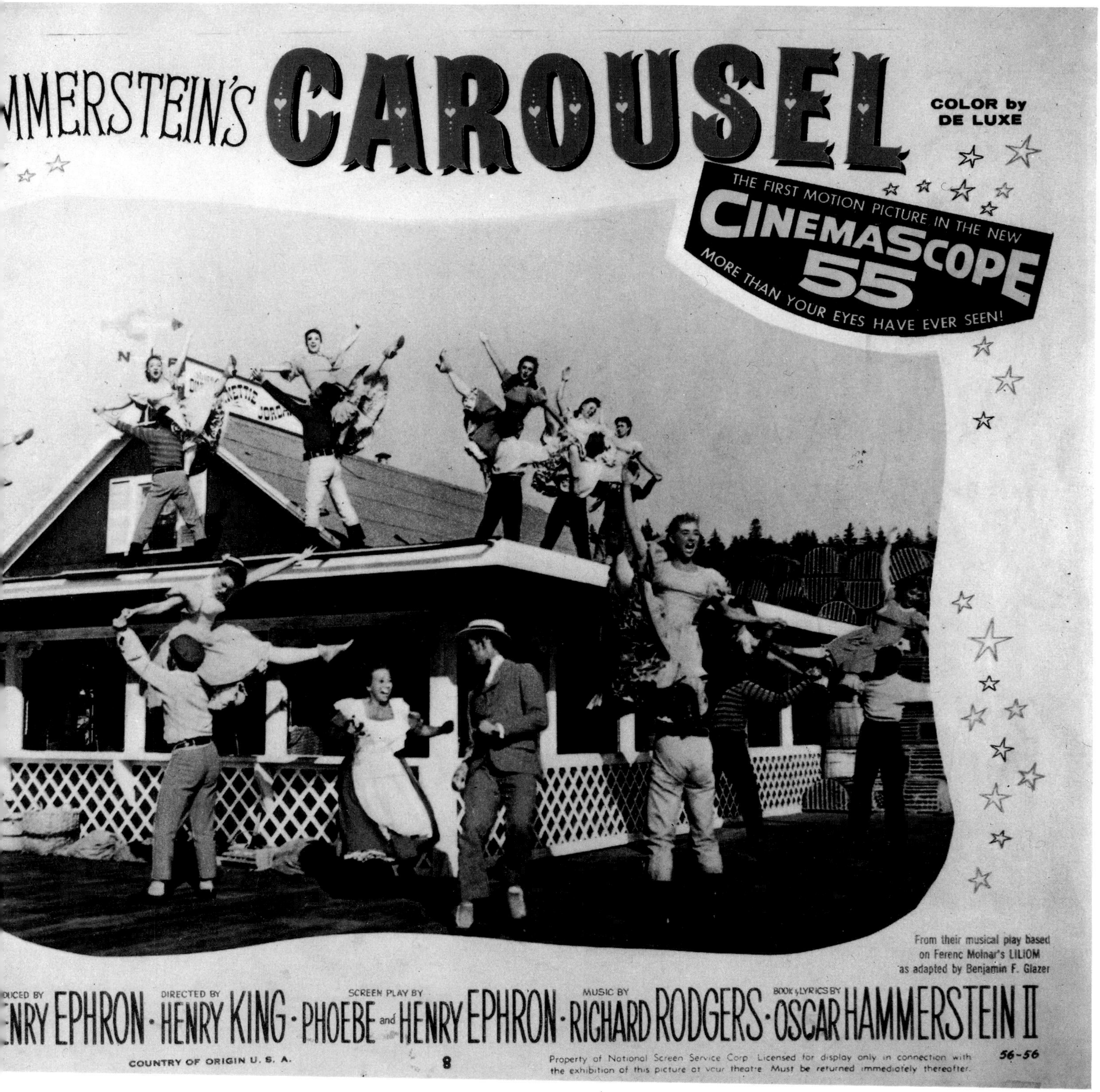
MMERSTEIN'S CAROUSEL
COLOR by DE LUXE
THE FIRST MOTION PICTURE IN THE NEW
CINEMASCOPE 55
MORE THAN YOUR EYES HAVE EVER SEEN!
From their musical play based
on Ferenc Molnar's LILIOM
as adapted by Benjamin F. Glazer
DUCED BY
NRY EPHRON · DIRECTED BY HENRY KING · SCREEN PLAY BY PHOEBE and HENRY EPHRON · MUSIC BY RICHARD RODGERS · BOOK & LYRICS BY OSCAR HAMMERSTEIN II
COUNTRY OF ORIGIN U. S. A.
8
Property of National Screen Service Corp. Licensed for display only in connection with the exhibition of this picture at your theatre. Must be returned immediately thereafter.
56-56

Goes to the Movies" and "Hollywood: The Gift of Laughter," and the series for which Haley produced and co-wrote the pilot, *Entertainment Tonight*. Haley had also produced several of the Academy Award shows and "The American Movie Awards," all of which made him the foremost writer-producer of documentaries about the motion picture industry. Clearly, if anyone was going to put together a film about the history of dancing in the movies the logical choice was Haley. And, in partnership with Niven, that is what he did.

Says David Niven, Jr.: "The first thing Jack and I did was to bring in an expert to help with the choice of footage —

Gene Kelly became our executive producer. Gene is not only one of filmdom's foremost dancers, directors, and choreographers but he is highly knowledgeable about all forms of dancing, its history and development, and about everything that currently goes on in the dance world. He shared our passion but he also brought a clear, judgmental eye."

Something like fifteen hundred musicals and countless short subjects have been made in Hollywood from the beginning of the sound era to the present, and most of them contain dancing. "The choice was mind-boggling," says Haley. "The amount of dancing that has been done on film is incredible. Even to narrow down a choice from the work of Kelly, Astaire, Eleanor Powell, and Ann Miller was difficult, let alone the hundreds of other talents. Eventually, for viewing purposes, we transferred from film to videotape well over one hundred hours of material. The old saying that the difficulty in life is choice became painfully apparent on this particular project. In order to pare it down to a two-hour film we found ourselves dropping things we loved. But the fine, firm hand of Kelly was always there, pointing out the difference between what was very good and what was superb. The big problem was balance — to show as many kinds of dance as possible and not overload with the powerfully spectacular nature of some of the material. Eventually we decided on segments, such as the great stylists of the 1930s, ballet, team dancing, etc., and have Mikhail Baryshnikov, Ray Bolger, Sammy Davis, Jr., Liza Minnelli, and Gene Kelly introduce them."

David Niven, Jr.: "It was an unusually difficult picture to put together. In a strange way it was infinitely harder than a so-called normal film. Certainly more complicated. One starts off by looking at about nine hundred movies, selecting the musical numbers, then transferring them to videotape and allocating the clips into categories. The one hundred or so hours of tape then became our bible. Next came the agonizing business of choice, followed by a semblance of order, a concept, a shape, a clear framework, plus the scripting and the filming of the new material. *That* was the artistic side of the endeavor. The other side was the legalistic one, including the clearance of material, restrictions, dealings with unions and publishers, artists' contracts, the negotiation of video synchronization rights, not to mention matters of pure cost. All of this can be, in a word, nightmarish. Now, assuming one has got this far without shooting oneself, one spends months tracking down the original film negatives and ordering interpositives of the clips, together with composite positive prints. Once these multifarious elements were finally assembled we edited in much the same way any film is edited — with hope, prayers, and the lighting of candles."

That's Dancing! is the largest and most comprehensive overview of film dancing ever attempted. In writing this book it was decided not to stay within the demarcations of the movie but to go beyond it and give a broader account of the history of dancing in the American sound film, told through the stories of those individuals who had most conspicuously contributed to its success. When it came to listing those individuals, we felt the most politic way to do it was to present them alphabetically. In so doing it just happened that the name at the top of the list turned out to be Fred Astaire. The poetic justice of this is not likely to meet with any contention.

Sammy Davis, Jr., one of the hosts of *That's Dancing!,* limbers up at MGM while waiting to film his part. Opposite: Choreographer George Balanchine directs his wife, Vera Zorina, in *I Was an Adventuress* (Fox, 1940).

The first star dancer to grace the movies was Marilyn Miller. She was brought to Hollywood by Warners in 1929 to appear in its version of the Jerome Kern musical *Sally* (above), in which she had starred on Broadway nine years earlier. At that time Marilyn was twenty-two and already a veteran of vaudeville. Once she signed with the great Florenz Ziegfeld, she became *the* musical star of Broadway.

The film *Sally* did well, and a year later Warners brought Marilyn out west to film another Jerome Kern musical in which she had triumphed, the 1925 *Sunny*. But both films suffered from Hollywood's still-primitive approach to filming musicals, and the star was less than happy with the way she appeared on the screen. After her third picture, the limp and dull *Her Majesty Love* in 1931, she gave up on movies and returned to the medium in which she was truly a star, the stage.

The first Hollywood hoofer to have her tap-dancing recorded on a film track was Joan Crawford. This was for MGM's *Our Dancing Daughters* in 1928 (right), in which she played a Roaring Twenties flapper. The role came naturally, for five years previously Crawford's career had begun when she won a dance contest doing the Charleston, the Black Bottom, and the Varsity Drag.

Joan Crawford had been under contract to MGM for four years when the studio put her in its all-star *Hollywood Revue of 1929*. She had one number, "Gotta Feeling for You" (below), which could easily have headed her toward a career as a dancing star, except that is not what she wanted. Joan wanted to become a dramatic actress. Although she starred in *Dancing Lady* in 1933 — becoming the first lady to dance with Fred Astaire on film — from then on it was glossy melodrama all the way.

There have been children who could dance, who could sing, who could act, and who could charm, but there has been only one who combined all those talents—Shirley Temple. She was four years old when she first appeared on the screen and six when Fox signed her to a contract, starring her first in *Stand Up and Cheer* (1934), with James Dunn playing her song-and-dance father. Together they did "Baby, Take a Bow!" (opposite), a well-calculated title that Fox used later that year for its first film with her name at the top of the cast.

It was somebody's bright idea to bring in Bill Robinson, the great Bojangles, to dance with Shirley in *The Little Colonel* (Fox, 1935), a story of the Old South, with Robinson as a genial plantation slave. This was the film in which they did "The Stair Dance," a routine that was a specialty with Robinson throughout his long career. And it charmed audiences so thoroughly that a sequel became inevitable. In *The Littlest Rebel* (opposite), Shirley and Bojangles were caught up in the Civil War, but he was still genial and still teaching her dances. Robinson was by this time a man of fifty-seven; according to the racial strictures of 1935 the only way he could dance with a white lady was if the lady happened to be seven.

Shirley Temple's ability to pick up and master dance routines was almost inexplicable for a child of her age. And, because of her rapport with Bill Robinson, he was the one who taught them to her—this in addition to his on-screen appearances in her films. In *Rebecca of Sunnybrook Farm*, which they did together in 1938, the big production number was "The Parade of the Wooden Soldiers" (below).

Bojangles was not the only dancer with whom 20th Century-Fox partnered its most valuable asset. When Darryl F. Zanuck merged his 20th Century Pictures with Fox in 1935 and became head of production, he realized that Shirley was far and away the studio's biggest money-maker, and her pictures were crafted around her. In *Captain January*, her first release in 1936, young Buddy Ebsen was hired to dance "At the Codfish Ball" with her (above), and it was an absolute charmer. Ebsen and his partner, his sister Vilma, had been successful in New York, and their first screen appearance was in MGM's *Broadway Melody of 1936* with Eleanor Powell. After Buddy danced with Shirley, he returned to MGM, with Vilma, for Powell's *Born to Dance*.

In *Little Miss Broadway* (Fox, 1938; above), Shirley's co-star was George Murphy, who, after four years in the movies, had established himself as a pleasant actor in light comedy and a nifty hoofer whenever given a chance in a musical. In this one Shirley played an orphan—as in almost all of her pictures—living in a home for retired vaudevillians, and she manages to save them from foreclosure. George lent a helping hand, as well as his feet.

Bill Robinson danced for the last time on film in 20th Century-Fox's all-black *Stormy Weather* in 1943 (right), doing several numbers with Lena Horne, including "I Can't Give You Anything but Love." He was then sixty-five and in fine fettle—in fact, he danced almost until the time of his death six years later. As a youngster, he danced for coins in taverns. As a teen-ager, he joined a traveling colored revue, and this led to vaudeville bookings. By the start of World War I he was a headliner, earning four thousand dollars a week. A friend gave him the nickname "Bojangles" because its happy-go-lucky sound matched Robinson's sunny personality.

Critics said Robinson's dancing was not spectacular but that it was done with such cheerfulness and conviction that it made him seem like the greatest tapper there ever was. He was different from most others in that he did not use metal on his shoes; he instead employed wooden soles, and included steps derived from clog dancing. With Robinson it was all footwork and not a great deal of body movement, but no one developed tapping with greater refinement: he could do running trills with his taps and rolls of varying volume, sometimes with a machine gun-like staccato. He said, "What I have to say, I say with my feet," and what Bojangles had to say was always cheerful.

The art of tap-dancing is an American contribution to the arts, and it was largely a black invention. Bill Robinson helped make it popular, but many others picked it up and took it several steps further, especially the Nicholas Brothers, Harold and Fayard. Born in 1918, Fayard is ten years older than Harold. They began as youngsters in vaudeville. Their appearances at the famed Cotton Club in Harlem led to offers from Hollywood, and in 1940 they became the first black act to be contracted to a studio. They made their film début in 20th Century-Fox's *Down Argentine Way*, in which they dazzled the customers with their interpretation of the title song (opposite, above; Fayard is the one doing the leap).

Fox used the Nicholas Brothers next in *The Great American Broadcast* of 1941 (left). In a train station sequence, they play porters who beat out the rhythms of "Alabamy Bound." With nothing more than a floor and a few suitcases as props, they dance up a tapping storm and leap all over the place.

The most famous number done by the Nicholas Brothers in the movies was "Chattanooga Choo-Choo" (opposite, below) in *Sun Valley Serenade* (Fox, 1941), in which they were joined by eighteen-year-old Dorothy Dandridge and accompanied by Glenn Miller and his Orchestra. Again they did gravity-defying leaps, landing in the splits position and then snapping back up to attention. They also did the amazing split slides beneath each other's legs. Says Fayard, "We never called our dancing 'hoofing.' That's when you concentrate on your feet and don't care about your body and hands. We use it all."

31

Hollywood's most acclaimed team of white tap dancers was the Condos Brothers, Nick and Steve, who won the reputation of having the fastest legs in show business. They first appeared on screen in the Alice Faye-Jack Haley musical *Wake Up and Live* (Fox, 1937; left), doing two numbers, "It's Swell of You" and "I'm Bubbling Over." What amazed moviegoers was not just their graceful movements and their precision tapping but the astounding trick they did with their feet, known in the business as *wings.* In these movements the Condos Brothers flipped their feet sideways and beat out five rapid taps with each foot. According to other dancers these wings are close to impossible to do—and no one in the movies came close to matching the wings of the Condos Brothers.

The Condos Brothers were among the many enjoyable elements of Betty Grable's *Moon over Miami* (Fox, 1941). The most prominent song in the Ralph Rainger-Leo Robin score, "You Started Something" (below), forms the background of a nightclub sequence in which Betty challenges the boys to a tap routine.

Betty Grable became an overnight star with *Down Argentine Way* in 1940 (above), but, as in most cases, this instant stardom was arrived at only after a long apprenticeship. She had first appeared in a film as a fourteen-year-old in 1930, and later that year she was one of the girls chosen by Busby Berkeley for the chorus numbers in *Whoopee*. Four years later she had a solo in *The Gay Divorcee*, singing and dancing "Let's K-nock K-neez." Paramount signed her to a contract in 1937 and gave her leads in minor movies, but by 1940 she realized nothing much was happening.

She accepted an offer to appear on Broadway in the Cole Porter musical *Du Barry Was a Lady*, starring Bert Lahr and Ethel Merman. It drew rave notices, and Betty got plenty of attention for her dancing. Now Hollywood could hardly wait to get her back. Darryl F. Zanuck signed her to a long-term Fox contract and starred her in the spirited Technicolor romp *Down Argentine Way*—and the spectacular movie career of Betty Grable was launched.

33

The Betty Grable musicals were light, frothy things, but as long as Betty sang, danced, smiled, and showed her legs, the silly story lines drifted into the background. A typical example, *Springtime in the Rockies* (Fox, 1942; left), was a show-biz yarn that somehow took her to Canada's beautiful Lake Louise. Harry James and his Band were also featured, and not long after the film's completion Betty became Mrs. James, causing servicemen all over the world to sing, "I want a girl just like the girl who married Harry James." Also in the picture was the suave Cesar Romero, who seldom got to dance in movies—a pity, because he was excellent at it.

Betty Grable said her favorite movie was *Mother Wore Tights* (Fox, 1947; opposite), the story of a vaudeville family, with Betty and Dan Dailey as the parents. In Dailey she found an ideal partner. Dailey had started in pictures in 1940 but never got a chance to show how fine a dancer he was. When he returned to Hollywood after his war service he soon realized that the one kind of performer in short supply was the leading man who could dance. He auditioned at Fox and he was accepted immediately—and it touched off Dailey's career as a Hollywood name.

In 1949 Fox gave Dailey a chance to shine in his own light with *You're My Everything*, the story of a vaudeville hoofer who becomes a movie star. For Dailey fans the highlight was his energetic version of "Chattanooga Choo-Choo" (below), accompanied by the Berry Brothers (Nyas and Warren). It is possibly the best bit of hoofing the superb Dailey ever did in a film.

And then there is the case of Mickey Rooney, probably the finest all-around talent in Hollywood history. He is certainly the entertainment industry's best exponent of survival. Born in 1920, the Mighty Mick was two when he first went on stage, with his parents, in vaudeville and four when he first appeared in a film. In 1933 MGM gave him a part in *Broadway to Hollywood* (opposite) — as a little song-and-dance man, of course.

It was in his MGM films with Judy Garland that Rooney came into his own as a hoofer, starting with *Babes in Arms* (1939) and continuing with *Strike Up the Band* (1940; below) and *Babes on Broadway* (1941), all of them directed by Busby Berkeley, which had a lot to do with their happily frenetic dance quality.

According to Gene Kelly, Judy Garland could pick up a set of dance steps in minutes. Her sense of music was innate, as was her sense of rhythm. In the delightful *Meet Me in St. Louis* (MGM, 1944), she stepped to the old cakewalk "Under the Bamboo Tree" (right), with little Margaret O'Brien doing her level best to keep up.

James Cagney IN "Yankee Doodle Dandy"

Based on the story of GEORGE M. COHAN

Country of Origin U.S.A

Presented by WARNER BROS. Pictures, Inc.

James Cagney's ability as a hoofer may have surprised moviegoers when they saw him step in *Footlight Parade* (Warners, 1933; opposite, above), but it was no surprise to anyone who had seen young Cagney on Broadway in the twenties. He cut his teeth as a hoofer in vaudeville and gradually got work as an actor. He was thirty by the time Hollywood caught up with him, and then it capitalized on his feisty personality by turning him into a little tough guy. As such, Cagney became engagingly pugnacious. In *Footlight Parade* he was the worried and harassed producer who kept interrupting his dance director (Frank McHugh), "No, no—it goes like this."

The triumph of James Cagney's career found him not as a tough guy but as a song-and-dance man — George M. Cohan in *Yankee Doodle Dandy* (Warners, 1942; opposite, below, and above). Cohan was the first important creator of purely American musicals; he wrote the words and music and the plots, he directed and produced them, and he starred in them. He was also a fine hoofer, whose style had been greatly influenced by Irish folk dancing. Irish New Yorker Cagney fully understood that style, and to it he brought his own slightly antic style, based upon his by-then familiar body movements, the characteristic use of his arms and shoulders, and his bursting sense of energy.

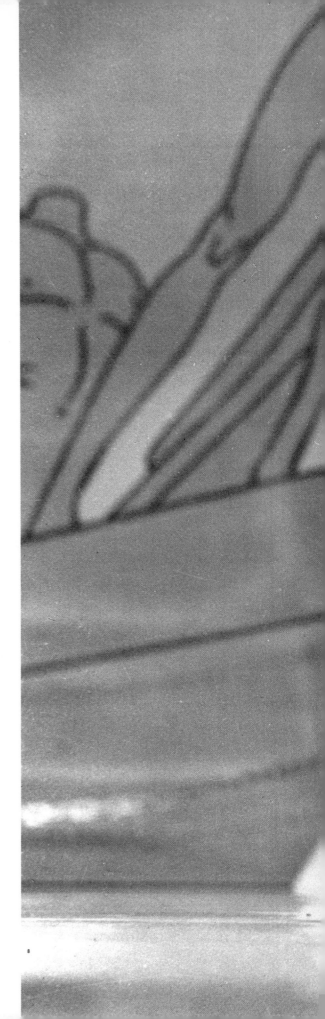

Margarita Carmen Cansino came to the movies with the best of dancing credentials. Both her grandfather and her father had been professional dancers in Spain, and her father, Eduardo, was dancing with the *Ziegfeld Follies* in New York in 1915 when he met *Follies* beauty Volga Haworth. Their daughter was born in 1918, and she was a mere four when they started to give her dancing lessons. As a teen-ager she joined the Dancing Cansinos, and it was with them that she first appeared in Hollywood. She got some small movie roles, but it was not until she changed her name to Rita Hayworth in 1937 that things started to happen, including a contract with Columbia, the studio where she would make most of her best films.

Dancing did not play much part in her movie career until she became Fred Astaire's partner in *You'll Never Get Rich* in 1941, which turned out so well that he gladly chose her the following year for *You Were Never Lovelier*. When Rita next danced on the screen it was with Gene Kelly in *Cover Girl* (1944). After that came *Tonight and Every Night* (1945), in which she danced "You Excite Me" (above) and "What Does an English Girl Think of a Yank?" (right). The choreographer of *Tonight and Every Night*, the remarkable Jack Cole, performed this number with Rita. Cole had been trained in ballet, and his interest in Oriental and Hindu dances led him to combine those influences with American jazz. Among the many Broadway shows choreographed by Cole are *Kismet* and *Man of La Mancha*, in addition to dozens of movies.

Ballerinas have seldom become movie stars; the art of the ballet has always been—and still is—a little too rarefied for the mass movie-going public. A lovely lady who at least had a good chance on film was Vera Zorina. Because of her beauty as well as her dancing she was chosen for Samuel Goldwyn's venture into culture, *The Goldwyn Follies of 1937*. The acclaimed George Balanchine was brought in as choreographer; he was so impressed with Zorina that he married her. She also appeared in Warners's film version of *On Your Toes* (1939), again with choreography by Balanchine. Vera was among the dozens of stars Universal used in its wartime extravaganza *Follow the Boys* in 1944 (both pages), in which she danced with George Raft. This possibly surprised a great many people, who had grown up with Raft's image as a flippant tough guy, often in gangster guise. Actually, Raft had started his career — or so he claimed — as a dance-hall gigolo, and graduated to the stage as a legitimate dancer. However, the public would never buy him as a dancer—his dead-pan, hard-eyed look and his flat New York accent seemed to work best when surrounded by crime. But make no mistake about it, George Raft could dance.

In putting together the ballet segments of *That's Dancing!* co-producers Jack Haley, Jr., and David Niven, Jr., chose one that was beautifully obvious: Tamara Toumanova's impression of the great Anna Pavlova's most famous dance, "The Swan" (above) by Camille Saint-Saëns, re-created in *Tonight We Sing* (Fox, 1953), with Leo Mostovoy as her partner. The film was a tribute to impresario Sol Hurok, the man who brought all the great European stars of opera, concert, and ballet, including Pavlova, to America in the years following World War I. The Russian-born Toumanova had danced in the Ballets Russes de Monte Carlo before she came to Hollywood to play opposite Gregory Peck in his first film, *Days of Glory,* which was about guerrilla warfare, not the ballet. Since a career as a dramatic actress did not open up, she returned to ballet.

One ballet dancer who did especially well for herself was Vera-Ellen, who was eighteen when she was hired to dance in Danny Kaye's *Wonder Man* in 1945. The next year she was in his *The Kid from Brooklyn,* which led to starring roles in two 20th Century-Fox musicals, *Three Little Girls in Blue* (1946) and *Carnival in Costa Rica* (1947). Her career advanced a giant step when Gene Kelly chose her to dance "Slaughter on Tenth Avenue" with him in *Words and Music* (1948), and she was his partner in his *On the Town* (1949). Fred Astaire picked her for *Three Little Words* (MGM, 1950), and they worked a ballet sequence (below) into the film especially for her. Vera-Ellen then went to England to star in *Happy Go Lovely* (1951) and upon her return went into *The Belle of New York* (1952) with Astaire. She danced delightfully with Donald O'Connor in *Call Me Madam* (1953) and with Danny Kaye in *White Christmas* (1954). The British picture *Let's Be Happy* in 1956 turned out to be her last; she retired at the age of thirty.

Although June Allyson's movie career officially began with MGM's *Best Foot Forward* in 1943 (above), when she was twenty-six, she had started dancing on film in 1937. Born Ella Geisman in the Bronx, as a child she studied dancing in order to strengthen her fragile health. Soon she was a dance addict, and she resolved to become another Ginger Rogers. Her career took a giant step forward when, as Betty Hutton's understudy in *Panama Hattie* in 1940, she went on one night for the ailing Betty and producer George Abbott happened to be in the audience. He gave June a part in his upcoming *Best Foot Forward*, and when MGM made it into a movie she was in that, too. People immediately took to her bright and breezy manner, husky voice, and wide smile, and even though her dancing was less than expert, it at least had bounce and vitality — especially doing "The Three B's," which melded Brahms, Beethoven, and Bach with Boogie-Woogie, Barrelhouse, and the Blues. Kenny Bowers and Jack Jordon were the boys who helped her bounce the Barrelhouse.

If *Best Foot Forward* personified youthful exuberance, then *Good News* (MGM, 1947) was only half a tap beat behind. With songs and dances that had been popular since the original stage hit of 1927— "The Best Things in Life Are Free," "Just Imagine," "Lucky in Love," and "The Varsity Drag," this last danced by June and Peter Lawford as well as the entire student body of Tait College (center) — the film was a big hit.

June Allyson was one of the many stars with which MGM populated its all-star tribute to the careers of Richard Rodgers and Lorenz Hart, *Words and Music* (1948), and her performance with the Blackburn Twins of "Thou Swell" (below) stood out as one of its highlights.

In *Two Weeks with Love* (1950) Jane Powell and Ricardo Montalban danced the tango (above), directed by Busby Berkeley. The petite and charming Jane — possessed of a soprano voice that ranged over almost three octaves — had enjoyed several years at MGM by this time. Ricardo Montalban, after several years of stardom in Latin movies, had been imported from Mexico in 1947. Because of his training in dancing and his handsome looks, the movie moguls tried to turn him into another Valentino — he danced in *Fiesta, On an Island with You, The Kissing Bandit,* and *Sombrero* — although Montalban's ambition was to prove his mettle as an actor.

Jane and Ricardo performed well in the bouncy *Two Weeks with Love,* but the performer who stole the picture was young Debbie Reynolds. This was the one in which she sang, with Carleton Carpenter, "Aba Daba Honeymoon." (The sound-track recording of it sold over a million copies.) This was the breakthrough for the then eighteen-year-old Debbie Reynolds. A year or so later Gene Kelly chose her to star with him in *Singin' in the Rain.* Although she had done a little dancing before, she really had to get into training for this picture. The tough Kelly drilled her in the art of tap-dancing until, she claims, her feet bled. It was worth the effort, because long after they stopped making movie musicals Debbie was able to go on with successful acts in the top Las Vegas spots and on the stage. In 1953 MGM starred her with Donald O'Connor in *I Love Melvin.* In one fantasy sequence, "A Lady Loves" (below), Debbie imagines herself a famous movie star, dancing not only with Fred Astaire but with three Astaires.

Give a Girl a Break (MGM, 1953; left) was a pleasant and well-titled little musical that gave Debbie Reynolds the break of having Stanley Donen as her director and Gower Champion both as choreographer and dancing partner. She played a girl looking for a break on Broadway; no one doubted that she would get it.

When MGM made a film of Meredith Willson's exuberant musical *The Unsinkable Molly Brown* in 1964, it cast the unsinkable Debbie Reynolds in the lead, partly because she campaigned for the part with undaunted determination. But it was hard to think of anyone better suited to play the Colorado hoyden who struck it rich and battered her way to the top of Denver society. Peter Gennaro was the choreographer, and he and Debbie had a veritable field day with "Belly Up to the Bar, Boys" (above).

As a dance team, and a very attractive one at that, Marge and Gower Champion belonged in a class of their own. The first MGM musical in which they danced together was *Show Boat* (both pages) in 1951; their sprightly hoofing to "Life upon the Wicked Stage" (below) proved a genuine crowd-pleaser. By that time they had been married for four years, following half a year of partnership as Gower and Bell. Gower Champion first danced on screen in MGM's *Till the Clouds Roll By*, before he met Marge, but as a couple they first appeared in Paramount's Bing Crosby musical *Mr. Music*. Both started their careers in Los Angeles. Marge danced as a child, and at fourteen she became the model for Disney's *Snow White*. Gower won a dance contest at the age of fifteen, in partnership with Jeanne Tyler, which led to their teaming professionally. After the war he needed another partner and found one when ballet master Ernest Belcher introduced him to his daughter Marge. Belcher himself deserves mention in any discussion of dancing in Hollywood musicals, because he was the coach for just about every actor or actress who ever needed to do a ballet step in front of a camera.

The Champions' last MGM film was *Jupiter's Darling* (1955), the strangest Metro musical of them all. This one had Howard Keel as Hannibal, the Carthaginian general who led his army and his elephants over the Alps to conquer the ancient Romans, and Esther Williams as the aristocrat he wooed. Marge and Gower played a pair of Roman slaves named Meta and Varius. All of this may not have made much sense, but it allowed for some unusual dance settings. One of them, "The Life of an Elephant" (left), required the cooperation of several well-trained pachyderms.

In 1952, MGM gave the Champions a starring vehicle, *Everything I Have Is Yours* (below), in which they played a dancing married couple. The critical consensus was that the dances were the only valid parts of an otherwise pedestrian show-biz yarn, and that as hoofers the Champions were irresistible.

The last film in which Marge and Gower Champion danced was Columbia's *Three for the Show* (1955), which headlined Betty Grable and Jack Lemmon. The estimable Jack Cole was still at Columbia, and he choreographed a stylish setting of Gershwin's "Someone to Watch over Me" for the Champions. With no further offers from Hollywood they took to the nightclub circuit and television. After Marge retired, Gower became a noted choreographer and director on Broadway. He achieved a major success with *42nd Street* in 1980, but, tragically, he died of a heart attack the day before the show opened.

The plot seed of Cole Porter's *Can-Can* (above), which Fox turned into a lavish picture in 1960, was the introduction of the can-can in the Paris of the late nineteenth century and its subsequent banning as being lewd. Fox received some unexpected publicity when the studio invited visiting Soviet Prime Minister Khrushchev and his wife to watch Shirley MacLaine, Juliet Prowse, and a horde of beautiful girls in the filming of the can-can sequence. Khrushchev was not amused, and said he agreed with the original French verdict.

The sight of Shirley MacLaine (right) doing so well as a dancer surprised some moviegoers, but Shirley had actually started her career as a dancer in New York. The South African–born Juliet Prowse (left), a top-flight dancer, made her film début in *Can-Can* and went on to considerable success. And, for anyone wondering why the hoofing in *Can-Can* was so brilliant, the answer is Hermes Pan.

Columbia had filmed the play *My Sister Eileen* in 1942 with Rosalind Russell, and Russell starred in the musical version that appeared on Broadway eleven years later, with a score by Leonard Bernstein. Then, to make matters confusing, Columbia did its own musical version of *My Sister Eileen* in 1955 (right), with Janet Leigh as Eileen and a score by Jule Styne and Leo Robin. While the score was not as impressive as Bernstein's, it was a charming musical in its own right. It has an important place in the Hollywood catalogue because Bob Fosse not only choreographed it but appeared in it as a dancer. He found Janet Leigh an easy pupil for their "There's Nothing Like Love" dance.

One of Bob Fosse's biggest successes on Broadway as a director-choreographer was *Sweet Charity*, with his wife Gwen Verdon in the lead. When Universal decided to make it into a supermusical in 1969, it was not willing to take a chance on Verdon and the part went to Shirley Mac-Laine. Such a part, that of a good-hearted, gamin-like taxi dancer in the seedier regions of Manhattan, was well within the MacLaine range, and Fosse—there was no question about his directing the picture—found her a breeze to choreograph. Somewhat ironically, he assigned his wife Gwen to help Shirley, but Gwen, well known in the business as being friendly and generous, showed no signs of spite at having lost out on such a good movie part. Shirley showed to advantage in "I'm a Brass Band" (left) and "There's Gotta Be Something Better Than This" (overleaf), although the title could not be applied to what Paula Kelly, Shirley, and Chita Rivera did with it.

Sammy Davis, Jr., presides over the fun in this scene (opposite) from *Sweet Charity* (Universal, 1969).

Bobby Van had the distinction of doing the oddest dance ever done in the movies, which might have had something to do with the fact that it was choreographed by the bizarre Busby Berkeley. In *Small Town Girl* (MGM,1953), he cheerfully hopped like a rabbit for about five minutes to the tune of "Take Me to Broadway." MGM kept him busy in 1953, casting him next as one of the whirlwind dancers in *Kiss Me Kate*, and then giving him a leading role in *The Affairs of Dobie Gillis* (above), a trifle about college life, with Bobby as one of its more exuberant students. His film career ended with this picture and he then became successful on the stage, noticeably in the 1970 revival of *No, No, Nanette*, with Ruby Keeler. Still an amazingly youthful-looking fifty, Bobby Van was stricken with a brain tumor, and in 1980 his life came to a sudden end.

Gwen Verdon starred in only one movie, *Damn Yankees* (opposite), which Warners filmed in 1958, three years after it opened on Broadway with Gwen as its star. As Lola, the sexy witch who, while doing the Devil's bidding, turns a middle-aged baseball fan into a husky, handsome baseball player (Tab Hunter), she sang "Whatever Lola Wants" — and no one could doubt that she gets it.

Mitzi Gaynor, who still combines a flair for dancing with a cheeky sense of comedy, began her career as a teen-ager, dancing with the Los Angeles Light Opera Company, which led to her getting a Fox contract at the age of nineteen. Mitzi did especially well as vaudeville star Lotte Crabtree in *Golden Girl* in 1951, and the following year she starred in *Bloodhounds of Broadway* (above), as a hillbilly girl whose sights are set on Broadway. As in all movies of this kind, there was never any question about the girl's success. And there was never any question about Mitzi Gaynor's success.

Carol Haney was another dancing lady who had only one major crack at the movies—in *The Pajama Game* (Warners, 1957)—and she, like Gwen Verdon, owed it to George Abbott and Stanley Donen, both of whom had done the Broadway original. On Broadway Carol Haney had won a Tony Award as the Best Supporting Actress of 1955; she had delighted audiences with her two big numbers, "Hernando's Hideaway" and "Steam Heat." In the film she also dazzled the viewers with the spirited ensemble number "Once-a-Year-Day" (right). Partnered with Buzz Miller, the two of them leaped all around Los Angeles's Hollenbeck Park.

Russ Tamblyn was a natural choice to play Riff, the street-gang leader of the Jets (above) in *West Side Story*, when the superb Leonard Bernstein-Stephen Sondheim musical was made into a superb movie in 1961, released by United Artists. The role of Bernardo, the leader of the rival Puerto Rican gang, the Sharks (opposite, above), went to twenty-eight-year-old Greek-American dancer George Chakiris, who won an Oscar as Best Supporting Actor. Rita Moreno (opposite, below), playing Bernardo's fiery girlfriend Anita, also won an Oscar, for Best Supporting Actress. The Puerto Rican dancer-actress clearly knew the territory.

Jerome Robbins, who had choreographed the Broadway original, was hired as co-director, with Robert Wise, to further develop the brilliant dances he had created. Using the streets of New York and beautifully agile photography, Robbins somehow made sense of the spectacle of tough street kids expressing their feelings in modern dance form. *West Side Story* swamped the Academy Awards show in 1962, with ten Oscars, starting with Best Picture and including a pair for Robert Wise and Jerome Robbins. Robbins was also given a special Oscar for his achievements in the art of film choreography.

Robin and the Seven Hoods (Warners, 1964), despite a clutch of talented stars in Frank Sinatra, Bing Crosby, Dean Martin, and Sammy Davis, Jr., was a so-so musical. But it gave Sammy Davis, Jr., one of his rare chances to hoof on film, principally in "Bang-Bang" (below), in which he tap-danced on a bar and sprayed machine-gun bullets around. Sammy had previously danced as a ten-year-old in a picture called *Rufus Jones for President*, which the producers of *That's Dancing!* managed to dig up and include. He is perhaps better remembered for his strutting in the 1959 *Porgy and Bess*, and he had another dancing opportunity in *Sweet Charity*. But, for the most part, his fans had to go to Las Vegas to see the best of Sammy Davis, Jr., as a hoofer.

Ann-Margret is another fine singer-dancer whose best work has been done in Las Vegas. Had she come along sooner in the heyday of the Hollywood musical she would surely have been a major name in this league. She was twenty when 20th Century-Fox put her in its 1962 remake of *State Fair*; she sizzled in her one big production number, the aptly titled "Isn't It Kind of Fun?" She then went to Columbia to star in *Bye Bye Birdie* (1963) and sizzled again, as a sexy teen-age fan of an Elvis Presley–like rock star. When she and Bobby Rydell (above) sang and danced "A Lot of Livin' to Do," it was not a statement to doubt.

Janet Leigh, who had earlier worked with Bob Fosse in Columbia's musical version of *My Sister Eileen* in 1955, got another chance to kick up her heels in *Bye Bye Birdie* (Columbia, 1963). Choreographer Onna White gave her a workout in this number, the wild "Shriners' Ballet."

With *Viva Las Vegas* (MGM, 1964), Ann-Margret graduated from being an admirer of someone like Elvis Presley to Presley's co-star, in what some consider to be his best musical. In this one she was a swimming instructor who falls for racing driver Elvis, but the occupations did not preclude singing and dancing. Fortunately. As for her dancing in *Viva Las Vegas* — a man would have to be dead not to respond to such fiery sexiness.

Russ Tamblyn began his movie career at the age of twenty playing one of the bursting-with-vigor brothers in *Seven Brides for Seven Brothers* (1954). Running up walls and doing back flips from them was just one of the Tamblyn stunts. He seemed to have spring coils in his heels. After leaping around in *Hit the Deck* (1955), he starred as *Tom Thumb* in 1958 (both pages), for which MGM built sets full of greatly oversized things for the tiny little fellow to cavort around. Tamblyn's Tom may have been tiny, but his energetic dancing was colossal.

Barbra Streisand's dancing is far from being on a par with her singing, but she has always been able to hold her own with a song-and-dance routine. However, she had to work a little harder than usual when 20th Century-Fox brought in Michael Kidd to do the choreography for *Hello, Dolly!* (1969). Kidd staged the title number in a replica of the famous New York restaurant Delmonico's and turned the waiters into a virtual *corps de ballet*.

In *Hello, Dolly!* (Fox, 1969) Barbra Streisand also danced "Put On Your Sunday Clothes," with a young man from Texas with the mellifluous name of Tommy Tune, all six-foot-six of him. This was the first film appearance for the then-thirty-year-old Texan. Soon afterward, he established himself as one of the most vital of new dancers and choreographers in the American musical theater.

The Boy Friend (MGM, 1971) starred Twiggy and Christopher Gable, both new-comers to the movies, although the public had already heard a lot about the very slim and winsome Twiggy because of her career as a model. Christopher Gable was formerly a dancer with the Royal Ballet in London and he was hired to choreograph *The Boy Friend* as well as dance in it as the charming hero.

Tommy Tune was prominent in MGM's *The Boy Friend* (1971), which enlarged Sandy Wilson's little English musical by giving it a fantasy sequence à la Busby Berkeley. The original was a homage to musicals of the twenties, and cinematic fantasy made it even more so. Tommy, with his incredibly long legs, was well in evidence in "Won't You Charleston with Me?"

The Boy Friend (MGM, 1971) not only included a Berkeley-like fantasy sequence, it also had this airplane number distinctly reminiscent of *Flying Down to Rio* (1933)—a movie that, inspired by the success of *42nd Street*, tried to top Berkeley in outrageousness and fantasy.

The biggest impact on film dancing in a great many years was made by John Travolta in Paramount's *Saturday Night Fever* (opposite), which became a box-office smash in 1977. Born of an Italian family in Englewood, New Jersey, in 1954, Travolta took dancing lessons as a boy from Fred Kelly, Gene's brother. Travolta was eighteen when he first appeared on stage, which led to television work and a part in the movie *Carrie*. Next came *Saturday Night Fever* and instant stardom.

John Travolta's role in *Saturday Night Fever* (Paramount, 1977) as the underprivileged, inarticulate Tony Manero, who finds articulation on the floor of a disco, touched a great many people. To understand the role Travolta visited many New York discos and to get in shape for the film he did two hours a day of running and three hours of dance practice. Charismatic, sexy, and very physical in his dance movements, Travolta seems to ignite on those disco floors. *Saturday Night Fever*, indeed.

In *Pennies from Heaven* (MGM, 1981), Bernadette Peters played a schoolteacher who falls from grace. Before she goes, she indulges in this wonderful Berkeleyesque fantasy, backed up by her pupils.

Comedian Steve Martin may not have given much thought to dancing before he was assigned to *Pennies from Heaven* (MGM, 1981), but once he accepted the part he learned how hard it is and how long it takes to step like Astaire. The part was that of a sheet-music salesman in the years of the Depression, who wishes life was as rosy as the lyrics in the songs he sells—which was reason enough for the film to slip into lovely song-and-dance fantasies of the Busby Berkeley kind. The expensive *Pennies from Heaven* failed in its attempt to combine these fantasies with the misery of the Depression—the contrast was just too stark—but whenever it became Fantasy Time it became wonderful. The reason it became wonderful was director-producer Herbert Ross, who had been a choreographer on Broadway before coming to Hollywood, where he choreographed such films as *Carmen Jones*, *Dr. Doolittle*, and *Funny Girl*, before turning to direction with *Goodbye Mr. Chips* in 1969. If all of *Pennies from Heaven* had been dance fantasy it would have been manna from heaven.

And for the first and last word on the subject of hoofing in Hollywood? It's not so much a word as a name — Astaire.

FRED ASTAIRE

The only person who does not enjoy being nostalgic about Fred Astaire is Fred Astaire. In an industry awash with scrapbooks, he apparently has none, and any attempt to engage him in reminiscences about his career is likely to prove unproductive. Anyone who assumes that this is merely a stance of modesty on his part will soon find that it is not. Astaire does not enjoy talking about the past. References to "the good old days" may provoke the rather testy response, "*These* are the good old days." The Astaire past is something for the admirers and the historians to deal with, not for him.

Astaire makes his Hollywood début dancing "Heigh, Ho, the Gang's All Here" with Joan Crawford in *Dancing Lady* (MGM, 1933). Page 82: *Daddy Long Legs* (Fox, 1955). Fred dances with drumsticks to "The History of the Beat."

The Astaire past, both in terms of the man's accomplishments and his place in the history of dance, is quite incredible. There still exists a photograph of Astaire at the age of five doing a routine at the Claude Alvienne dancing school in New York. The year is 1904. As this book goes to press Astaire is a healthy eighty-five. Between the two lies the story of a man who made dancing interesting and appealing to more people than anyone had ever before affected. The millions who have watched him — and there are millions who will continue to watch him — have been persuaded, if any persuasion was needed, that dancing is a wonderful thing to be able to do — and that it is also amusing and exhilarating, romantic and sexy.

No matter where and when he had been born Astaire would have been successful, but it was his fortune to be born in a country that was slowly emerging in the arts, a development that would come to full blossom in his lifetime. In 1899, the year of his birth, the American musical theater was drawing its offerings mostly from London and Vienna. By the time Astaire arrived in New York in 1917, American composers had begun to add their melodies to the stage. After World War I, a turnabout suddenly became apparent: Europe was in low gear and America was in high. Broadway bustled with musicals, and the names of young men like Gershwin, Youmans, Berlin, Rodgers and Hart, Kern, and Porter shot up like rockets. Fred Astaire was a vital part of Broadway all through the twenties. Then when musicals finally found their feet in Hollywood in 1933 he became an even more vital part of this marvelous new outlet — and remained so throughout the thirties and the forties and the fifties. It is a track record that no one else even comes within sight of matching.

A flying Fred from *Top Hat* (RKO, 1935). Below: *Flying Down to Rio* (RKO, 1933). Fred dances "Orchids in the Moonlight"—not with Ginger Rogers but with Dolores Del Rio.

Talent cannot be explained, other than to say that it is some kind of predisposition that can be nurtured and developed and then enjoyed, provided luck becomes an ally. Luck, of course, has a lot to do with working hard and seizing opportunities. In regard to these generalizations, the Astaire story runs in a straight line. In regard to seeking out some explanation for his success as a dancer, the answer must lie in his love of music. Astaire is a musician, and possibly this fact has not been stressed enough. He is an excellent pianist. In *Follow the Fleet* (1936) he can be seen doing a barrelhouse version of Berlin's "I'm Putting All My Eggs in One Basket" on an upright. The playing is not faked. He is also a drummer. In *Daddy Long Legs* (1955) he flails away at a drum set to Johnny Mercer's "History of the Beat," then gets up and dances with the drumsticks, bouncing them off the floor and off the wall. Only a dancer who is also a musician could pull off such a routine. And it is this innate sense of music that is the basis of all Astaire routines. With every film he began by studying the songs—as they were handed to him by the composer, long before they were arranged and orchestrated. He understands music in terms of notation, timings, accents, and keys.

It is no secret that Astaire is a songwriter—and a far from successful one, although what he writes is respectable stuff. Perhaps his best is a song he wrote with lyricist Johnny Mercer, "I'm Building Up to an Awful Letdown," but there have been others on which he has written both the words and the music, like "You Worry Me" and "If Swing Goes I Go Too." Astaire's problem as a songwriter is unlike that of any other—simply that he is deeply in the shadow of the men who have written for him. These are the composers who have written music for Fred Astaire: George Gershwin, Vincent Youmans, Arthur Schwartz, Cole Porter, Burton Lane, Jerome Kern, Irving Berlin, Harold Arlen, Frank Loesser, and Harry Warren. It is a unique problem. No other person has had so many great songs written for him by so many great composers. And Astaire delivered them so memorably that he came to be identified with them. It is a truly astounding identification and it has much to do with Fred Astaire's success as a dancer.

Astaire was born in Omaha, but when he and his sister Adele, older by eighteen months, showed unusual ability as dancers, their mother took them to New York and enrolled them in the Alvienne school. Adele was the truly remarkable one at this time; Fred was the convenient partner. Their father, an ex-Austrian Army officer who had not been in America very long, gamely decided to stay in Omaha and support his family in their show business endeavors. Friedrich Austerlitz must have had some realization that his children were exceptional. By the time he died in 1923 they were well-known names in the theater (they were in fact appearing in a show in London at the time). But it was the mother who was the really remarkable parent. She lived to be ninety-five and gave advice to them until the end.

Fred and Ginger dance in *The Barkleys of Broadway* (MGM, 1949). Opposite: In *The Band Wagon* (MGM, 1953), Fred is the happy man with a shine on his shoes.

The Astaires appeared in vaudeville as children and traveled all over America. Schooling was picked up willy-nilly. When pressed to recall these years, Astaire shakes his head and says, "All I can remember is my worry whether or not we could do the act properly and the floor wouldn't be too slippery, and I'd fall on my ear or something." Others remember their act a little more passionately. Eddie Foy, Jr., recalled, "First time I saw Fred Astaire was in 1916, in the Middle West. We were doing some shows with my father as the Seven Little Foys and we ran into him some place outside Chicago. Pop was crazy about them two kids, but he kept saying to the family, 'Now watch this little boy. Now there's a good dancer. Watch his style.'"

Adele claimed that this was a turning point in Fred's attitude, which until now had been a little flippant toward dancing. When he was sixteen she noticed him tapping and dancing by himself. "Suddenly he began inventing things. I was more the clown. I mean I like to be funny, I couldn't be bothered learning all those steps. Many times Freddie brought me to task by making me do over a few steps I did wrong the night before. Oh, I had it from him, don't worry." What Adele actually saw was the emergence of Fred Astaire the perfectionist, the man who in his later years in Hollywood would become uncompromising with the demands he would make on himself and his partners.

The Astaires first appeared on Broadway in 1917, in the revue *Over the Top*. It was literally over the top for them in making the transition from vaudeville to the legitimate stage. They never went back. The Shuberts hired them for *The Passing Show of 1918*. The following year the esteemed producer Charles Dillingham signed them for *Apple Blossoms,* and he put them in two more of his shows after that. In all of them they were featured dancers, and in every case the reviewers searched for new ways to describe their pleasing work.

Their careers took another leap forward with the success of *Stop Flirting* in London. It ran for more than four hundred performances at the Shaftesbury Theatre and made them into London socialites. Their success in New York had drawn them into society there, but in London it became more apparent that Fred and Adele, despite their modest Omaha background, had a fondness for the upper crust. Fred now began to acquire some of the style that would mark him as a dapper figure in the movies: the expensive but conservative tailoring, the interest in racehorses, and the clear diction that served him so well with witty lyrics. He found himself courted by royalty; the Prince of Wales became a close friend, as did his brother George, soon to become king.

Back in New York, Fred associated with another kind of royalty—the songwriters who were in the process of lifting American music onto a new level. One of them was George Gershwin, who took a shine to Fred because Fred could talk music as well as dance it. Out of that friendship came a new

Top Hat (RKO, 1935). The image is set, once and for all.

direction in the Astaire career—real stardom and a growing importance in the American theater. The Astaires opened in Gershwin's *Lady, Be Good!* in December of 1924. Whatever music Astaire had performed prior to this has long dropped into obscurity; now began the identity of Astaire with a parade of great songs, the first of genuine importance being "Fascinating Rhythm." In 1926 the Astaires took *Lady, Be Good!* to London. Another long run. Then another Gershwin show, *Funny Face,* opened on Broadway in November 1927. They took that one to London, too. By the end of the twenties they were trans-Atlantic celebrities.

The Astaires began the next decade with a Vincent Youmans musical, *Smiles.* Unfortunately, it did not live up to its name; it closed after sixty performances. It merits a footnote in history, however, because in it Fred did a dance called "Young Man of Manhattan," equipped with top hat, white tie, tails, and cane. The image was beginning to form. It was also important because it was seen by a pair of young songwriters, Howard Dietz and Arthur Schwartz, who were moved to write a musical revue with the Astaires in mind, *The Band Wagon.* But by this time there had been a change in the private lives of the Astaires. During the last stay in London Adele had been courted by Lord Charles Cavendish, whose proposal she accepted. By the time she accepted *The Band Wagon* she and Fred knew that it would be their parting shot; Lady Cavendish would have no need to work. Because of this Dietz and Schwartz constructed their

show to give Fred much more of the spotlight. Even so, Adele could hardly have wished for a better exit vehicle, for *The Band Wagon* was a smash.

It was during the run that Fred, by some kind of natural compensation, met the lady who would become his wife, Phyllis Potter. Despite this he still had to face the fact that at the age of thirty-three he was about to start a new phase of his career—as a soloist, minus the partner with whom he had worked since childhood. He was far from happy about it. He opened in Cole Porter's *Gay Divorce* in November 1932; several critics could not resist commenting that Fred seemed at times to be looking off into the wings, hopefully waiting for his sister to arrive. The audience, though, fixed its sight firmly on Fred. *Gay Divorce* was another smash hit, and the birthplace of another song with which he would thereafter be identified, "Night and Day." A year after its Broadway opening Astaire took the show to London, and it was there that the stage career of Fred Astaire came to an end. For some time he had been making noises about being uneasy with life in the theater. The golden opportunity had arrived.

By the time *Gay Divorce* closed on Broadway Astaire had accepted an offer from David O. Selznick, then head of production at RKO Radio Pictures, to appear in *Flying Down to Rio,* with music by Vincent Youmans. The jinx against movie musicals—occasioned by the flood of "all-talking, all-singing, all-dancing" extravaganzas that finally drowned in

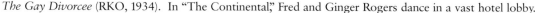

The Gay Divorcee (RKO, 1934). In "The Continental," Fred and Ginger Rogers dance in a vast hotel lobby.

the audiences' tears of boredom — had been broken by the Warner success with *42nd Street*. Once Busby Berkeley proved that the camera did not have to be nailed to the floor, other directors picked up the challenge. *Flying Down to Rio* went beyond even Berkeley's madness, with a sequence in which girls dance on the wings of airplanes in flight. Fortunately, Astaire did not have to concern himself with anything that bizarre.

However, *Rio* was so long in production that Astaire took time out to appear in MGM's gigantic backstage musical *Dancing Lady*, with Joan Crawford as the lady. It required him only to appear as himself, in two numbers with Crawford — the chipper "Heigh, Ho, the Gang's All Here" and the oom-pah-pah "Let's Go Bavarian." It was a thoroughly respectable start to a movie career. The only person who had doubts about it was Astaire, who did not like the way he looked. "I thought I looked like a knife on the screen. I was a weird-looking character anyway and I never liked the way I photographed." After completing his work on *Rio* the diffident, doubtful Astaire took off for London and the resumption of *Gay Divorce*. The public reaction to the film left no doubt about where Astaire was headed next. From here on it was life on celluloid.

Astaire had to be persuaded to see *Flying Down to Rio*. He had avoided it, convinced he had made little impression. In it, he danced two numbers, a tango with leading lady Dolores Del Rio, "Orchids in the Moonlight," and a lively Latin spot, "The Carioca," with Ginger Rogers. What the public responded to was not so much the former as the latter. Something about the sight of Astaire and Rogers intrigued them — they looked so right together.

Actually Rogers, who had already been in Hollywood for several years, did not know of her teaming with Astaire in "The Carioca" until the film was well into production. She and Fred were not strangers. He had been asked to help her with her dance steps when she appeared in Gershwin's *Girl Crazy* on Broadway in 1930. They had had some supper dates, but Astaire formed the impression that she was a girl interested only in her career, and they did not see each other again until the *Rio* casting.

RKO producer Pandro S. Berman took the positive response to Astaire and Rogers as a go-ahead signal. Needing a vehicle for them, he decided on a filming of the Porter musical, *Gay Divorce*, in which Astaire had recently enjoyed so much acclaim. (For the screen, the title had to be changed to *The Gay Divorcee*: the strictures of 1934 film censorship allowed for a divorcee — but not an actual divorce — to be gay.) Astaire now caused a strain by explaining to Berman that Rogers was wrong for the part. The leading lady should be English and genteel, and very, very graceful in dancing

"Night and Day." Ginger was, he thought, a little too earthy, the kind of girl who was marvelous doing the Charleston.

Berman agreed but pointed out to Astaire that he was now in Hollywood, which was in the business of getting people to place their money at the box office, and if it looked as if people might pay to see Rogers and Astaire together, that was what they would get. What Berman probably did not realize at the time was Astaire's reluctance to get locked into another partnership. The strain of the unraveling with Adele had been severe, and the thought of going through it once more scared him. Fate, however, was against him. *The Gay Divorcee* was a winner. Astaire was pleased to find Rogers highly adaptable as a dancer and that she could, and did, soften her rather brash image and become more refined. Years later it would be said that he gave her style and that in return she gave him sex appeal. It is probably as true and simple an assessment as can be made.

The Astaire-Rogers image was molded by their dancing of "Night and Day" in *The Gay Divorcee*. He wears a tuxedo, she a white evening gown, and they meet in a deserted ballroom. To Porter's sensual melody he courts her, gently and gracefully. She attempts to resist him but she soon surrenders, and glides with him in a feeling of mutual enchantment. It is a scene they will repeat, with different melodies and in different settings, many times in the following years. But the big hit of *The Gay Divorcee* was "The Continental," with music by Con Conrad, requiring an immense Art Deco set, supposedly a hotel esplanade, and a hundred back-up dancers. The routine goes on and on, with endless variations and camera angles, clocking out at over seventeen minutes. And it became the first piece of film music to receive an Academy Award. Like it or not, they were now Fred-and-Ginger.

Flying Down to Rio began another partnership for Astaire, with a young dancer with the elegant name of Hermes Pan (shortened from Panagiotopulos). Then twenty-three and with the peculiar advantage of resembling Astaire in face, build, and dancing style, Pan was an assistant to *Rio*'s dance director Dave Gould. Gould suggested to Pan that perhaps Astaire might need some help with a dance he was devising. Recalls Pan, "I was terrified because I knew his reputation. He was all by himself on the stage, going through some routine, and I introduced myself, and he said maybe I'd like to see what he was working on. He was very polite and gentlemanly, as always. He showed me this fantastic half a routine that wasn't finished. I was awed. I remember we got to one place and he said, 'I'm up the Swanee. I need a little break or something.' It just happened to come to me and I said, 'Maybe something like this,' and he said, 'That's not bad,' and he used it, so that gave

Fred and Randolph Scott take a break from filming *Follow the Fleet* (RKO, 1936)—but they keep right on hoofing.

Carefree (RKO, 1938) could be the title of the dance as well as the picture, but this nifty number is called "The Yam."

me confidence." The rapport was immediate. Hermes Pan became Astaire's assistant, and within a couple of years he was the dance director on all the Astaire-Rogers pictures. He continued to work with Astaire on many subsequent productions.

In Astaire, Hermes Pan found the personification of his ideas about film dancing. Pan took on a supporting role, often in encouraging a hesitant Astaire to try various moves. "I didn't influence his style because he was already a star when I was starting out. People naturally influence each other whether it's unconscious or not. Later on I could see certain moves or attitudes he would never have done before." If a great dancer can be said to have a right-hand man, then that is what Pan was to Astaire.

RKO, a studio on shaky financial ground in the early thirties, had obviously found a road to profit with Astaire and Rogers. Now they had to find the right vehicles for them. Next up was *Roberta* (1935), a filming of the Jerome Kern musical, with Irene Dunne as the star but with a build-up of the roles played by Astaire and Rogers. One of the songs, "I Won't Dance," gave Fred a chance to reveal his ability as a pianist. The important number was "I'll Be Hard to Handle," which further etched their image as bantering lovers, communicating messages through dance movements rather than words. The technique was not entirely new, but it had never before been so pleasingly choreographed in such subtly amorous terms. Audiences by the millions were entranced by it, and dancing schools found business picking up as men became eager students in the art of how to win girls by dancing with them.

The Astaire-Rogers teaming was now serious business, and RKO commissioned Irving Berlin to write a score especially for them. The result, *Top Hat* (1935), proved to be a work of art, and a movie musical still in a class of its own. Here was Fred with top hat, white tie, and tails, and, as Berlin's lines have it, "I'm steppin' out, my dear, to breathe an atmosphere that simply reeks with class?" Here was Fred in a hotel room, exuberantly tapping out "No Strings," waking an annoyed Ginger in the room below, and then courting her merrily during a storm in a park to the lilting tune of "Isn't This a Lovely Day (To Be Caught in the Rain)?" The plot called for her to resist him but the whole point of this and all their other pictures together is that it is impossible for her to resist him. Music, dance, romance — how could the public resist? How could they not respond to Fred gliding around a dance floor with Ginger in his arms and singing, "Heaven, I'm in heaven, And my heart beats so that I can hardly speak/And I seem to find the happiness I seek/ When we're out together dancing cheek to cheek?"

Irving Berlin was also in heaven. He had written five songs for *Top Hat* and they were all hits. He agreed straight away to write another score for Fred-and-Ginger. *Follow the Fleet* (1936) put Astaire in the navy and gave him a chance to tap-dance around the deck of a battleship. An ex-dancer turned sailor, he barges into a dance hall with his chums early in the film. There he meets his ex-partner (Ginger, of course), and they proceed to wipe up the competition in a dance contest. To the bounce of Berlin's "Let Yourself Go," they put on a performance that none of the other competitors can possibly match. As the plot steams on, Fred helps

Doing "The Shorty George" with Rita Hayworth in *You Were Never Lovelier* (Columbia, 1942).

Ginger and her sister raise funds to save a ship by (what else?) putting on a show. This allows Fred and Ginger to get into formal evening clothes to perform the finale of the fund-raiser — yet another Berlin classic, "Let's Face the Music and Dance." Some years later Berlin let it be known that he would rather have Astaire introduce his songs than any other performer. Jerome Kern felt much the same way. Kern was like Astaire in many ways — fussy, meticulous, painfully painstaking — and he once said, "Astaire *can't* do anything bad."

Kern was the next composer of an especially fashioned Astaire-Rogers musical, *Swing Time* (1936), which contained the gorgeous love song, "The Way You Look Tonight," that brought him and lyricist Dorothy Fields an Oscar. It also had the requisite bouncy number, "Pick Yourself Up," and a sad one called "Never Gonna Dance," which title still causes Ginger to wince because the last sixteen bars required forty-seven takes and ended with her feet bleeding. (On the other hand, "Waltz in Swing Time" was shot in its entirety in one take. Film dancing, particularly if it involves Astaire, is totally unpredictable.) Astaire ended the most ambitious number, "Bojangles of Harlem" — his tribute to Bill Robinson — by dancing in and out of sync with three silhouettes of himself. A born worrier, Astaire was always concerned about coming up with new dance ideas, fearing that the public would eventually become bored if he and Ginger simply trotted around a dance floor. He had no need to worry, but no one was ever able to convince Astaire of that.

Astaire's friendship with George Gershwin dates back to the days when Gershwin was a song plugger in a publishing house on Tin Pan Alley. Because of the success they had had on Broadway with *Lady, Be Good!* and *Funny Face*, Astaire expected the busy composer at some point to write a film score for him. It came with *Shall We Dance* in 1937, and the songs were tailored. Knowing his man, Gershwin wrote "Slap That Bass," which could only be done by a dancer who was also a musician, and knowing that a Fred-and-Ginger picture needed a bantering love song, he and Ira did "Let's Call the Whole Thing Off," which Fred decided to perform on roller skates. *Shall We Dance* was also the birthplace of "They Can't Take That Away from Me," one of the songs most indelibly associated with Astaire.

Afterward the Gershwins agreed to do another score, but Ginger threw a curve into the plans. Her desire to step out of the musical format and stretch her wings as an actress put a temporary end to the famous team. RKO decided to go ahead with an Astaire-minus-Rogers musical, *A Damsel in Distress* (1937), hoping that the Gershwin score would compensate for the drastic missing link. It did not, and the studio

Fred does his "Snake Dance" for the amusement of Robert Ryan in *The Sky's the Limit* (RKO, 1943).

worsened matters by giving Astaire as his leading lady young Joan Fontaine, who could neither sing nor dance. But the film gave us "A Foggy Day" and "Nice Work if You Can Get It." Tragically, by the time the film came out George Gershwin was dead, stricken with a brain tumor at the age of thirty-seven.

RKO persuaded Rogers to team with Astaire in *Carefree* (1938) and it signed Irving Berlin to write the songs. But the composer and the two stars had reached their peak with *Top Hat* and *Follow the Fleet*. *Carefree* proved only that they could not reach that high again as a team. The audience had to settle for some fine moments, especially the beguiling "Change Partners," with Fred dancing with the wrong woman and longingly looking at Ginger in the arms of another man. Berlin gave them a jaunty dance number with "The Yam," but for Astaire watchers the truly astonishing performance is his dance on a golf course, supposedly in Scotland. Golfers who watched Astaire teeing off a row of golf balls, one after the other, with an unbroken series of swings and with perfect musical timing, thought it was faked. It wasn't, but Astaire spent ten days rehearsing the dance and took two days to film it.

The Astaire-Rogers pairing came to an end in 1939 with *The Story of Vernon and Irene Castle*, the least typical of

their films and the only one in which they played actual people. The Castles, a celebrated dance team in the years before World War I, had introduced many fashionable dances. Clearly, Astaire and Rogers were the only ones who could play them on the screen. The public showed little interest, however, and the film earned the dubious distinction of being the only Astaire-Rogers venture not to make a profit.

The gossip reporters tried to imply that the team's break-up was due to feuding between the stars, which was definitely not the case. While they did not socialize, both were friendly and respectful. Both knew that any film cycle has to end, and the finale had been in sight for several years. They had done it all, and the last two films had proven that it was best to leave well enough alone. Rogers had also proven that she was a fine actress, and she had plenty of work offers. The problem was Fred Astaire: what was *he* going to do? It was the Adele business all over again, and it revealed to those who had not quite understood his reluctance to start a partnership with Rogers just what it was that had bothered him at the time.

In 1939, at age forty, Fred Astaire gave thought to retiring. He had already been a dancer for longer than most dancers manage to last and he was comfortably fixed, with a happy home, a wife, a son, a daughter, and a life style that had nothing to do with show business. It would take a twisting of an arm to get him to resume making movie musicals. Louis B. Mayer was the man with the twist. At a time when both RKO and Warner Bros., which had made a specialty of musicals in the thirties, opted to drop them, Mayer was the man who picked them up. With Arthur Freed as the head of his musicals department, Mayer made MGM the foremost film studio in the art of making musicals. He had long had Eleanor Powell under contract, so why not team the world's foremost female dancer with the world's foremost male dancer?

The result was *Broadway Melody of 1940,* with songs by Cole Porter. Astaire played a hoofer, half of a team — the other half being George Murphy—and Powell was a Broadway star. The irresponsible Murphy mistakenly gets a crack at being Eleanor's partner, with Fred teaching him the steps, but inevitably the misunderstandings lift like a fog from this movie. Just as inevitably, Astaire and Powell dance together, first with "I Concentrate on You," and then, for the finale, a magnificent version of "Begin the Beguine."

The idea of retiring now seemed a little silly. Yes, he would do more pictures, but he did not want to sign a studio contract and he definitely did not want to be locked into

Ziegfeld Follies (MGM, 1946). With Lucille Bremer in "This Heart of Mine."

another partnership. He accepted a Paramount offer to dance with Paulette Goddard in the mild *Second Chorus* (1940), which caused him to think about retiring again. Then Columbia came up with something enticing. *You'll Never Get Rich* (1941) promised a new score by Cole Porter and a teaming with a lady, Rita Hayworth, whose dancing he respected. He had worked with her dancing parents in vaudeville and was favorably impressed by the training they had given their daughter. He found she could do any dance routine he needed, ranging from the romantic "So Near and Yet So Far" to the snappy "Boogie Barcarolle." Although the public applauded, Fred shied away from committing himself to a continued teaming with Rita.

The idea of teaming up with Bing Crosby, on the other hand, appealed to him, even though it meant second billing. Irving Berlin had written the score, so that made it even more appealing. Astaire enjoyed having the opportunity to do a duet contest with Bing, the hoofer versus the crooner, in "I'll Capture Your Heart," and Virginia Dale was his dancing partner in the jaunty "You're Easy to Dance With." Astaire's most impressive number in *Holiday Inn* is the solo "Say It with Firecrackers," which is exactly what he does, taking them out of his pockets and exploding them on the floor to punctuate his rapid steps.

Columbia called: Would he do another picture with Rita Hayworth? The public was clamoring. Astaire thought it over and agreed, on the understanding that it would be the last. In point of fact, no partner did more than two films with

him after Rogers. *You Were Never Lovelier* (1942) also reunited him with Jerome Kern. His beautiful title melody was a perfect basis for a romantic dance with Rita, as were "I'm Old-Fashioned" and "Dearly Beloved." But there was also the fast-paced rhythm number, "The Shorty George," and the wild "Audition Dance," in which Astaire frantically dances all over the office, including the desk, of a hotel owner whose daughter he is trying to woo.

In these years, Astaire could only be wooed into a film if he felt it offered him something a little different. *The Sky's the Limit* (1943), which took him back to RKO, turned him into a heroic aviator who ducks out of the hero's welcome arranged for him and meets a photographer (Joan Leslie) in a service canteen. Although the dances with Leslie were pleasant, it is the songs of Harold Arlen and Johnny Mercer that give the film its distinction, especially the smoky "One for My Baby," destined to become another Astaire standard. But the experience did not convince him that there was much point in continuing with his movie career. Again it was Louis B. Mayer who came along to twist his arm. Mayer was going to make a supermusical involving all his stars to pay tribute to the great Florenz Ziegfeld. Astaire would have to be a part of it.

The enormous *Ziegfeld Follies* was begun in 1944 and it was not finished until almost two years later. It was a film of many parts, and some of the best parts involve Astaire. It called for him to talk directly to the audience about Ziegfeld and sing a song, "Bring On the Beautiful Girls," but it was not until he started dancing with Lucille Bremer in "This Heart of Mine" that the Astaire part of the film really began.

Opposite, left: Fred and Ginger dance "The Swing Trot" in *The Barkleys of Broadway* (MGM, 1949), the film that reunited them after ten years. Opposite, right: *Blue Skies* (Paramount, 1946). Here are "A Couple of Song-and-Dance Men," and the one doing the least dancing is a singer named Bing Crosby. Below: *Let's Dance* (Paramount, 1950)—with a piano? Pianist Tommy Chambers seems undisturbed.

The lovely melody was by Harry Warren and producer Arthur Freed provided the lyrics. The period of the great Metro musicals was blossoming full flower, thanks almost entirely to the taste and drive of Freed. For this number, he hired the artistic Vincente Minnelli as director and Robert Alton as choreographer, and their "This Heart of Mine" is a gem. Astaire plays a jewel thief at an elegant ball, enchanting Bremer with his singing and dancing as part of his plan to rob her, but love makes the robbery unnecessary. It is Astaire at the peak of seductive dance form.

Ziegfeld Follies did well by Astaire, and vice versa. He had two additional numbers in this film, the poignant and dramatic "Limehouse Blues" and a lusty revival of the Gersh-

win routine "The Babbitt and the Bromide," which he had done in *Funny Face* in 1927. This time his partner was Gene Kelly, and that made a whale of a difference.

Before *Ziegfeld Follies* was released, Astaire was seen in *Yolanda and the Thief*, which he had made following his stint in the former film. It was an extension of "This Heart of Mine," in the sense that it again teamed him with Lucille Bremer, she as an aristocratic girl in some South American convent and he as the slick Yankee con man out to rob her. Again love changes his heart. *Yolanda* is a beautiful fantasy; if Astaire wanted something different, this was it—but the public did not want it. Once more the resolve to retire welled up in his thoughts. More than a year went by. Hollywood seldom entered his mind, especially now that he was doing well with his beloved thoroughbred horses, one of which, Triplicate, was bringing home large winnings.

Then Paramount called; they were making another big Crosby picture, called *Blue Skies*, with a score by Irving

Berlin, and they had a problem. They had hired a famous dancer, Paul Draper, but it turned out he could not speak his lines very well. Astaire declined, but when Berlin himself called it became hard to stand back; besides, Irving had written a marvelous comic duet for him and Bing, "A Couple of Song-and-Dance Men." And Fred would get to dance to some grand old Berlin songs, including "Heat Wave," "A Pretty Girl Is Like a Melody," and the irresistible "Puttin' On the Ritz." A refusal was impossible.

Two years of happy retirement drifted by and then another phone call, this one from Gene Kelly, called him to action. Kelly was making a Metro musical with Judy Garland called *Easter Parade* (1948), and again Irving Berlin was the songwriter. The production was in dire straits because Kelly had broken his ankle. Astaire shook his head and suggested Kelly wait until he was well. Neither the tides nor MGM of 1948 was prepared to wait, and Astaire once more drove himself back to work. While Astaire characteristically tends to be a little difficult and grouchy, he also characteristically finds it hard to say no.

Easter Parade turned out to be to his pleasing. He got along well with Judy Garland, with whom he performed the memorable comic derelict song "A Couple of Swells" as well as several old Berlin ragtime numbers. The film also gave him the opportunity to create two amazing numbers: the drum dance in a toystore, in which he beats and bangs all kinds of drums while tap-dancing, and "Steppin' Out with My Baby," in which he achieves some incredible effects by dancing against a visual backdrop of men dancing in slow motion. Only those closely associated with Astaire can appreciate the time and labor that went into these routines.

Easter Parade's success prompted the studio to press for a sequel with Astaire and Garland. By the time the film was set for production, however, Garland's declining health set off a search for a substitute. Adolph Green and Betty Comden, who had written the script for *The Barkleys of Broadway*, had the bright thought of getting Ginger Rogers. Rogers liked the script and Astaire, after the usual head shaking, agreed. For the studio publicists the reunion was a natural — Fred-and-Ginger, back together after ten years. The emotional and nostalgic impact was enormous. Charles Walters, the director, admitted to breaking into tears when Ginger walked on the set for the first time and embraced Astaire.

Producer Freed set Harry Warren to write the music and teamed him, for the first time, with Ira Gershwin, resulting in some obviously expert numbers, of which "Shoes with Wings On" is an Astaire jewel. A "show within a show" piece, it has him as a cobbler who tries on a pair of dancing shoes and finds them magical. Then, à la *The Sorcerer's*

Opposite: *Three Little Words* (MGM, 1950). Fred dances with Vera-Ellen to "Nevertheless." *Royal Wedding* (MGM, 1951). Wildly in love, Fred dances all over the room to the tune of "You're All the World to Me" (above). Actually, he's hanging onto that chair. The delectable Jane Powell (below) was also in the film.

Apprentice, things get out of hand, with dozens of pairs of shoes becoming wildly animated, thanks to trick photography, and Astaire finally resorting to battle to quell them. *The Barkleys of Broadway* ended in a happily obvious manner, with Fred-and-Ginger in evening clothes, elegantly spinning to "Manhattan Downbeat." But as Astaire rather suspected, the film was not quite as successful as everybody else had believed it would be. While it was good and it did well, it is very hard to recapture magic.

Paramount's *Let's Dance* in 1950, with the frantic Betty Hutton, must have sounded interesting in concept, otherwise Astaire would never have entertained the idea of doing something that turned out so mild. Frank Loesser supplied the song score. The only memorable item is Astaire's "Piano Dance," which uses a baby grand as a dance prop. Hermes Pan, who was in charge of the dance routines, admits, "It was a case of very bad casting. I don't think Fred should have been subjected to a partner who would limit him."

Pan was also the dance director on the next project, MGM's account of the lives of songwriters Harry Ruby and Bert Kalmar, *Three Little Words* (1950), with Red Skelton as Ruby and Astaire as Kalmar. Astaire harbors particular affection for the film, for it gave him the chance to play a successful songwriter—a fantasy that, for him, never came true. He also enjoyed dancing with Vera-Ellen, the most expert of all his partners; as Pan says, "He could really dance instead of being limited by the girl."

Royal Wedding (1951) had leading-lady problems. June Allyson, the original choice, dropped out when she became pregnant. Judy Garland was considered for a while, but she was dropped when her health took a turn for the worse. The job finally went to Jane Powell, a delightful singer but a limited dancer. However, Nick Castle, the dance director, and Astaire found Powell a willing student. She did quite well paired with Astaire on the Latin routine "I Left My Hat in Haiti." The crowning piece in *Royal Wedding*, "You're All the World to Me," features an Astaire solo. It required a room to be built like a box that could be stood on all four sides. With the help of some very deft camera work and editing, the number displayed Astaire dancing on the sides and the ceiling of the room. It amazed everyone; even Astaire himself thought "it wasn't bad."

The Belle of New York (1952) was a disappointment. In this reworking of an old operetta, Astaire played a turn-of-the-century playboy, with Vera-Ellen as the prim girl with whom he finally settles down. Years later the director, Charles Walters, said he felt that although Vera-Ellen was a superb dancer she lacked warmth as an actress, and that in this particular film there seemed to be no chemistry working between her and Astaire. "Fred was never happy with it. I'd

be amazed at the lightness, the gaiety in a scene. Then I would say, 'Cut,' and his face would drop, the shoulders would drop, and he'd say, 'Oh, it's terrible. I can't stand it. I hate it.' It was a waste of time trying to convince him it was fine."

Another insight on the Astaire character comes from Harry Warren (this was the fourth Astaire film for which Warren had written the music): "He is unlike anybody else in the business. He's the most retiring, most polite, and quietest man I've worked with. We had discussions on his dances, on ideas for them. He would tell me what he had in mind, and I would play melodies for him. If he liked them I would write them down and he would take them away. Sometimes he would come back a few days later and almost apologetically explain that he had tried a piece out and couldn't get it to work. Could I write something else? With Fred it was a pleasure."

Astaire's increasingly pessimistic outlook on his film career brightened in 1953 when MGM assigned him to *The Band Wagon*. It turned out to be one of the great movie musicals, and one with which he could truly identify. In fact, writers Comden and Green constructed it around him, giving him the role of a celebrated song-and-dance man whose film career has run down and who returns to Broadway to recapture his former glory. In that respect it was fantasy — Astaire never at any time showed any interest in returning to the stage — but at least he could understand that kind of man.

The film had no relationship to Astaire's stage hit of 1931, except for the title and the songs of Arthur Schwartz and Howard Dietz, who supplied some new material as well as old hits that they lifted from some of their other stage shows. This *Band Wagon* is really a show-biz valedictory. In it, Nanette Fabray and Oscar Levant play characters based on Comden and Green; Jack Buchanan, the man often described as England's Fred Astaire, is the director who makes a mess of the show and finally settles for being a song-and-dance man. During her years in show business, Cyd Charisse came to know well the character she plays here, a snooty ballerina who looks with disdain on the pairing with a Hollywood hoofer.

An unlikely sideline commentator on *The Band Wagon* turns out to be Sir John Gielgud, whom MGM had brought from London to play Cassius in *Julius Caesar*. Sir John had enjoyed Adele and Fred when they appeared in London in the twenties, and he has a comment that is more pertinent than most: "I think he was obviously the leading spirit. As in so many partnerships, like for instance the Lunts, there was a curious feeling that the man had given the woman the feminine side of his talent, and developed it for her, and then

Daddy Long Legs (Fox, 1955).
Fred glides with Leslie Caron
to "Something's Gotta Give."

Silk Stockings (MGM, 1957). Cyd Charisse is Ninotchka, and the Cole Porter melody is "All of You." Below: In *Finian's Rainbow* (Warners, 1968), sixty-nine-year-old Fred does a merry set of steps to "When the Idle Poor Become the Idle Rich."

become a wonderful partner. I always think the best dancers are the best showers-off of a woman."

Sir John was invited to watch Astaire shooting a routine. "I rushed over and he was doing a shoeshine number. They said he had sweated his way through four gray flannel suits that morning doing the number over and over again. Of course the soundtrack had already been recorded and his singing was coming through the loudspeaker and he had to mime the words, and I was amazed that he could begin halfway through the shot. All timed to perfection without losing a beat of music or appearing to be put out by the fact that he wasn't really singing at all. The skill was amazing. I was amazed at his painstaking thoroughness and extraordinary accuracy."

The triumph of *The Band Wagon* was diminished for Astaire by the death of his wife, Phyllis, in September 1954. It had been an excellent marriage; Astaire had wanted, and got, a wife and home totally removed from the entertainment business. He had previously signed a contract with 20th Century-Fox to do *Daddy Long Legs* but he now felt it would be impossible. His sister and everybody close to him persuaded him that for his own sanity and for the sake of everyone concerned with the film he should do it. He did, and anyone seeing the film would have a hard time detect-

ing that it was made by a man stricken with grief. Leslie Caron, a graceful graduate of ballet, made the dancing easier than it had been in some of his other partnerships.

Two years went by before Astaire could be coaxed back to the screen, and again it had to be something that would really interest him. Paramount suggested a filming of the 1927 Gershwin musical *Funny Face*, in which he had had such a good time. He liked the idea, and he also liked the idea of having the elegant Audrey Hepburn as his leading lady. Under Stanley Donen's direction and with choreography by Eugene Loring, *Funny Face* (1957) became prime Astaire, and one of the most beautifully stylish musicals ever filmed. The story was set in the fashion world of New York and Paris, which Astaire and Hepburn fitted like expensive, exquisitely tailored models. When they sang and danced "'S Wonderful," it seemed the only possible comment.

Before he could start making his usual noises about retirement, especially from musicals, MGM signed him for its version of Cole Porter's Broadway hit *Silk Stockings*. Rouben Mamoulian directed and both Hermes Pan and Eugene Loring were brought in as dance directors. In this musical version of *Ninotchka*, Cyd Charisse was the logical choice to play the beautiful but haughty Russian whose heart needs to be melted. Although Astaire was now fifty-eight, no one watching the man leaping around to the demanding beats of "The Ritz Rock 'n' Roll" would have

After having vowed never to dance on screen again, Fred changed his mind and did some stepping with Gene Kelly
to introduce *That's Entertainment, Part II* (MGM, 1976).

guessed it. Nonetheless, this was truly the beginning of the end; *Silk Stockings* would be the high-water mark in his career as a dancer.

Now firmly resolved not to do any more movie musicals, Astaire let it be known that he was employable as an actor, if anyone was interested. Two years passed and Stanley Kramer offered him a supporting part in *On the Beach*, which proved that he could indeed turn in a respectable job of straight acting. However, Astaire's resolve to be free of dancing came to a halt that same year, 1959, when television producer Bud Yorkin faced him with the idea of doing a video hour called "An Evening with Fred Astaire," which would review highlights in his career. It was a case of *carte blanche*—Astaire could do the show on any terms, he could be the executive producer and hire anybody he liked.

The first person hired was Hermes Pan, who brought in a young lady named Barrie Chase. Her impact on both the show and Astaire was considerable. As Adele Astaire put it, "She vibrated him, as he'd say. Filled him full of vibes. I think that's what happened. She was so inspiring to him and was such a beautiful dancer. And a little temperamental too, which he liked. So they got along beautifully." Whatever it was, it resulted in the most critically and publicly acclaimed television production of 1959. A year later came "Another Evening with Fred Astaire," and the year after "Astaire Time." In all, the three shows garnered some forty awards.

What the three television shows proved, among other things, was that Astaire's career was a vital part of the history of American music. It was now clearly apparent that there were no less than thirty major standard songs with which he was identified; all he had to do was break into the first line of any of them and there was instant applause. In his song "You're the Top," Cole Porter had included the line, "You're the nimble tread of the feet of Fred Astaire." Perhaps it was his way of saying he was grateful, as were Kern and Berlin and all the others.

Any kind of praise embarrasses Astaire, and possibly the most embarrassment he has ever received in one sitting came his way the evening of April 10, 1981, when he was awarded the American Film Institute's Life Achievement Award. Much of Hollywood's royalty attended the gala, televised gathering. The master of ceremonies, Astaire's friend David Niven, began the evening by saying, "Fred, this is going to be hell for you—but it's going to be heaven for us." The remark was followed by two hours of proof. But nothing said that evening could beat the opening lines of the song Harry Warren and Johnny Mercer had written for him in *The Belle of New York*:

> *I wanna be a dancin' man,*
> *While I can,*
> *Gonna leave my footprints on the sands of time...*

BUSBY BERKELEY

The man who made the most electrifying and lasting impact on motion picture choreography was not a qualified choreographer or even much of a dancer. But he had in plenty the most essential attribute of a choreographer: inventiveness. Basically, the choreographer must come up with ideas and figure out ways to present them — and, in that respect, Busby Berkeley carved his own niche in the movie business. Besides being copious, his ideas were ornate, florid, amusing, and sometimes bordering on the vulgar. They were also astonishingly geometric. Had he operated in the academic community Berkeley would probably have been a master mathematician.

In later years, when retrospective showings of his movies developed a cult following, Berkeley found his work—those weird and wonderful dance numbers in pictures like *Gold Diggers of 1933, 1935,* and *1937*—described as surrealistic. Berkeley, a man of very ordinary education, would probably have had to look the word up. Upon learning that it had something to do with art being affected by the activities of the subconscious mind, he then would have sagely agreed with this critical assessment of his talent. Berkeley had bluffed his way into fame and, in those last years when admiring attention finally put him in the spotlight's glare, he was not about to change.

A brash and breezy kind of man, Busby Berkeley always operated on nerve, sometimes on sheer gall. By the time he became dance director for the Rodgers and Hart musical *A Connecticut Yankee* in 1927, he was known on Broadway as a man with endless ideas for dance routines — yet even by that time in his career he had never studied dancing or even taken a dancing lesson. Working on his first major show, he began to worry that his bluff might be called. Years later Berkeley confessed, "The second act opened with Queen Guinevere's dancing class in the castle. I thought it would be a good ploy to start the scene with the Queen teaching the class the first five positions of dance. The trouble was I didn't even know the first position, let alone the others. So I walked around the stage rubbing my head and pretending I was thinking up something. I said to one of the girls, 'I think I'll have the Queen start off by showing the first position.' She said, 'Oh, you mean this,' and pointed her feet in a certain way. I looked out the corner of my eye to see what she was doing and then pointed to another girl, 'Second position,' and so on. In this way, and without their knowing it, I learned the first five positions of dance."

One of the first reviews of *A Connecticut Yankee* informed its readers, "A new dance director has been born on Broadway." Berkeley doubtlessly chuckled to himself. He was then thirty-two and he had long learned that the best way to get ahead in life is to learn by doing, and, more important, to give the impression that there is no doubt that one knows what one is doing. Born to theatrical parents in Los Angeles in November 1895, Berkeley grew up trailing around with touring companies. It was not a life that either parent recommended, and at the age of twelve Busby was enrolled in the Mohegan Lake Military Academy, near Peekskill, New York, where he was to remain for five years. Little did they

Dames (Warners, 1934). This overhead shot, possibly Berkeley's most famous, was just one of several in his staging of "I Only Have Eyes for You." Page 104: Berkeley (in white) lines up his shots for "The Lady in the Tutti-Frutti Hat," possibly the weirdest of his lavish production numbers, in *The Gang's All Here* (Fox, 1943).

"Those dancing feet" take over the avenue known as *42nd Street* (Warners, 1933).

know that this move would have the most profound influence on his life as a choreographer. It takes very little study of Berkeley's work to realize that it is basically military—it is all based on drill formations.

Berkeley joined the army when America went to war in 1917 and became a lieutenant in the artillery. While stationed in France, Berkeley discovered the talent that would make him famous years later. One of his duties was to conduct parade drill, and it was typical of Berkeley to go beyond regulation lines. He asked for permission to try something new. "I had worked out a trick drill for twelve hundred men. I explained the movements by numbers and gave the section leaders instructions for their companies and had them do the whole thing without any audible orders. Since the routines were numbered the men could count out their measures once they learned them. It was quite something to see a parade square full of squads and companies of men marching in patterns in total silence. The French Army asked if it would be possible for me to do the same for them but our people refused permission."

Following the armistice, Berkeley's parade-ground talents were utilized in entertaining the now largely idle troops before they could be shipped home. The YMCA sent over groups of entertainers and Berkeley helped organize shows in the camps. This convinced Berkeley that being a stage director was what he really wanted to do. He was in the right place at the right time. The officer put in charge of entertainment admitted to Berkeley that he knew nothing about show business and asked him to take over the program. For more than a year Berkeley toured with his army show throughout France and Germany, getting a good apprenticeship in show business at army expense.

Once back in New York as a civilian Berkeley quickly found work, not as a director but as an actor in a road company production. He was not so much an actor as a personality — breezy, feisty, the kind of man who would tackle anything. For years he bounced from show to show, mostly in comedic parts. If nothing else was available, he was not averse to taking a job as an assistant to the director. Berkeley might not have been much of an actor but he could always

Filming the opening number of *Gold Diggers of 1933* (Warners, 1933), "We're in the Money," with Ginger Rogers front and center.

be counted on to come up with ideas, as well as the nerve to put them through. In the summer of 1923, while directing a show in Paterson, New Jersey, to spike up flagging business he flew over the city with a stunt pilot, releasing balloons that contained free tickets. The real attention-getter, though, was Berkeley himself: with his legs locked around a wing strut, he hung upside down. This fearlessness served him well in Hollywood, when he would stroll sixty feet up along the rafters of sound stages to plot his bizarre choreography.

Berkeley's career during the first half of the twenties included all manner of jobs as performer and director in the New York hinterland. In 1925, he finally won a Broadway assignment, as the dance director for a musical called *Holka-Polka*. By now he had earned a reputation for choosing and working with chorus lines of attractive girls. Several such assignments followed, until *A Connecticut Yankee* brought him a new level of recognition.

He worked on five Broadway musicals in 1928, including Rodgers and Hart's *Present Arms,* in which he played a lead-

ing role besides organizing the dances. The talent for organizing dances — a talent that Berkeley himself could never explain — received high praise with his next job, *The Earl Carroll Vanities of 1928,* in which he now started to deploy girls in the fanciful phalanxes that would mark his movies a few years later. One New York critic noted, "He creates none of these dances in advance; in fact his inspiration seems to come from having the girls in front of him on the stage ready for work." It would be the same in Hollywood.

By the end of the twenties Berkeley was considered one of the four top dance directors on Broadway, along with Bobby Connolly, Seymour Felix, and Sammy Lee. Then Berkeley got his first job as the sole director of a musical, the Shubert production of *The Street Singer,* which opened in September 1929 and ran for several months. The notices began to get a little more prestigious. Gilbert Seldes wrote, "The dances Busby Berkeley arranged for *The Street Singer* were so numerous, intricate, exciting and well done that nothing else in the show mattered...."

When sound came to the movies, Hollywood sent all its

scouts to raid Broadway of the talent it needed to make the musicals that it churned out in those infant years. The William Morris Agency asked Berkeley if it could represent him for films. He declined, saying that he was not only doing well in New York but that he had not been impressed with what he had seen on the screen. Only when he was promised the position of dance director on Samuel Goldwyn's filming of the Eddie Cantor stage musical *Whoopee* did Berkeley head for the West Coast.

Goldwyn told Berkeley that he was pleased to have him on this first musical to be made at his studio, and asked him what the first step should be. Berkeley replied, "Girls," to which Goldwyn blushed and assured him of open choice. Berkeley went on to explain that it was not simply a matter of picking girls with pretty faces and shapely limbs, they more importantly had to have intelligence, coordination, the ability to execute intricate routines, and stamina — especially the latter, since the work was long and tiring. Goldwyn advised him to take whatever time he needed to get his girls and his bearings, to wander around the studio and observe.

Berkeley's observations of picture-making caused him to shudder inwardly at how complicated it was and how little he knew about it. He said, "I realized, of course, that the technique was entirely different from the stage. In pictures you see everything through the eye of the camera. Unlike the theater, where your eyes can roam at will, the director and the cameraman decide where the viewer will look. It was obvious to me that film musicals so far had been disappointing because no one thought of imaginative things to do with the camera. With my reputation as a man who came up with unique ideas, I now desperately tried to think of some. My total ignorance of photography and the completely alien environment made it difficult to keep up a facade of assurance."

It was Richard Day, the art director of *Whoopee,* who gave Berkeley the advice that moved him out of doubt and into the kind of inventiveness for which he soon became acclaimed. Day pointed out that the camera has only one eye, not two, and that if Berkeley held a hand over one eye he could get a clear idea of what the camera saw. This was enough to trigger Berkeley's concept of how to focus on the dancing and how to make the camera a participant in the action, not simply something that sat back from a distance and observed. So far in the making of movies the job of the dance director had been to devise the routines and then let

Footlight Parade (Warners, 1933). "By a Waterfall," a lavish piece of cinematic, aquatic fantasy.

the film's director shoot them. Berkeley told Goldwyn that this was not the way he wanted to work; he wanted to direct his material. Goldwyn hedged and asked Berkeley if he thought he could handle such a job. Replied Berkeley, characteristically, "Mr. Goldwyn, I don't *think* I can — I *know* I can."

Berkeley's learn-by-doing process received a jolt on the first day of shooting *Whoopee*. He recalled, "When I walked on the set I saw four cameras and four crews. This was something else I didn't know about, and I asked my assistant for an explanation. He told me the standard technique was for a routine to be shot from four directions and that the cutter would assemble the shots, make a selection and put the scene together. With another show of confidence I announced, 'Oh? Well, it's not my technique. I use only one camera, so let the others go.' I finally got my way, and during my entire career in films I have never used more than one camera on anything. My idea was to plan every shot and edit in the camera."

Samuel Goldwyn looked on with some trepidation as Berkeley plowed ahead with his own ideas. He could not understand why Berkeley moved in for close-ups of the chorus girls, until Berkeley explained, "Well, we've got all these beautiful girls in the picture, why not let the public see them?" Goldwyn immediately grasped this logic. It was also in *Whoopee* that Berkeley first used his overhead shots, bringing the camera up high to look down on the routines as if they were moving diagrams. Those Berkeley diagrams became more and more complicated in the films that followed, resembling somewhat — well ahead of its time — the stop-frame photography of blossoming flowers.

By the time *Whoopee* was released in late 1930, the vogue for movie musicals was already beginning to peter out. They were more expensive and difficult to make than the average movie, and the public, having sated itself on the glut of musicals, found them increasingly harder to stomach. With fewer job offers coming his way, Berkeley went back to New York to work on *Sweet and Low*. Goldwyn called him again to Hollywood to devise the dance numbers for two more filmings of Eddie Cantor shows, *Palmy Days* and *The Kid from Spain*. Similar assignments on a few more pictures followed, all with squads of dancing girls and ingenious camera movements, but Berkeley was getting tired of it. By 1932 movie musicals had reached the inglorious status of box-office poison, and Berkeley considered a permanent return to Broadway.

Wonder Bar (Warners, 1934). Berkeley's octagon of mirrors multiplies the dancers doing "Don't Say Goodnight" to infinity.

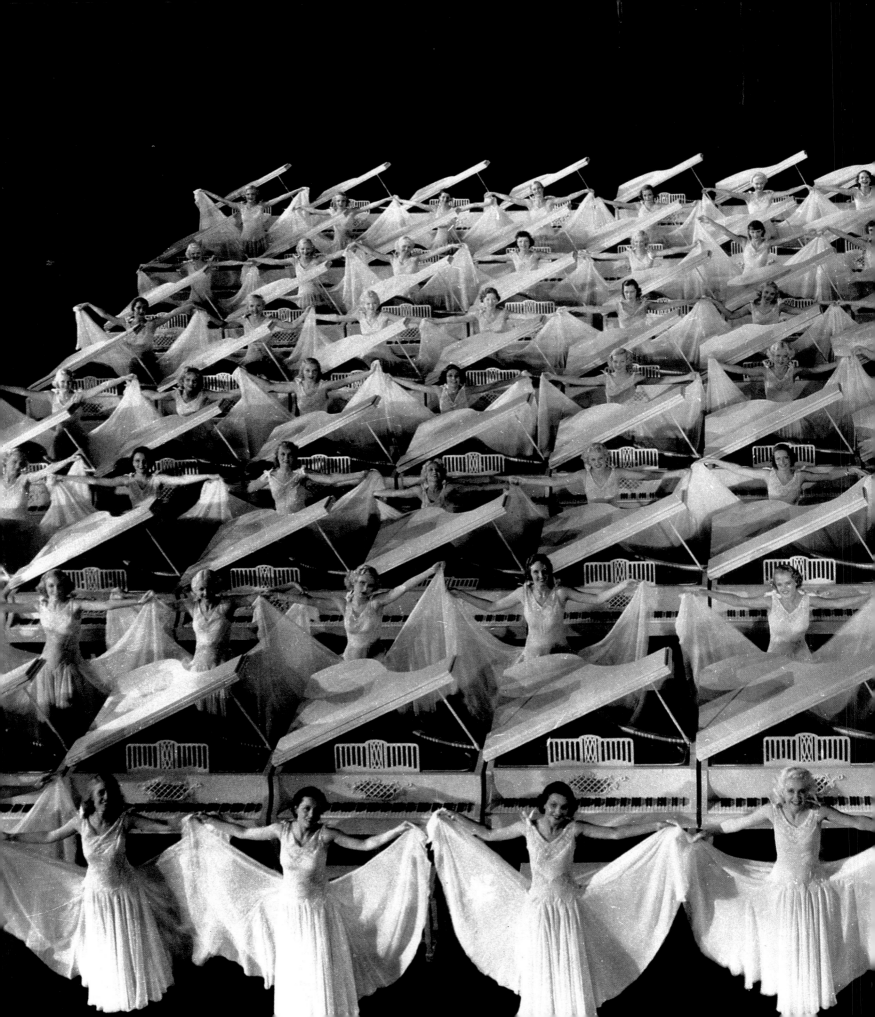

But the big turning point in his career was on hand — a turning point that affected not only him but the whole concept and future of musicals on film. Darryl F. Zanuck, the dynamic young head of production at Warners in 1933, had bought the studio a property called *42nd Street*. Although it was all about theater people and show biz, Zanuck convinced his employers that it was not really a musical but a good, solid, romantic, dramatic story. It would, of course, contain some dancing, so why not get the best dance director in town? The brothers Warner decided to take a chance. *42nd Street* not only pulled them out of the red and into the black but it launched them on a series of large-scale musicals, almost all of them involving Berkeley and the songwriting team of composer Harry Warren and lyricist Al Dubin. By the time *42nd Street* was edited, Berkeley, Warren, and Dubin had pocketed seven-year contracts.

Having a big budget and plenty of resources on hand triggered ever more fantastic ideas from Berkeley. In *42nd Street* he devised a finale for the title song with a device he would use over and over again, that of telling a story with people and places, like a little film within the film. Ruby Keeler comes on the screen in close-up, then the camera pulls back to reveal her tap-dancing not on a stage but on top of a taxi. The camera keeps pulling back, disclosing an enormous set filled with all the bustle and hubbub of the intersection of Broadway and 42nd Street. All kinds of people are doing all kinds of things — traffic goes by, vendors ply their goods, people look out of windows and go in and out of buildings, courting couples go hand in hand, and the police keep their eyes on the rich, the poor, the crooked, and the innocent. To

Gold Diggers of 1935 (Warners, 1935). Berkeley weighs the girls chosen for the chorus as his assistant Eddie Larkin notes the poundage (above). In the production number "The Words Are in My Heart" (left), fifty-six lovely pianists waltz with their mobile pianos.

end the sequence, Berkeley has his fifty girls banked on a giant staircase, each girl holding a huge card in the shape of a glittering building. The whole skyline of Manhattan seems to dance in rhythm.

The cost-conscious executives of Warners got some idea of what the fertile imagination of Busby Berkeley was going to do to their budgets when they watched him devising his ideas for "Shuffle Off to Buffalo." Not about to settle for a nice, big dance number, he insisted on another scenario. "Since it was a honeymoon song, I had them build me a Pullman train carriage, one that would split down the middle as I moved my camera into the interior. I was then stuck for an idea of what to do once I got inside. I sat for three days in front of the set, and then during a lunch break it came to me, and what you see on the screen—the action inside the Pullman—was staged that afternoon."

Berkeley neglected to mention that as he sat around for three days so did all the dancers and technicians — and Warner executives, biting their nails. The studio invested four hundred thousand dollars in *42nd Street,* then a large budget, and had the film failed the studio would have been in danger of closing. But the success was enormous and not only revitalized the studio but touched off the era of the Hollywood musical, an era that would enjoy a good twenty years of creativity and productivity.

For *Gold Diggers of 1933,* an immediate follow-up, Berkeley was expected to come up with some more bright ideas. They exceeded anyone's expectations. The film opens with Ginger Rogers leading several dozen girls, dressed in skimpy costumes seemingly made out of silver dollars, as they trot around singing "We're in the Money"—which is possibly what the Warner executives were singing in their offices. Impressive as it was, it was dwarfed a reel or so later by "Pettin' in the Park," in which squads of amorous boys and girls do just that. Like so many of his routines, this one — which includes girls changing their underwear in silhouette — is pleasingly vulgar, but for the next number he opted to be classy. "The Shadow Waltz," with Harry Warren's beguiling melody, is perhaps the nearest Berkeley came to ballet in his movie career.

Twenty-four girls gracefully swirl around in three-quarter time, all the while pretending to play violins, as Berkeley photographs them from a variety of angles, including, at one point, a vertical split screen in which the girls appear to be dancing up the middle on both sides. Then Berkeley turns out the lights and we find that the violins are neon-lit around the edges, as are the bows. Somewhat surrealistically, the violins waltz to the melody and inevitably form geometric patterns, photographed from above. The idea came to Berkeley when he recalled a girl dancing while playing the violin at the Palace in New York. When he found out from a studio electrician that it was possible to wire his girls with portable batteries and place neon strips around the frames of the violins, the idea blossomed into what would result in a startlingly visual production.

Footlight Parade was next, another backstage musical and a natural for Berkeley's concepts of what a stage director might come up with if he had a theater the size of Central Park. "By a Waterfall" required an entire sound stage to be turned into an Art Deco swimming pool, complete with glass sides so that Berkeley could film the girls in their rhythmic contortions under water. This elaborate aquacade involves a hundred girls and runs close to a quarter of an hour, climaxing with a huge human fountain. It would have made a splendid ending for the film, but Berkeley had another idea in mind for that: "Shanghai Lil."

Happily, this brought James Cagney onstage to dance (as the director who has to replace his drunken leading man at the last minute). Playing a sailor, among many, he swaggers into a Shanghai bar, where he joins Ruby Keeler in some nifty tap-dancing on top of a bar. Then the bugle blows, calling the men to arms, and Berkeley really comes into his own, using for the first time on film the military drill he had concocted in France. A fair portion of the United States Navy then marches in kaleidoscopic patterns all over the set.

At this point, Berkeley acquired the title "The Million-Dollar Dance Director." This referred not to the money his film routines cost Warner Bros. but to a court case brought by Samuel Goldwyn against Warners. Goldwyn rightly claimed that he had Berkeley under contract for one more picture and that his Warner work was keeping him from it. The settlement called for Berkeley to go to the Goldwyn studio to do *Roman Scandals.* Then back to Warners and *Wonder Bar* (1934), which involved an incredible piece of cinematic imagination on his part. For the song "Don't Say Goodnight," he dreamed up a set made up of eight huge mirrors facing inward, in which he placed one hundred dancers. With reflections stretching into infinity, they seem like thousands. He was told by ace cameraman Sol Polito that it would be impossible to film inside this octagon of mirrors without the camera being seen. Berkeley explained the way to do it, and it was done.

By now Busby Berkeley was looked upon as a kind of mad fool from whom wildly wonderful ideas sprang with ease. He claimed that some of the ideas came to him as he lay in his bath in the early morning, with the result that when he bounced into the studio with some fantastic concept the cry would be, "Oh, Buzz has just had a bath." The ideas certainly were fantastic; in *Fashions of 1934,* a pageant

The most acclaimed of all Berkeley's numbers, "The Lullaby of Broadway," in *Gold Diggers of 1935* (Warners, 1935).
Below: Berkeley's busy finale for *Varsity Show* (Warners, 1937).

of ostrich plumes decorated with fifty lovely girls form a Hall of Human Harps, a Web of Dreams, and Venus with her Galley Slaves; in *Gold Diggers of 1935,* fifty-six white grand pianos, each played by a pretty girl, waltz across a black floor in graceful, curving arcs; and in the same film, squads of tap dancers gradually fill the screen like a slow tidal wave, until finally there are a hundred of them beating out "The Lullaby of Broadway," photographed in serried ranks on a vast set of wide stairs and photographed in a torrent of camera angles. It is, perhaps, the best thing Berkeley ever did. (It was his own favorite.) It brought Harry Warren and Al Dubin an Oscar for the best song of the year. In the same year, the Academy of Motion Picture Arts and Sci-

Ziegfeld Girl (MGM, 1941). Tony Martin sings "You Stepped Out of a Dream," and among those emerging are Hedy Lamarr (left) and Lana Turner. Opposite: In *Strike Up the Band* (MGM, 1940), Mickey Rooney, Judy Garland, and many similarly energetic youngsters "Do the Conga."

ences instituted a new category, one for Dance Direction. Berkeley was nominated for his "Lullaby of Broadway" number, but to the amazement of many in Hollywood he lost to Dave Gould, who was given the Oscar for his work on two pictures, *Moulin Rouge* and *Broadway Melody of 1936.*

Despite the accolades, Berkeley was not content to be known merely as the inventor of elaborate pieces of cinematic choreography. He wanted to be a full-fledged director of movies, and he kept after Jack Warner until he was given an assignment as such, a minor musical with Dolores Del Rio titled *I Live for Love* (1935). It did not live long at the box office. In the four remaining years of Berkeley's Warner contract, he had several other directing jobs, but it was still

as the concocter of dance numbers that both his employers and the public looked to him.

In 1936 he was given his first job directing a major musical, *Stage Struck,* which capitalized on the fact that its stars, Dick Powell and Joan Blondell, had just become man and wife in real life. Dick and Joan were next shunted into *Gold Diggers of 1937,* for which Berkeley was assigned to invent a spectacular finale, although with the caution that it was not to cost too much. Berkeley picked up the challenge by using a sound stage that required nothing more than a shiny black floor and seventy girls — in white, of course — marching around with flags and drums in almost endless military drills while singing "All's Fair in Love and War." Replete with some trick photography, it became yet another stunner.

The last truly stunning Berkeley invention for Warners was the finale of *Varsity Show* in 1937, and he was proud of it. "The set covered a whole sound stage. It centered on a giant staircase fifty feet high and sixty feet long, on which I paraded my entire company of several hundred girls and boys. The object of the number was to salute the leading colleges and universities, and in my overhead shots I had them form the initials and insignias as Fred Waring and his band played the appropriate music. It was an exhausting number to rehearse and stage but well worth the effort because it brought down the house almost everywhere it was shown."

Possibly as a reward for *Varsity Show,* Warners next gave Berkeley his biggest job yet as a director, *Hollywood Hotel* (1937), which contained a lot of songs but no spectacular settings. The film is mostly remembered for introducing the Johnny Mercer-Richard Whiting "Hooray for Hollywood," which remains the best song ever written about the movie business. The following year he devised some fairly impressive dance routines for *Gold Diggers in Paris* (1938), as well as directing other kinds of pictures. This, however, did not satisfy Warners. As far as the studio was concerned, the wave of the musical film had crested and plunged down. It was content to let other studios pick up the musical ball and carry it in other directions. Berkeley's contract was not renewed, and neither was Dick Powell's. Powell, who had appeared in some thirty Warner musicals, ten with Berkeley, was happy to leave and look for different types of pictures. Composer Harry Warren, with a Fox contract waiting for him, had nothing to worry about.

The kind of wildness that marked Busby Berkeley's film work also spilled over into his private life. By the time he left Warners he had been divorced three times — with another three wives upcoming — and he had been charged in a well-publicized manslaughter case of killing three people in a car accident in September 1935. Accused of drunken driving, he

Babes on Broadway (MGM, 1941). The title song. Not exactly Broadway, this is part of the MGM backlot that always passed for New York.

was acquitted when his lawyer convinced the jury that the crash had actually been caused by a blowout of one of Berkeley's tires. It was, however, a harbinger of more personal chaos to come. Berkeley enjoyed living well but was not provident with his money and assets. However, his career showed no sign of letup when he left Warners in 1939; MGM immediately offered him the assignment of creating the finale for the Jeanette MacDonald musical *Broadway Serenade,* which led to a contract with the studio.

In joining MGM Berkeley stipulated that he wanted work as a director as well as a choreographer, and that he wanted films other than musicals besides. MGM obliged, but Berkeley got no further in his directing career than he had at Warners. He was a good but not outstanding director; it is only his large-scale musical numbers that have lasting value.

He got off to a good start directing Mickey Rooney and Judy Garland in *Babes in Arms,* resulting in two more simi-

The finale of *Girl Crazy* (MGM, 1943), to the strains of Gershwin's "I Got Rhythm," with Tommy Dorsey, Judy Garland, Mickey Rooney, and fifty or so dancers.

larly buoyant musicals with them, *Strike Up the Band* and *Babes on Broadway.* All three films are fast-paced and full of movement, and all are about youngsters putting on shows. As such, they are the best of their kind. However, When MGM had a really big musical lined up it did exactly as Warners had done and asked Berkeley to come up with some lavish, spectacular creations. At MGM money was no object, and, unlike at Warners, whose more frugal executives paced the edges of his sets, Berkeley was given free reign.

The Rooney-Garland musicals contained more dancing than the massive Warner production numbers, and the putting-on-a-show numbers made much more sense in terms of logistics. The charm of these films is the kinetic energy with which Berkeley charged them, the best example being the "Hoe Down" routine in *Babes on Broadway.* Mickey, Judy, and several dozen other high-spirited youngsters step, bounce, and leap around minute after minute.

Berkeley's own level of energy must have been at an all-time high during this year, 1941, because he also created and directed the dance numbers for two of MGM's biggest musicals, *Ziegfeld Girl* and *Lady Be Good.* In the former he directed Judy Garland and an ensemble of two hundred in the elaborate calypso "Minnie from Trinidad," and for the grand finale he came up with a flight of fancy built around the song "You Stepped Out of a Dream."

Berkeley was especially proud of this creation. "We saw this as a chance to present beautiful girls as visions in dreams. Adrian outdid himself with his costumes for this number, as did Cedric Gibbons with his set — immense sixty-foot-high spiral staircases in gold and silver, adorned with massive cut-glass chandeliers and fantastic trimmings. Each girl emerged from a misty cloud effect, dripping with silver sequins. With all due respect to the master, Ziegfeld could never have done on a stage what we did in that finale."

Lady Be Good brought Berkeley into contact with Eleanor Powell, and MGM looked to him to come up with something wonderful for their super dancer. He did. For her "Fascinatin' Rhythm" routine he devised a set that called for huge silver-beaded curtains zig zagging all over the place, eight grand pianos on various levels, and one hundred male dancers in top hats and tuxedos and carrying canes. Berkeley and Powell disappointed no one with this union. The studio rewarded him with the direction of the film that brought Gene Kelly to the movies, *For Me and My Gal,* and then assigned him the job of inventing a finale for its production of *Girl Crazy* (1943), starring Rooney and Garland in an updating of the 1930 Gershwin musical. He built the finale around the song "I Got Rhythm," turning it into a terpsichorean rodeo.

In *Gold Diggers of 1933* (Warners, 1933), Berkeley's beauties do "The Shadow Waltz."

Girl Crazy completed Berkeley's contract at MGM. He next accepted an offer from 20th Century-Fox to take on the complete direction of *The Gang's All Here* (1943), with the understanding that it would include some lavish production numbers. It was the first time Berkeley had the chance to work with Technicolor, and he met the challenge with the enthusiasm of a toreador getting a crack at the world's best bull. People had often wondered what his fantastic Warners routines might have looked like had they been shot in color. They now had the chance to find out. It was the era of wartime escapist entertainment and Berkeley was in his glory. *The Gang's All Here* is the most characteristic of all his work on film, and it is also a tribute to the talent of cinematographer Edward Cronjager that he was able to implement Berkeley's incredible ideas.

For his opening number, "The Lady in the Tutti-Frutti Hat," Berkeley built a set resembling a South Seas island and sprinkled it with sixty lovely girls in undulating lines. At one point he uses huge bananas to make strange, erotic formations. The star off this routine, the tiny but abundantly energetic Carmen Miranda, had her immense headdress knocked off by Berkeley's swooping camera crane in an accident that might have badly injured her. Berkeley liked to ride his huge camera boom like a dive bomber coming in for attack. It resulted in some stunning photography but it understandably made the actors nervous. After the narrow miss, Carmen yelled, "That man ees crazee," which no one so far had reason to doubt.

The finale of *The Gang's All Here* is the apex of the Busby Berkeley film career. Here his love affair with the kaleidoscope found its full expression. "The Polka Dot Polka" uses incredible photographic devices, including water curtains tinted with changing colors and, as in *Wonder Bar*, effects devised with the use of huge mirrors. "I built a set with two mirrors fifty feet high and fifteen feet wide which together formed a V design. In the center of this I had a revolving platform eighteen feet in diameter and as I took the camera up between these two mirrors, the girls on the revolving platform below formed an endless design of symmetrical forms. In another shot I dropped from above sixty neon-lighted hoops which the girls caught and used in their dance maneuvers."

The Gang's All Here should have led to more and equally good opportunities. That it did not was due to the chaotic nature of Berkeley's private life. In early 1944 he returned to Warners to direct the insignificant *Cinderella Jones*, but he spoiled his relationship with Jack Warner by arrogantly demanding that on all future projects he be the producer as well as director. Warner canceled the contract.

Berkeley then returned to Broadway to direct *Glad to See You*, a title that turned out to be bitterly wrong. It flopped. So too did his fourth marriage. On top of all this, his eighty-year-old mother, to whom he had always been very closely attached, contracted pneumonia and then cancer. By the time of her death in June 1946, Berkeley had not worked on a film in two years and had spent a great deal of money trying to keep her alive. Also by that time a fifth marriage had gone by the boards, a situation greatly aggravated by his lapsing into debt on his income taxes. Berkeley attempted suicide by slashing his throat and wrists, but he was found and rushed to a hospital. Long periods in psychopathic wards followed as he slowly recovered his health.

It was not until 1948 that Berkeley was able to resume his film career. Through the aid of George Amy, who had been Berkeley's editor on most of his Warners hits, he was hired by Warners as an assistant on *Romance on the High Seas*. With the apparent recovery of his abilities he received a call

During the shooting of "Fascinatin' Rhythm" in *Lady Be Good* (MGM, 1941), Berkeley has a little fun pretending to be Eleanor Powell's partner.

from Arthur Freed at MGM, who decided to take a chance and hand him the director's chair on *Take Me Out to the Ball Game.* Despite the success of the film and the praise for his work—it even brought him the Exhibitor's Laurel Award for 1949—the film turned out to be his final work as a director.

Again Berkeley was dogged by misfortune. Freed gave him a rich assignment, directing *Annie Get Your Gun,* with Judy Garland. After years of neurotic behavior and drug-taking to give her energy and to enable her to sleep, her health had gone from bad to worse. She had always been a little in awe of Berkeley's commanding manner, and now her behavior on the set became increasingly erratic, exacerbated by an apparent fear of Berkeley. The production collapsed; both Berkeley and Garland were replaced. For two people playing touch-and-go with mental health, it was a shattering experience.

MGM was more sympathetic toward Berkeley than toward Garland. After her *Annie* fiasco she never again worked for the studio, whereas Berkeley was called upon from time to time to devise production numbers. He occasionally worked for other studios as well. He did well with two Esther Williams extravaganzas — *Million Dollar Mermaid* in 1952 and *Easy to Love* the following year. For *Mermaid* he dreamed up a sequence to rival the aquatic wonders of "By a Waterfall." Here he had Esther rising from a huge water tank, under a canopy of four hundred streams of water that shot up thirty feet to form a massive waterfall. In another and even more spectacular number he had a hundred swimmers cavorting with flaming torches, swooping down large chutes, and leaping from overhead swings. Later he dropped Esther into a mass of swimmers from a height of fifty feet, with the swimmers exploding into a ferris wheel on the water. When Esther emerges from the water she is on a platform with ten lovely girls and hundreds of lighted sparklers.

For *Easy to Love* Berkeley took a large production team to the Cypress Gardens in Florida, where he applied his genius for military drill to squads of water-skiers whizzing all over in bizarre formations. For his most spectacular stunt, he put Esther on a trapeze hung from a helicopter (he also photographed it from a helicopter), from which she dives eighty feet into a V-shaped formation of skiers traveling at thirty-five miles per hour. Finally, after hurtling over innumerable ramps, Esther skies right up to the camera. It is amazing to think what effects Berkeley might have managed had 3-D been available to him at this time.

With the exception of a job in 1962 devising numbers for

Million Dollar Mermaid (MGM, 1952). Shades of "By a Waterfall," but this time in gorgeous Technicolor and with a gorgeous mermaid— Esther Williams.

Jumbo, Berkeley's movie career came to an end in 1954 after he staged the "Totem Tom-Tom" number in *Rose Marie.* This choreographic spectacle involved Joan Taylor and a hundred male dancers in an Indian ceremonial dance, but of a kind no Indian tribe had ever imagined. Said its proud creator, "We rehearsed this number for a month and used Stage 15 at MGM, then the largest sound stage in the world, turning it into a mountain stronghold. We tried to make the number as dramatic and frenzied as possible, and as the climax I had one of the Indians grab Joan, lift her over his head, and throw her from a cliff fifty feet high into the outstretched arms of the Indians below, who then bound her to a great totem pole. It was an exciting number to stage."

Having emerged from his personal troubles, Berkeley, at the age of sixty, was obviously in fine form as far as choreographic invention was concerned. The Esther Williams numbers and the *Rose Marie* dance had proved that quite clearly. Unfortunately, the times were now against him. By the mid-fifties the movie musical was a dying duck. Television had siphoned away the audiences, costs were rising, and, possibly worst of all, the film studios created their own toughest competition by leasing their old movies to television. Hollywood found it hard to compete with its past, and Busby Berkeley found it impossible to get work. It is difficult to think of any other industry in which a man so gifted and experienced could end up unemployed.

Berkeley had little luck in trying to adapt his talents to television. He did, however, finally find luck in marriage with wife number six, Etta Judd, who had been a friend for many years. With whatever funds he had left, and he had never been careful with money, they bought a modest home in Palm Desert, a few miles east of the celebrated Californian resort town of Palm Springs, and settled into retirement. With the passing of the years, Berkeley became a largely forgotten man.

But life still held some surprises in store for him. His past caught up with him in the wave of nostalgia that started to rise in the late sixties. In 1965 he was invited to attend the San Francisco Film Festival as part of a tribute to film directors. Requested to bring his favorite film, he chose *For Me and My Gal,* which met with great applause. Then the Museum of Modern Art in New York staged a full-scale tribute to him alone and called it "The Master Builder of the American Musical." Made up of clips from his most spectacular numbers, it put him squarely in the spotlight. It suddenly became apparent, as never before, just what Busby Berkeley's impact had been on the motion picture musical. The tribute was followed by others, not only in America but also in Europe, and suddenly the forgotten man became a cult figure.

Despite the adulation, Berkeley received no offers of work — until late 1970, when a group of New York producers and backers decided to test the nostalgia wave by refurbishing the 1925 Vincent Youmans musical *No, No, Nanette.* It was someone's inspiration not only to ask Berkeley to be the dance supervisor but also to hire the long-retired Ruby Keeler to head the cast. The seventy-five-year-old Berkeley was not in good health, and it quickly became apparent that not much could be demanded from him in the way of services. His supervision was largely confined to choosing the twenty-two chorus girls, after auditioning more than three hundred, and he was consulted about various matters regarding the staging of the dances. In truth, he was mostly used for name value. According to some sources, he was treated rather shabbily by the producers, who gradually ignored him when they realized he had little left of the vitality that had made the name they were now waving from banners.

Within a week of its opening on Broadway, *No, No, Nanette* was a certified smash hit. At the end of the first Broadway performance, comedienne Patsy Kelly led the white-haired, slow-moving Berkeley onstage — and the house exploded with applause. The audience chanted his name over and over and cheered. She hugged him and he cried, and it is possible that his mind was flooded with memories of the old Broadway and the old Hollywood.

If the producers of *Nanette* had been somewhat coldly calculating in using the Berkeley name, it did not much matter. More important was that it had brought him to the Broadway where he had started fifty years before and it had enabled him to end with a smash. Now he could go back to Palm Desert and really retire. After the hubbub had died down he did just that, until the end — March 14, 1976. That he had managed to make it to eighty, after a lifetime of bouncing between the heights and the depths and carving a name for himself in the most unlikely sort of way, probably surprised him a little. No one could have planned such a career and no brain other than his could have come up with all those incredible, surrealistic, fantastic ideas.

Busby Berkeley's contributions to the art of the movies, specifically to the art of film choreography, have been praised whenever the subject is discussed. Gene Kelly has this to say: "Berkeley showed what could be done with a movie camera. A lot of that is made fun of nowadays; sometimes laughed at. But he was the guy who tore away the proscenium arch. He tore it down for movie musicals. Many get credit for that but it was Berkeley who did it. And if anyone wants to learn what can be done with a movie camera, they should study every shot Busby Berkeley ever made. He did it all."

Small Town Girl (MGM, 1953). Ann Miller and the subterranean orchestra doing "I've Gotta Hear That Beat": Berkeley by way of Kafka. Below: The last of the lavish Berkeley production numbers, his staging of "Totem Tom-Tom" with Joan Taylor and scores of pseudo-Indians, in *Rose Marie* (MGM, 1954).

RAY BOLGER

When putting together *That's Dancing!*, producers Jack Haley, Jr., and David Niven, Jr., made a point of tracking down the almost legendary "lost" numbers that were edited out of certain MGM musicals of the Golden Era. Some of them were indeed lost and gone forever, probably stolen by zealous admirers, but quite a few of them still exist in unedited form in cans stored away in the MGM vaults. With the various changes in command over the years, and the subsequent economy measures brought in by new managers to clean up and clear out, the deleted numbers became ever harder to find. Loyal, veteran, film-loving employees took devious steps to save material that the new managers might not have valued.

The Great Ziegfeld (MGM, 1936), and the great Bolger's first time up in the movies. Preceding page: *Four Jacks and a Jill* (RKO, 1941). Bolger in his characteristic dance position.

By dint of long and patient searching, Haley and Niven managed to unearth quite a lot of missing footage. After viewing it they decided that little of it really merited inclusion in a compilation of the finest dancing sequences in the history of Hollywood. Says Haley, "It was interesting to look at all these forgotten, and for the most part unseen, numbers, but you could grasp immediately why they weren't used. They were good, sometimes very good, but they fell short of the excellence of the rest of the material. In collecting a vast amount of really fabulous material for *That's Dancing!*, David and I found ourselves making the same kind of decisions. And we ended up using only about four minutes or so of this previously unused footage."

In looking through footage long considered lost, Haley and Niven came across something on which they instantly agreed, even before the number had run its course. It was a dance Ray Bolger had done as the Scarecrow in *The Wizard of Oz*, after he meets Dorothy on the Yellow Brick Road and tells her about his woes, "I haven't got a brain—only straw." In this knockabout dance, the Scarecrow expressed his amiable brainlessness by hopping around on the road, bouncing off fences, and (aided by a wire) flying through the air. Bolger himself had forgotten about the dance, and, although he was pleased to have it included in *That's Dancing!*, he could understand why it had been taken out of *The Wizard of Oz*.

"The point about this or any film dance is that it fits the story, especially if it's a well-worked-out story like this one. What happened here was that the dance stopped the story for a couple of minutes. The Strawman had said all he had to say about himself in the song, and once Dorothy had agreed to take him along with her to see the Wizard, the dance wasn't necessary. It interrupted the flow—you couldn't go from the dance to the next piece of action without a jolt. If I'd been the producer I would probably have edited it out myself. But then, I'm the original Face on the Cutting Room Floor."

Film actors are prone to wail that some of their best work ends up on the cutting room floor. Bolger has genuine reason to groan about this factor of filmmaking, for a number of his dances, especially those done at MGM in his early years, did end up being edited out. This is particularly regrettable because Bolger has appeared in only a dozen films. That in itself is a sad fact, because he is undoubtedly the finest of American comic dancers. More to the point, he is the only American comic dancer to have gained star status. Bolger is quite unlike any other dancer.

Bolger has often been described as the past master of the art of being gracefully awkward. The humor of his dancing comes from his apparent confusion and lack of complete control of his body, especially of a pair of legs that seem unusually long in comparison with the rest of the body. The legs sometimes buckle, he seems to lose a little balance, his feet slip as if he had just trod on a banana skin, or he comes out of a spin somewhat in a tizzy. He smiles sheepishly. But it is, of course, all part of the Bolger act, an act that succeeds only because it is completely in control. It is comedic dancing, eccentric dancing, and Bolger has done it so well that it draws away from the fact that on occasion he has performed brilliantly as a straight dancer. His tap-dancing in *Stage Door Canteen* is among the finest pieces of tap work ever done in a film, and his dances with Anna Neagle in *Sunny* are not far short of Astaire caliber.

Identification has been a problem for Bolger. Dancers tend to regard him as a comedian and comedians look upon him as a dancer. He describes himself as a "dancing comedian," and he feels that not enough is understood about the correlation between dancing and acting. Bolger believes that all good acting, involving as it does body movement, is a form of dancing. He analyzes some of the great comedians in terms of dance: "Charlie Chaplin did every kind of dance to express comedy. The others were more specialized. To me Bobby Clark was pure tango; W. C. Fields was the old-fashioned shuffle; Eddie Cantor was an eccentric, quick with the feet; and Ed Wynn always reminded me of a little girl doing the 'Pizzicato Polka' at a recital and breaking down and giggling before she's through. Jack Benny was the hesitation waltzer, and Milton Berle is the fast buck-and-wing

man, trying to get as many steps as possible into a two-minute routine." This is how Bolger thinks of comedy as applied to dancing, and it is a valuable key to understanding his own work.

Because of his long legs and his slim build, Bolger gives the impression on film of being taller than he is. He is a fraction under five-foot-eleven, and in his heyday he danced at around one hundred and forty pounds. His face determined the course of his dancing career: ears large, parrot-like nose, chin receding toward the Adam's apple. It is an eccentric face, perfect for comedy. Bolger's feet are unusually small for a dancer (he wears a size seven-and-a-half shoe) and have been well cared for. In his dancing days he wore only cotton socks and threw each pair away at the end of the day, thinking that if washed and worn again they might shrink and irritate his toes. Taking advantage of the extremely long legs, Bolger devised the trick of projecting himself in the air, pulling up the legs, and seemingly remaining airborne for an improbable length of time. This made him a favorite subject for photographers, who loved to catch him in flight.

Ray Bolger was born in Dorchester, near Boston, on January 10, 1904, to what he describes as an ordinary, "non-show-biz" family. In his last years of high school he worked in the evenings and during the summers as a messenger for the First National Bank in Boston. After graduation he took on a succession of jobs, including working for the New England Life Insurance Company and the Kelly Peanut Company, plus a short interval trying to sell vacuum cleaners door to door. His interest in dancing came from seeing shows in theaters, but being unable to afford lessons he stood in the alley outside the O'Brien School of Dancing and did steps to whatever music he could hear coming through a ventilator.

This impressed a friend, who advised him to see an old gentleman who used to be a dancer but who was now employed as a watchman at the Boston Horticultural Hall, one Dinny Haley. Bolger learned the rudiments of dance from Haley and practiced at night on the marble floor of the Horticultural Hall. Haley was encouraging a number of young men at the same time; Bolger claims he was not the most promising pupil. "As a matter of fact, I was the slowest. My ears could hear the rhythms and I could do them, but I didn't want to do what the others did. I felt it in a different way. I imagine it was my build and my nervous temperament."

Bolger's first step in the direction of a career came when he was spotted by Senia Roussakoff. This man, who ran a ballet studio, suggested that Bolger take lessons. Since he could not pay for them but had had some experience work-

Opposite: *Rosalie* (MGM, 1937). Bolger rehearses with Eleanor Powell. Unfortunately, this dance didn't get into the picture. *Sweethearts* (MGM, 1938). In "Nanette and Her Wooden Shoes," Bolger leaped in the air (above) and danced with Jeanette MacDonald (below).

The Wizard of Oz (MGM, 1939). Judy Garland, Bolger, Bert Lahr, and Jack Haley encounter danger in the Land of Oz.

131

ing for a bank, Bolger performed bookkeeping services in exchange for free lessons. At a recital given by the more advanced Roussakoff students in 1922, Bolger, at the age of eighteen, got his first experience in front of an audience. He did a dance of his own invention, portraying an Oriental dope fiend in what he thought was a serious, solemn interpretation. The audience, however, found it funny and laughed, which fortunately impressed an impresario who was there looking for talent for his company, the Bob Ott Musical Comedy Repertory Company, a troupe that toured forty weeks a year throughout New England and neighboring states. Bolger spent two years with Ott, until one of the other actors, Ralph Sanford, suggested they break away and try their luck as a team on the vaudeville circuit. Calling themselves "A Pair of Nifties," they struggled through some miserable experiences before getting an audition and a short stay at the Rialto Theatre in New York.

The team disbanded when Sanford was offered a job as a single elsewhere. Bolger was able to stay on at the Rialto, which gave him enough nerve to continue as a single, and which led to vaudeville bookings in Buffalo. There he found a friend in Harold Arlen, then a musician and budding songwriter (some years later he would provide the music for *The Wizard of Oz*). They returned to New York together, and both found work in the same nightclub, Arlen in the band and Bolger as a dancer. There he was discovered by the Shuberts, who hired him for *The Merry Whirl* (afterward retitled *The Passing Show of 1926*). This brought him a mention, although without name, in a newspaper review: "A very baggy suit of clothes came out and whirled fantastically around. I never found out whether there really was anyone inhabiting the suit."

Several months later Bolger was chosen by the Shuberts for another show, *A Night in Paris*. He recalls, "In this one I was in a position where the audience had to be terribly alert to see me at all. I was placed behind a line of tall, stately chorus girls. For a fleeting moment, the line would open up, I would dance, and then the girls would close in on me again." He was, however, seen by someone of theatrical importance — Gus Edwards, who hired him for his revue *Ritz Carlton Nights*, a stint that lasted two years. The show brought about two major improvements in his life: it enabled him to develop as a comic, and while it was playing in Los Angeles Bolger met Gwen Rickard, who became Mrs. Ray Bolger in 1929. "I haven't made a move without her since."

Bolger's first Broadway appearance of importance was in *George White's Scandals of 1931*, and the show of 1932 also employed his talents. A bigger role in *Life Begins at 8:40* in 1934 advanced his identity as a distinct theatrical figure. One New York critic noted, "He is an engaging comedian whose dancing never fails to steam up the audience." Now came the big step — being hired by Rodgers and Hart for their *On Your Toes*, which opened at the Majestic Theatre in November 1936 and ran for 315 performances. *On Your Toes* was the first musical to introduce a modern ballet on Broadway, the arresting "Slaughter on Tenth Avenue," and the prestigious choreographer George Balanchine was brought in to direct it. And Ray Bolger danced it.

On Your Toes deals with a young hoofer whose vaudevillian parents persuade him to give up this kind of entertainment and take up serious ballet. His efforts at classical ballet are ludicrous until a composer friend hands him a modern work, and with this he scores a success. "Slaughter" is a satire on gangster stories. The hoofer and his girlfriend, running away from murderous crooks, take refuge in a Tenth Avenue café. The mobsters catch up with them and shoot the girl. The hoofer, dancing to elude the gangsters' bullets, keeps on with increasing desperation, rising to a frenzied climax, until the arrival of the police.

With a running time of eleven minutes, it was an exhausting number to perform. Bolger says he fainted a number of times backstage: "It was exhausting, not so much in the legs but in the stomach; it was hard to breathe correctly. Your legs you don't feel until afterward. They give way last." But it was worth all the effort, for *On Your Toes* was a major career breakthrough. Critics called him "the foremost eccentric dancer on our stage," and said that "the show is his from curtain rise to curtain fall." Someone also referred to him as "the jazz Nijinsky."

Ray Bolger was first seen on screen in *The Great Ziegfeld* (1936), in which William Powell played the acclaimed Flo Ziegfeld, the producer who, among other things, glorified the American Girl. MGM certainly glorified him in this lavish accounting of his career, with restagings of many of the songs and dances that had highlighted his own shows on Broadway. Seymour Felix was the choreographer. Bolger appeared in a single number, an elaborate stage re-creation of "You Gotta Pull Strings," doing his antic taps, splits, spins, and skids, surrounded by a flock of lovely chorus girls.

This number for *The Great Ziegfeld* was filmed before *On Your Toes* opened. After Bolger's great success with the Rodgers and Hart show, MGM brought him back and signed him to a contract, which allowed him to return occasionally to the stage but not to work for other movie studios. His first assignment was *Rosalie* (1937), which gave him third billing after Nelson Eddy and Eleanor Powell. If this prospect excited him, he was soon to learn about the ways of picture-making, which could reduce third billing to a small part, especially in a mammoth musical accenting a lot of Eddy singing and Powell dancing.

The Wizard of Oz (MGM, 1939). On that Yellow Brick Road, with Judy Garland.
The Wicked Witch (Margaret Hamilton) keeps an eye on them (below).

Bolger played a West Point cadet, the comic sidekick of the hero, but he found himself heavily cut from the two-hour film in the editing. What remained were a few bits of military hoofing and one dance around some crates of fireworks, which causes them to go off. At the Hollywood première of *Rosalie* Bolger was surprised to find himself missing from the parts he had most enjoyed doing, and that with the editing he seemed to be constantly shooting in and out of the picture. This was noticed by a woman sitting in front of him, who asked after one fleeting appearance, "Where'd he go?" Bolger leaned forward and said, "Back to New York, lady."

The Jeanette MacDonald-Nelson Eddy musical *Sweethearts* (1938) was his next assignment. The first of the team's pictures in Technicolor, it used the Victor Herbert operetta of the same name as the basis for a backstage story about a happily married pair of musical comedy stars, whose long-running hit is *Sweethearts*. Bolger was given not a running part but a single production number. In the Herbert original it was called "Jeanette and Her Wooden Shoes," but because of MacDonald it was changed to "Nanette..." George Wright and Robert Forrest provided the new lyrics, which had Bolger as a Dutch boy courting Nanette: "Nanette and I have got a plan/ Here's hoping nothing wrecks it./ While you make all the music you can/ Nanette and I will exit." The stage consists of a large windmill, surrounded by tulip gardens on a hill and paths plunging down to center stage. In company with two dozen girls, Bolger enters and shoots down the main path, then out into the theater on a runway, doing his aerial leaps. He returns to the stage for a staccato tap dance. MacDonald enters and sings, and then joins Bolger in a jaunty trot dance. This pleasing number was choreographed by Albertina Rasch, the resident mistress of ballet at MGM and the wife of composer Dimitri Tiomkin.

Despite the success of *Sweethearts* and his "Wooden Shoes" number, Bolger found himself with a lot of time on his hands between pictures. MGM had nothing for him until *The Wizard of Oz* went into production in late 1938. In the spring of that year he had been informed that the studio wanted him for the film, which came as no surprise, but he was disappointed to learn that it wanted him to play the Tin Woodman. Bolger was well acquainted with L. Frank Baum's classic children's story, largely because he had long idolized Fred Stone, who had played the Strawman in the original Broadway presentation, which Bolger had seen as a child.

Bolger argued that playing the Tin Woodman, in a metal suit, would restrict his essentially loose style of dancing but that the soft costume of the Strawman was stylistically right

for him. In fact, he had done a strawman dance in a previous stage show. It took a while to persuade the executives. Finally Bolger devised a dance to prove his point. They had assigned Buddy Ebsen to the role of the Strawman, but Ebsen readily agreed to switch to the part of the Tin Woodman, saying that he was so pleased to be in *Oz* that he did not much care which part he played. Sadly for him, it was a disastrous decision. When Ebsen was made up for the part he found he was severely allergic to the aluminum powder used to cover the tin suit. Particles of aluminum got into his lungs and he was rushed to the hospital. The role went to Jack Haley.

Bert Lahr was brought in to play the Cowardly Lion, completing the trio of character players who join Dorothy on the Yellow Brick Road as she goes to see the Wizard. If the film is a classic, it is due not only to Judy Garland's lovely performance as Dorothy but also to the work done by Bolger, Haley, and Lahr, all of whom were ex-vaudevillians. However, none could ever look back on the filming without recalling the great discomfort they underwent because of the difficult costumes they were required to wear throughout the lengthy filming of the picture. *The Wizard of Oz* is one of the most magical movies ever made, but this magic was arrived at only through enormous efforts on the part of its planners, its manufacturers, its crews, and its cast.

The costumes and the makeup worn by Bolger, Haley, and Lahr required more than an hour to put on when they arrived at the studio early in the morning, sometimes at seven, and they took almost as much time to remove late in the afternoon or evening. A plaster cast was made of Bolger's face in order to construct a cloth mask, which was then glued to his face. "It was a miserable experience, and by the time we finished filming the mask had made some permanent lines in my face. Bert and Jack and I worked very, very hard and we all had respiratory problems because of the makeup. And we all looked so horrible that we were embarrassed to go to the commissary for lunch, so we had our lunches sent to the set. But what made it really hard was the heat. In those days they were using the old three-strip Technicolor, which was beautiful, but it needed huge lights and it was unbearably hot. They've refined the process since then and they don't need that kind of lighting, but then it was really hot, especially wearing that makeup. We did a lot of kidding around during the long waits between the shots — the three of us knew all kinds of stories and jokes — and I think if we hadn't laughed we'd have gone mad."

Bolger received third billing in *The Wizard of Oz*, but unlike in *Rosalie*, this time it meant something. It allowed him a complete, sustained characterization as the nice, floppy Strawman in search of a brain. The only regret was

Sunny (RKO, 1941).
Bolger demonstrates a
flair for the elegant
with Anna Neagle.

that the dance Bobby Connolly had devised for him had to be cut. But in a film like *Oz* the whole was more important than parts that did not quite fit, no matter how charming they might be.

Following *The Wizard of Oz* Bolger returned to New York to do the short-lived *Keep Off the Grass.* Once back in Hollywood he asked to be released from the confining MGM contract and then proceeded to make two pictures at RKO. British producer-director Herbert Wilcox and his wife, Anna Neagle, who had already made *Irene* and *No, No, Nanette,* were then at the studio. They hired Bolger to star with Anna in the Jerome Kern musical *Sunny* (1941), which had first been filmed in 1930 with Marilyn Miller, the star of the original Broadway presentation. The Wilcox-Neagle version was a mild success, its best parts being the dancing done by Neagle and Bolger, both solo and together. They obviously enjoyed doing a knockabout nautical number, and in the ballroom routines Bolger revealed himself to be a graceful dancer.

The second RKO film quickly sank from sight. *Four Jacks and a Jill* (1941) is the kind of movie known only to ardent film buffs. Bolger played a musician (one of the jacks) who joins his pals in adopting a pretty waif (Anne Shirley). She poses as a European aristocrat in order to get work for herself as a singer, which helps the musicians get work, too. Bolger was the leader of the band, who, fortunately for this minor musical, also happened to be a dancer. It gave him two good numbers, a frenetic "Boogie Woogie Conga" and the amusing routine "I'm in Good Shape for the Shape I'm In."

The Hollywood studios seemingly had nothing more to offer Ray Bolger by the end of 1941, but back in New York Rodgers and Hart had written a musical for which they thought he would be perfect. They were perfectly right, and *By Jupiter* turned out to be a theatrical highlight of Bolger's career. Rodgers and Hart wrote the script as well as the songs, basing it on the play *The Warrior's Husband* by Julian F. Thompson, all about Amazon women at war with the men of ancient Greece. Bolger was Sapiens, the cowed husband of Queen Hippolyta. In a maze of plot complications that gradually turn the Amazon ladies docile, Sapiens ends up king. The critics were not impressed with the plot, but Bolger drew rave notices. Typical was *Time:* "It is Ray Bolger's show…as the simpering, ladylike husband he is deft enough to draw many a laugh, skirt many a snicker. As a dancer he is superb—inexhaustibly inventive, unfailingly comic."

By Jupiter opened at the Shubert Theatre in June 1942 and ran 427 performances. Sadly, it proved to be the last of the Rodgers and Hart shows, as Lorenz Hart died a year later.

Opposite, left: At the *Stage Door Canteen* (United Artists, 1943). Opposite, right: *Look for the Silver Lining* (Warners, 1949). June Haver plays Marilyn Miller, and Ray portrays the great Jack Donohue. Below: *Sunny* (RKO, 1941). A pair of comic sailors, Bolger and Anna Neagle.

Bolger's own association with it came to an end only because he had made a commitment to the USO to go to the South Pacific to tour military bases and entertain service personnel. Prior to the Rodgers and Hart show he had made a Caribbean tour for the USO, and by the end of the war he had traveled tens of thousands of miles for the USO.

Bolger was one of the most conspicuous entertainers of the armed forces during World War II, and he was among those who organized the American Theatre Wing, which sponsored the Stage Door Canteen in New York's Times Square. When a feature film was made and titled *Stage Door Canteen* (1943) he was, of course, one of the dozens of stars who contributed their services. The film is a reminder of a remarkable outpouring of generosity and patriotism on the part of the American entertainment industry in those years, as stars of every medium appeared at the USO canteens across the country to wait on tables, chat, and perform for the servicemen and women.

For *Stage Door Canteen,* Bolger used a piece that Rodgers and Hart had written especially for him, a song-and-dance number titled "The Girl I Love to Leave Behind." For his USO tours Bolger had developed a character the servicemen found endlessly amusing, his Sad Sack, a woeful private who finds military life confusing and hard to grasp. Bolger performs this characterization in the film—a man bullied by an unseen drill sergeant and who makes a mess of handling a rifle. But when he puts the rifle down, and after he sings about the girl he does not miss, he launches into a brilliant tap dance. It is the kind of dance that led critics to refer to him constantly as "double-jointed" or "rubber-legged."

Actually, Bolger is neither; skill and practice, not some strange physical ability, and sheer concentration on mood and expression create that effect. Bolger has always striven to convince his audience that he is feeling and doing something and not merely hoofing. His work is that not simply of a dancer but of a comic actor.

After the war Bolger found himself back at MGM, which, to his pleasure, assigned him to the Judy Garland musical *The Harvey Girls* (1946). Again given third billing, it again, as with *Rosalie,* turned out to be a disappointing rank. So much was cut from the film in order to bring it down to one hundred minutes that Bolger ended up almost as a bit player. Three numbers were dropped, including Bolger's big one, "Hayride," done with Judy. (Composer Harry Warren later used the melody in *Pagan Love Song,* where it emerged as "The House of Singing Bamboo.") What remained for Bolger were his three-minute solo segment of "On the Atchison, Topeka and the Santa Fe" and the ensemble dancing in "Swing Your Partner Round and Round." Although it amounted to good exposure in a popular film, it was brutal to have so much material end up on the cutting room floor.

Once again, a call from Broadway picked Bolger up, both in spirits and in career. Frank Loesser had written the songs and George Abbott the script for a musical version of *Charley's Aunt,* called *Where's Charley?* They offered it to Bolger, who was less than enthusiastic about it. As written, it would have called for him, as the friend of Charley who agrees to masquerade as the aunt, to perform most of the play wearing a voluminous Victorian lady's dress. Says

Bolger, "Tossing things around, I came up with the idea, 'Why doesn't Charley play the aunt?' and once we figured out how to do the rapid changes of costume, we were on our way."

Where's Charley? opened on Broadway in October 1948 and settled in for a long run. Among other things, it provided Bolger with a hit recording. In the theater he had thought of drawing the audience into singing the reprise of the infectious "Once in Love with Amy," the first time a star of a Broadway musical had ever done that, and the recording proved almost as compelling as the live performance. In every performance, whether in the theater, in the film, or on the record, Bolger quickly yells out the lines,

"Once in love with Amy, always in love with Amy / Ever and ever, fascinated by 'er, sets your heart on fire to stay...." It was, and remains, Ray Bolger's finest moment in American musical comedy. "It is the only Broadway show within my memory to appeal to all, from the very young to the very old. I had a letter the second year from a teacher who had written in for a sizable block of tickets, telling us that she had brought her seventh-grade pupils shortly after the opening, and now she was bringing this year's seventh grade."

Because Frank Loesser did not want to release the film

rights until the stage version had run its course, the movie version of *Where's Charley?* did not get the go-ahead until 1952. Warners bought the rights and decided to make it in England, using frozen funds it had accumulated there. This turned out to be to the film's advantage, for it enabled the picture to be shot partly in Oxford, the actual setting of the story, and to employ English character actors, singers, and dancers to play the college students and their girlfriends. A similarly good decision was made in hiring Michael Kidd as the choreographer, as well as bringing over Allyn McLerie, who had played Amy opposite Bolger on Broadway. Although Bolger was forty-eight at the time of the filming, there is nothing in the performance to suggest middle age as he quickly darts in and out of scenes, leaping, running, vaulting, skipping, scampering, and flouncing, all in addition to mere dancing. In short, it proved a field day for Bolger.

Bolger was seen in three other films before *Where's Charley?* made its appearance. In 1949 he was hired by Warners to play Jack Donohue in *Look for the Silver Lining,* a fanciful account of the life of Marilyn Miller, one of the most alluring singer-dancers on Broadway in the twenties. June Haver, not the most vital actress, did not fill Miller's shoes all that well, but Bolger was a perfect choice as Donohue, who had been not only Miller's partner in many of her shows but also her mentor, as well as an influential force in theater dancing in general. LeRoy Prinz staged the dancing for the movie. In the opinion of most critics, the highlight of the film was Bolger's tap-dancing to Jerome Kern's "Who?"

Bolger was also seen in 1949 in RKO's *Make Mine Laughs,* a compilation movie that used sequences from a number of musicals the studio had made over the years. They lifted a dance he had done in *Four Jacks and a Jill* without asking his permission; neither did they offer payment. Bolger was among a number of artists who sued RKO and won settlements, but when the legal complications became too burdensome, RKO withdrew the film.

Where's Charley?, in the theater and on the screen, kept Bolger busy for three years, after which Warners again brought him back to Hollywood. In 1952 the studio starred him with Doris Day in *April in Paris,* a title that did not make a great deal of sense since most of the action took place on a boat crossing the Atlantic. It did, however, enable Bolger to do something he had seldom done in his career—win the leading lady. In this improbable plot he plays a minor government official, J. Winthrop Putnam, an assistant to the Undersecretary of State, whose job it becomes to correct a blunder made when showgirl Doris receives the invitation to an international festival of the arts intended for

Above: *Look for the Silver Lining* (Warners, 1949). Bolger shows June Haver a few steps. Opposite: *The Harvey Girls* (MGM, 1946). Virginia O'Brien sings of her disenchantment with "The Wild, Wild West," which seems to include blacksmith Bolger. Below: *Where's Charley?* (Warners, 1952). "Once in Love with Amy"—always in love with Amy.

April in Paris (Warners, 1952). Dancing with Doris Day in "I'm Gonna Ring the Bell Tonight" (top), and with two presidential Bolgers (above). Opposite: *Babes in Toyland* (Disney, 1961). Fifty-seven years old, and still leaping!

Ethel Barrymore. By the time their ship docks in France, stuffy Winthrop, after a giddy night drinking champagne, has been loosened up and finds himself a new man, and in love with Doris.

But all that really matters about this silly picture is the singing of Doris Day and the dancing of Ray Bolger. Early in the film he has an unusual number dancing with Lincoln and Washington when their portraits in his government office come to life — an interesting device, since Bolger also plays the great presidents. The really memorable dance in *April in Paris* takes place in the gallery of the ocean liner. Bolger high leaps and taps out "I'm Gonna Ring the Bell Tonight," and then Doris joins him for some nifty footwork for two.

April in Paris was no milestone in the history of movie musicals, except in the unfortunate sense that it was the last one in which Bolger appeared. No other studio came up with a vehicle that would make use of his highly individualistic talents as a dancing man. In fact, no film of any kind came his way again until the Disney production of *Babes in Toyland* in 1962. This reworking of the venerable Victor Herbert operetta offered him the role of the villainous Barnaby, which, if nothing else, gave him top billing. Tommy Sands was Tom, the Piper's Son, and Annette Funicello was Mary Quite Contrary, who, at one point, is courted by landlord Barnaby as he sings and dances "Castle in Spain," to which he will take her if she gives in. Done with fountains of dancing water, the number is visually one of the better things about the film. At another point he joins with an equally greedy villain, Henry Calvin, to sing "We Won't Be Happy Till We Get It." *Babes in Toyland,* really a kiddy show, did not do much for the talent involved.

The demise of the movie musical in the fifties removed Ray Bolger, like so many musical stars, from the screen. He was more fortunate than many others in that it did not drastically affect his livelihood. He had long been known as a comic actor, and in time he accented that aspect of his ability more and more. He found many opportunities in television as well. His own love of dancing, however, did not diminish; even at the age of seventy he was still doing an hour of dance practice every day to keep the body in shape.

When, in 1984, Bolger reached the age of eighty, he had to curtail the exercises. Even a body as remarkable as his has its limitations. But he is still available for work, provided he is not required to leap up and down. When he was offered the role of a host in *That's Dancing!* he was pleased to find that he could do it sitting down. When asked if he is satisfied with his long career, he replies in the affirmative, "I've been very lucky." There are, however, a great many people who feel that Hollywood could have done more with the dancing talent of Ray Bolger.

CYD CHARISSE

In his book *The Great Movie Stars: The International Years* (St. Martin's Press, 1972) David Shipman writes, "If you were in an air-force cinema *circa* 1972, you'll never forget the sound which greeted the appearance of Cyd Charisse half-way through the climactic ballet in *Singin' in the Rain*. The audience to a man greeted this sinuous leggy beauty with a loud and prolonged 'Ooooaah'. As she slithered around an understandably bewildered Gene Kelly, there was uproar in the cinema. Cyd Charisse didn't do more than dance in *Singin' in the Rain* and people remember her for it."

Ziegfeld Follies (MGM, 1946). Fred Astaire performs "Bring On the Beautiful Girls," and the one in the solo spot is young Cyd Charisse (upper left), in her first Metro musical. Page 142: *Brigadoon* (MGM, 1954). Cyd plays an enchanting Scottish lass from an enchanted village.

Ballet never gained much of a foothold in the movies. It was, and to a large extent it still is, regarded by the mass public as a somewhat elitist dance form — just a little too classy. From time to time a film about ballet has done well at the box office — *The Red Shoes* (1948) and *The Turning Point* (1977) are beautiful examples — but in the main ballet has been a visitor to the screen, never a permanent resident. And the only lady, other than Leslie Caron, with a formal ballet background to have become a movie star is Cyd

Charisse. Her graceful dancing accounts only partly for her success; she also had going for her a sex appeal that was both appealingly dignified and smoldering. It is significant that she was chosen to perform in *Silk Stockings*, the musical version of Greta Garbo's *Ninotchka*. The sexual images are similar. Both are ladylike and both could do more with the look in their eyes than many a voluptuous girl could do with a striptease.

The name Cyd Charisse was arrived at after she had used

Till the Clouds Roll By (MGM, 1946). Dancing "Smoke Gets in Your Eyes" (right) with Gower Champion.

and then found expression in lessons she took with Constance Ferguson, who had been with a Russian ballet company. Recalls Cyd, "Her classes were held in the Paladuro Hotel ballroom. There was a bar and mirror, of course, and I can still remember those first lessons in that drafty old ballroom. I went to the bar and within a week or so I had mastered the first five positions. I found I loved it. I couldn't wait until it was time for my next lesson." Her father later built a bar and mirror in his home, and his little girl spent a lot of time working in front of it. "You can't become an accomplished dancer without that dedication."

The Finklea family spent the summer of 1935 in Santa Monica, California. Twelve-year-old Cyd was enrolled in the best dance school available, the Fanchon and Marco Dance Studio on Sunset Boulevard in Hollywood. One of the teachers was a dashing Frenchman named Nico Charisse, and his young pupil became impressed with both his dancing style and his personality. The family returned to Amarillo when summer ended, but two years later Cyd came back to Los Angeles as a resident and a full-time student at the Fanchon and Marco studio. By this time Nico Charisse had left to join a ballet company. She now studied under Adolph Bolm, who had once partnered the great Pavlova.

When ballet companies came to Los Angeles, some of the cast members usually visited Bolm. In late 1937, when the famed Ballets Russes performed in Los Angeles, its director, Colonel W. de Basil, came to see Bolm. He watched Cyd with growing interest and asked Bolm to have her repeat certain routines. He then asked her to join his company. Before accepting, Cyd returned to Amarillo and discussed

a number of others. She was born Tulla Ellice Finklea in Amarillo, Texas, on March 8, 1923, and she quickly came to be called Sid because it was the nearest her baby brother could come to saying the word "sister." Her father owned a jewelry store and the family circumstances were comfortable but not affluent. He was a man who enjoyed ballet, and he took his family to see productions whenever they arrived in the vicinity.

His daughter's fascination grew from these exposures

the prospects with her parents. Some weeks later, Ernest Finklea took his daughter to Cincinnati, Ohio, where the Ballets Russes was performing, and signed the contract that made her a member of the company. Unimpressed by her name, Colonel de Basil decided that she should be known as Felia Siderova. Her formal education continued by means of correspondence courses, and between those and her dancing lessons she found time for almost nothing else.

After a year with the Ballets Russes Cyd left the company to return to Amarillo and her ailing father. After he died she went to Los Angeles to continue her studies, and there again met Nico Charisse, with whom she took lessons. At this time she also studied with Madame Bronislava Nijinska, the sister of the great Nijinsky. The family grief had caused Cyd to miss the Ballets Russes's Australian tour. When the company returned to America she rejoined it, and she was with them when they were engaged to perform at Covent Garden in London in the summer of 1939.

Among other things, this brought her into contact with the great Michel Fokine, who invited her to dance a small role in *Paganini*, the last ballet he would ever choreograph. Her notices were good. By now she was known as Maria

Fiesta (MGM, 1947). Doing "The Flaming Flamenco" with Ricardo Montalban.

Istomina; English interviewers were delighted to find she could speak English. At this point, she faced another change in her life — in the form of Nico Charisse, who arrived in London and proposed to her. He took her to France and they were married in the town of Virchinny. She was sixteen, half the age of her husband.

From the romantic, picture-postcard Virchinny they returned to the reality of Amarillo, where Cyd's surprised mother asked that they be married again. After this formality the couple went to Los Angeles, where Charisse ran a dancing school, with his bride as a helper-teacher. Pregnancy curtailed her dancing activities; she gave birth to her son Nicky in 1942. The hopes for a career as a dancer diminished with domesticity and the running of a small business, but a year or so later, her friend David Lichine, who had been a fellow member of the Ballets Russes, turned up in Los Angeles and received an offer from Columbia to choreograph and perform a ballet in its filming of the Cole Porter musical *Something to Shout About* in 1943.

Something to Shout About, which Porter had written directly for the screen, was nothing much to shout about, except for one hit song, "You'd Be So Nice to Come Home To," and David Lichine's staging of the dance "Hasta Luego," for which he asked Mrs. Nico Charisse to perform with him as his partner. Columbia liked everything about her but her name and asked her to come up with something different. She picked Lily Norwood, Norwood being her mother's maiden name. The idea of working in the movies had never occurred to her, but after *Something to Shout About* came out, she received a call from Robert Alton, who was head of the dance department in the Arthur Freed unit at MGM.

Freed was producing the mammoth *Ziegfeld Follies* and Alton needed a beautiful dancer to do a few steps with Fred Astaire in the opening number, "Bring On the Beautiful Girls." Freed agreed with Alton that he had made a good choice, but he did not like the name Lily Norwood, which he felt was not interesting enough for such an exotic-looking girl. Up until now she had been called Sid by her friends and family. Freed liked it but suggested that it be spelled in a more intriguing manner. How about spelling it Cyd? And he liked the name Charisse. Cyd Charisse — Freed thought that sounded just right.

Cyd Charisse signed a contract with MGM and gained the benefits then available to contractees at major Hollywood studios: she was groomed in deportment, singing, speech, acting, and general dance. She realized that a career in pictures, even as a dancer, required some acting, in which she had no training. Her first chance came as one of *The Harvey Girls*, the story of the restaurant chain that brought waitresses out West to staff its expanding empire.

The Unfinished Dance (MGM, 1947). With Margaret O'Brien. Below: *On an Island with You* (MGM, 1948). Another dance with Ricardo Montalban.

Cyd teamed with Judy Garland and Virginia O'Brien, as the girls who room together, and with them she sang the winsome song "It's a Great Big World," expressing the trepidation of the innocent young girls facing life in the Wild West. The plot called for Cyd to fall in love with a handsome young barroom pianist played by Kenny Baker, and in one of the film's quieter moments she gracefully glided around an empty saloon as he serenaded her with "Wait and See." She was also conspicuous in the ensemble "Swing Your Partner Round and Round." *The Harvey Girls* did well, and Cyd had reason to feel good about her new career. At the same time, unfortunately, she had little reason to feel good at home, where her marriage was running down. Nico Charisse's dancing school came to a close and so did the marriage.

Despite the unhappy ending to her first marriage, Cyd looks back on it with some gratitude. "I'll always be grateful to Nico. I think he gave me a certain quality that set me apart from the run-of-the-million dancers. It is relatively easy for a dancer to acquire the technical ability to dance, to perform all the steps in a pure textbook fashion. But I watched Nico dance — and he could be positively brilliant — and some of what he did rubbed off on me. He had a very fluid way of dancing. He never came to a full stop, he was always in motion. He imparted that quality to me."

Shortly after *The Harvey Girls* was released in 1946, Cyd was seen playing a small, dramatic role as Margaret O'Brien's sad older sister in *Three Wise Fools*, which did nothing for her except give her more experience. But she was used to much better advantage in MGM's all-star tribute to Jerome Kern, *Till the Clouds Roll By*, in which she danced a graceful duet with Gower Champion to "Smoke Gets in Your Eyes." It was Champion's first crack at the movies, beginning an association with movie musicals that proved of value both to him and to film dancing.

Next came *Fiesta* (1947), which introduced Mexican movie star Ricardo Montalban to the American audience. Esther Williams co-starred as his sister. This movie, filmed in Mexico, dealt with the art and honor of bullfighting. Montalban played a toreador who would much rather be a composer, and Cyd was the dancer who backed him up. They did "The Flaming Flamenco" together, choreographed by Eugene Loring, who also directed the spectacular "Fantasia Mexicana," adapted from Aaron Copland's "El Salón México."

Cyd's ballet background came to the fore in *The Unfinished Dance* (1947), in which little Margaret O'Brien, idolizing the ballet star played by Cyd, causes another dancer to be injured in case she might become a rival. As drama it was limp stuff, but it gave dance enthusiasts some insights into the world of the ballet and the kind of hard, applied discipline its followers undergo. It was a perfect vehicle for Cyd, and all the more pleasurable in that the dance episodes were choreographed by her friend David Lichine. They included excerpts from *Swan Lake*, *Prince Igor*, and *Coppélia*, as well as a new piece by David Rose that would become his most popular work, "Holiday for Strings."

On an Island with You (1948), an Esther Williams aquatic musical, gave Cyd Charisse the opportunity to be seen and enjoyed by millions. It brought her together again with Ricardo Montalban, with whom she always enjoyed dancing, and it also had the advantage of the famed Jack Donohue as its dance director, although the big production piece he had devised for Cyd was abandoned when she injured a leg in the filming. She spent three weeks in the hospital and several more at home wearing a cast.

After recovering, she joined Montalban and Ann Miller in a "Dance of Fury" — a number devised by Stanley Donen to add some flair to the Frank Sinatra musical *The Kissing Bandit*, which, MGM realized, needed help. The Charisse-Montalban-Miller dance deserved better than to be sunk in this ludicrous picture. MGM then produced another all-star musical tribute, this one to Rodgers and Hart, calling it *Words and Music*. Again the stars were assigned special material, and Cyd did well doing an interpretive dance as Perry Como sang "Blue Room." She also appeared in a sprightly ballet, the title song from Rodgers and Hart's *On Your Toes*. Her private life was also sprightly; during 1948 she was courted by both Howard Hughes, whose eccentricities made him a doubtful catch, and by the greatly popular singer Tony Martin. On May 15, 1948, Cyd acquired yet another name — Mrs. Tony Martin.

Cyd received her first star billing in the 1949 murder mystery *Tension*, with Richard Basehart, then a good supporting role in *East Side, West Side*, with James Mason and Barbara Stanwyck. She was then off the screen for more than a year, during which time she gave birth to her second son, Tony, Jr. MGM had nothing for her when she returned, so it loaned her to Universal to co-star with Ricardo Montalban in *Mark of the Renegade*, a minor swashbuckler about early California à la *The Mark of Zorro*. Back at MGM they still had nothing musical in which to use her, so she found herself playing a half-breed Indian girl opposite Stewart Granger in *The Wild North* (1952). Cyd was beginning to wonder about the drift of her career when something really good came her way.

After Gene Kelly had finished shooting *Singin' in the Rain* he agreed with producer Freed that a spectacular dance production number would increase the picture's obviously good prospects at the box office. It was decided to build an extended piece around two songs for which Freed had sup-

Above: *Words and Music* (MGM, 1948). With Dee Turnell, Cyd dances a ballet to the sprightly "On Your Toes" (left), and, as Perry Como plays and sings "Blue Room," Cyd glides to the music (right). Below: *Singin' in the Rain* (MGM, 1952). Cyd introduces herself to Gene Kelly in "The Broadway Ballet."

plied lyrics years before for Metro musicals, "Broadway Melody" and "Broadway Rhythm." The scenario concerned a hopeful young hoofer who arrives in the Big Town looking for luck in his career; before finding it, he undergoes a few adventures. One sequence would take place in a flashy nightclub and bring him in contact with a sexy girl, the moll of a gangster.

Kelly wanted to use his assistant, Carol Haney, as the moll, but Freed and others felt she was not sexy enough for the part. Kelly felt uneasy about accepting Cyd for the part because she was slightly taller than him and because her balletic style was somewhat at variance with his more athletic and bravura movements. Rehearsals brought the desired

The Band Wagon (MGM, 1953). "Dancing in the Dark" with Fred Astaire. Opposite: *Singin' in the Rain* (MGM, 1952). Another moment from "The Broadway Ballet" with Gene Kelly.

effects, including a method of photographing the couple so that she did not seem taller than Kelly. The complicated number was in production for a month, filmed in two weeks, and edited to thirteen-and-a-half minutes at a cost of a little over six hundred thousand dollars, somewhat more than the production costs of the ballet in *An American in Paris*.

Whatever the efforts and the costs, it was worth every penny in the careers of Kelly and Charisse. As the flirtatious but mercenary moll, Cyd was the personification of sexual temptation. When the young hoofer first sees her she flirts with him, but is soon drawn back to her gangster when he flashes her diamonds. Later, when the hoofer has become a dancing star he sees her again and he imagines what it would be like to dance with her in a love duet. When he actually approaches her she spurns him, and he shrugs his shoulders.

Opposite: *The Band Wagon* (MGM, 1953). In "The Girl Hunt Ballet" with Fred Astaire (above), and demonstrating a ballet movement with James Mitchell to a puzzled Astaire (below). Left: *Deep in My Heart* (MGM, 1954). A *pas de deux* with James Mitchell to Romberg's "One Alone."

Cyd did not learn of Carol Haney's disappointment until she started rehearsing, but Carol showed no resentment. "I'll always remember Carol fondly for the way she helped me, when her heart must have been breaking. If it had been me I think I might have just walked out. She was truly fond of Gene, so she stayed and worked with me. I think most girls who knew Gene felt the same fondness for him."

Cyd was next assigned to *Sombrero* (1953), another Latin American romance with Ricardo Montalban. In its one dance routine, the superstitious heroine dances around an idol and then rolls down a hillside in a thunderstorm. This bizarre piece was choreographed by a man she had long heard about, Hermes Pan, whom she found delightful to work with. Pan was then in the process of helping Fred Astaire devise his dances for *The Band Wagon*, a circumstance that probably had something to do with Cyd being considered for Fred's leading lady. Astaire, like all dancers of medium height, was a little concerned about her height, but he was relieved to find her just a shade shorter. The steps they had done together in *Ziegfeld Follies* seven years previously were so brief he had forgotten about them.

clinch. The sophisticated dancing in this twelve-minute jazz ballet made tough demands on both Astaire and Charisse, requiring days of exhausting rehearsal. Anyone who has ever danced with Astaire knows that exhaustion is part of the salary.

"It has become a cliché to say that Fred Astaire is a perfectionist but it must be said because it is his essential quality. I think he came to appreciate my work, too, because I'd work just as hard and long as he did. Long after everybody else had gone home, we'd stay and work with Hermes in anticipation of the next day's shooting. He liked that. He never said it, of course, because that's not his style. But neither does he say anything critical to your face, I'm sure for fear of hurt feelings . . . he was always very considerate that way. Fred is the most perfect gentleman I have ever known."

Cyd was one of the many stars MGM gathered for its elaborate tribute to the life of composer Sigmund Romberg, *Deep in My Heart* (1954). To the melody of "One Alone," she and James Mitchell danced a sensuous *pas de deux*. Although somewhat more erotic in feeling than Romberg may have had in mind when he wrote it, it is doubtful that he would have raised any objections. Husband Tony Martin also appeared in the film, singing "Lover Come Back to Me" with Joan Weldon, and this is the closest he ever came to being in a movie with his wife. In terms of work hours, Gene Kelly was the man who saw a great deal of Cyd Charisse in 1954 and 1955, first with *Brigadoon* and then with *It's Always Fair Weather*. She looks back on both films with affection even though neither of them did as well at the box office as they deserved.

Gene Kelly's hopes of shooting *Brigadoon* in Scotland were quickly shot down by an increasingly cost-conscious MGM when it was realized how severe and unpredictable Scottish weather can be. But even though it was confined to the studios, there is no denying the beauty of the dancing in Kelly's version of *Brigadoon*. Since neither he nor Cyd were singers, much greater accent was placed on the dancing. (Kelly did his own singing but Cyd was dubbed by Carol Richards.)

The gossamer story is about an American who, while wandering in Scotland, comes across a village that is lost in history and which comes to life one day every hundred years. After meeting the enchanting Fiona Campbell, he falls in love with her, and soon they are dancing through "The Heather on the Hill." Although he returns to New York he cannot stop thinking about her, and finds himself drawn back to the village. There she is waiting for him, and he becomes a part of the legend as they sing and dance "From This Day On." Despite the lack of great success, *Brigadoon* remains one of Cyd's favorite movies.

The Band Wagon gave Cyd her best role yet, that of a famous New York ballet dancer who reluctantly agrees to star in a musical with an equally famous Hollywood hoofer, whom she regards with disdain. It took little research on her part to come up with the kind of character she was supposed to play; she had seen many of them in her own experience and she could easily adopt the necessary hauteur. The film was filled with the finest talent of American musical theater — the songs of Arthur Schwartz and Howard Dietz, the script of Betty Comden and Adolph Green, the direction of Vincente Minnelli, and choreography by Michael Kidd, to say nothing of the cast.

Needless to say, the dancing was of the highest caliber, including the beautiful, beguiling dance duet for Cyd and Fred, "Dancing in the Dark," and several pieces seen as rehearsals for the show they are working on in the story. The most extensive piece, a new number called "The Girl Hunt Ballet" with music by Schwartz and a text by Minnelli (unofficially aided by Alan Jay Lerner), was inspired by the popular private-detective stories of Mickey Spillane. Astaire impersonates the typical tough private eye, full of flip quips, and Cyd is the girl he always seems to run into, whether as a blonde suspect or a brunette who eludes him until the final

Opposite: *It's Always Fair Weather* (MGM, 1955). The boys at Stillman's Gym have reason to tell Cyd "Baby, You Knock Me Out." Right: *Meet Me in Las Vegas* (MGM, 1956). The "Frankie and Johnny" ballet. Below: *Silk Stockings* (MGM, 1957). "Paris Loves Lovers," Cyd and Fred Astaire.

It's Always Fair Weather (1955) was the third of the films Kelly co-directed with Stanley Donen. Even had it been better it still would have had a hard time matching *On the Town* and *Singin' in the Rain*. The songs by André Previn, Betty Comden, and Adolph Green were good but not outstanding, although one of them, "Baby, You Knock Me Out," provided Cyd with a dance she particularly enjoyed. Kelly choreographed it for her in a boxing gym called Stillman's, the plot device being that Kelly is a slick fight promoter and Cyd is the girl he is trying to impress — except that her knowledge of boxing turns out to be encyclopedic, causing all the rugged old pugilists to join in praising her. "It was a tough number to do but fun to be with all those ex-champs in a prize-fight ring…. I think 'Baby, You Knock Me Out' showed the Kelly touch at its peak—inventive, daring, totally worked out in his head before we began working together. When he's right, he's very right."

Meet Me in Las Vegas (1956) is another of Cyd's favorite films, because writer Isobel Lennart had her in mind when she wrote it. But MGM's change of guard at the top drastically affected the way it was made. Louis B. Mayer, who loved musicals, was gone, and the new commander-in-chief, Dore Schary, did not particularly like musicals. As a result, budgets and schedules were tightened, which meant bad news for those involved in choreography. Cyd Charisse is in line with every dancer in pointing out that no one other than a dancer can understand the amount of time and work needed to get the results for which they strive: "Long after everybody else has gone home, you'll still find dancers rehearsing."

Despite the strain of making the film caused by the new management, *Meet Me in Las Vegas*, filmed largely at the Sands Hotel, offers Charisse admirers much to study, especially the thirteen-minute ballet "Frankie and Johnny," based on the folk song. The new lyrics by Sammy Cahn were sung off-screen by Sammy Davis, Jr. Choreographer Eugene Loring set the number in a St. Louis waterfront bar, circa 1900. Cyd is Frankie, John Brascia is Johnny, and Liliane Montevecci is Nelly Bly, the girl for whom Johnny spurns Frankie, resulting in Frankie shooting him. The song sends Frankie to the gallows; in this sultry ballet version she woos the arresting sheriff and slinks off with him.

Aside from the ballet, *Meet Me in Las Vegas* provided Cyd with several kinds of dances, one of them being the hoedown "The Gal with the Yaller Shoes," done with the excellent Dan Dailey. Since she played a ballet dancer, Cyd also got to do bits of Tchaikovsky's *Sleeping Beauty* and Mendelssohn's "Rondo Brillant."

In covering the press showing, Jack Moffitt of *The Hollywood Reporter* wrote: "From a fan standpoint, I suppose the greatest emotional appeal of the picture lies in the advance toward secure stardom made by Cyd Charisse. Cyd is so beautiful, her life has been such a credit to Hollywood, her dancing is so lovely and her body is such a perfect medium of expression that everyone who enthuses over the movies wishes her well. It is therefore something of a joy to see the skill with which Roy Rowland's direction, by discovering an unsuspected potential of the actress for comedy, succeeds in loosening the stiffness out of her and warming up her personality. The sequences in which she gets tipsily jealous and barges into a burlesque show's top number to strut her stuff brought the house down. Rowland shows what he really can do when he pulls out all the comedy stops, and this is by far the best work Cyd has done to date."

The one criticism that had dogged Cyd in her career was the coolness in her personality, a quality of natural reserve that her acting had so far never been able to master but that completely disappeared when she danced. Had she received the same training in acting as she had had in dancing this would not have been a problem. In her dances of an amorous nature, she easily and excitingly communicated a sensuous, almost feline, womanly mystique. In 1957 she finally came close to overcoming the coolness. In her portrayal of

Silk Stockings (MGM, 1957).
Going into "The Red Blues."

Above: *Party Girl* (MGM, 1958). The dance with the bongo drums. Opposite: *The Silencers* (Columbia, 1966). As Sarita, the stripper-spy. Below: *Black Tights* (Eagle Lion, 1961). Dancing the ballet "A Merry Mourning" with choreographer Roland Petit.

the Russian envoy in *Silk Stockings* she gave her best definition of a woman whose cool nature is transformed by love, both in her acting and in her dancing. Cole Porter's musical treatment of *Ninotchka* needed an actress-dancer with this kind of facade, and in 1957 few doubted that the role would go to Cyd Charisse.

Silk Stockings teamed Cyd for the last time with Fred Astaire, a sad fact made even sadder when it was realized later that there would be no more great movie musicals for either of them. That realization is an uncomfortable part of the pleasure in seeing the film today. For Astaire, *Silk Stockings* capped a long and distinguished career that was bound to end soon in any case, but in the case of thirty-four-year-old Cyd such an ending seemed unreasonable. It is not a thought to dwell upon. Better to think instead of the joys of watching Cyd being slowly won over by the charming Astaire to the ways of what she at first considers the decadent West, especially Paris. He tells her about love and she replies that it is merely a chemical reaction. Then he plies her with Porter's seductive words, "I love the looks of you, the lure of you, / I'd like to make a tour of you. / The arms, the eyes, the mouth of you, / the East, West, North and the South of you." He pulls her to her feet—her leg curves into an arabesque — and she is slowly whirled into a transformation.

Some time later she joyously expresses her engagement in the more spirited "Fated to Be Mated." Plot circumstances take her back to Moscow, where she gets together with friends who yearn for Western decadence as much as she, and they close their doors and dance to the frenzy of "The Red Blues." The marvelous dances more than live up to the talents that put them together: Astaire, Charisse, and two top choreographers, Hermes Pan and Eugene Loring. Although Garbo's *Ninotchka* remains a classic, those who have become enamored of *Silk Stockings* cannot help feeling when they see it today that something is lacking: music.

With nothing in which to use her, MGM loaned Cyd to Universal in 1958 for the nautical adventure *Twilight for the Gods*. Back at the home studio she was starred opposite Robert Taylor in *Party Girl*, Taylor's last MGM film after being with them for twenty-four years. He plays a crooked lawyer in Chicago of the early thirties and she is the dancing girl who persuades him to go straight. At least the plot called for a little dancing, although by this time the budget cuts were so deep that in one dance Cyd had to perform with only a drum accompaniment. After a year or so of inactivity, Cyd and MGM decided to terminate the contract. She discovered that for her, as for most free-lance musical stars, the best prospects were television, the more expensive nightclubs, and the occasional movie.

In 1961 Cyd made two films in Europe. One was *Five Golden Hours*, a crime comedy with Ernie Kovacs. The other, *Black Tights* — to which she gladly contributed her talents — was a grouping of four modern ballets choreographed by Roland Petit. Petit used his ballerina wife Zizi Jeanmaire in two of the pieces, "The Diamond Cruncher" and "Carmen," along with Moira Shearer in "Cyrano de Bergerac" and Cyd in "A Merry Mourning," which had something of the "Gaieté Parisienne" spirit about it. For this segment, Maurice Thiriet wrote the music and Petit provided the story. He also played the part of the dashing young man who flirts with a lovely lady (Cyd), resulting in her husband (Hans Van Manen) challenging him to a duel. The husband is killed and the widow mourns, but the lover consoles her so charmingly that she soon happily dances away with him.

The director of *Black Tights* was Terence Young, and Cyd says of him, "Young was an excellent director for a dancing film. Ballet is, I think, one of the hardest things to capture on the screen. So many directors I've worked with, in television as well as movies, just say 'Dance,' and turn on their cameras and start shooting, and think they are making a ballet film. You lose seventy-five percent of the dance that way. To do ballet or any form of dance correctly, you have to shoot it using camera angles carefully and painstakingly, and Young was one of the few directors who understood that. I would compare him with Minnelli, Donen, and Kelly. They all have a tremendous eye for really knowing how to photograph dancing."

The only dancing on film Cyd has done since *Black Tights* is her guest-star appearance in *The Silencers* in 1966, one of a series Dean Martin made as superspy Matt Helm. She played a sultry stripper named Sarita, a double-crossing counterspy between dances. It was nothing of consequence, but by this time Cyd had faced the fact that her film career was over and that there were other things to do. After a good deal of doubt and trepidation she agreed to co-star with her husband in Las Vegas — the first time she had faced a live audience since her days with the Ballets Russes — and the success touched off many such appearances. In time she also overcame her doubts about starring in stage musicals, and she accepted offers, including *No, No, Nanette* in Australia, playing the role Ruby Keeler had done in the Broadway revival. "Tap dancing is not my forte, but I had to learn it, and I did. I still prefer other forms of dance, but one does what one has to do." Indeed.

The beautiful, elegant Cyd Charisse has done very well. Any form of compliment is redundant, except one made by Fred Astaire. "That Cyd! When you've danced with her you stay danced with."

RUBY KEELER

If the Academy of Motion Picture Arts and Sciences had ever offered an Oscar for modesty, the only probable nominee would be Ruby Keeler. When called upon to look at the celebrated musicals she made at Warner Bros. in the thirties she is often seen smiling a little ruefully and shaking her head at her own image. At one retrospective showing of Busby Berkeley movies — and she appeared in four of them — Ruby remarked, "I couldn't act, I couldn't sing very well and now it occurs to me I wasn't the greatest dancer in the world either." While there are many who agree with her, the agreement is of a peculiar kind, a warm and embracing kind, as if to say, "It doesn't matter — you were wonderful anyway."

Page 160: *42nd Street* (Warners, 1933). New showgirl Ruby has just been admonished to "pick up" her feet. Right: *Footlight Parade* (Warners, 1933). Ruby again plays the new showgirl, this time impressing Joan Blondell and James Cagney.

It is not only modesty that separates Ruby Keeler from most other entertainers but also an innocence of personality and an ingenuousness that is at odds with the rather brittle and nervous nature of the entertainment industry. Little about her could be described as *show biz*, despite her years of stardom and despite being married for a decade to Al Jolson, perhaps the most forcefully *show-biz* man ever to strut before the footlights. Keeler is one of those who have fame thrust upon them, and a classic example of the luck of being in the right place at the right time.

Her celluloid fame centers upon having been chosen to appear in *42nd Street*, generally regarded as the film that gave birth to the movie musical as a separate and genuine entity. (The many that preceded it can be regarded as pro-logues.) Thanks to Busby Berkeley, *42nd Street* proved what imaginative, cinematic choreography could do to make songs and dances vital and alive. In this film, truly about show business, Ruby Keeler was Peggy Sawyer, the chorus girl called upon to replace the injured star at the last moment — a situation that gave rise to some lines of dialogue beloved by all film buffs. The frantic scene is laid backstage at a Broadway theater. The highly strung, over-worked director, Julian Marsh (Warner Baxter), grabs Peggy by the shoulders and looks into her sweet face:

> *"Sawyer, you listen to me and you listen hard. Two hundred people, two hundred jobs, two hundred thousand dollars, five weeks of grind and blood and sweat depend upon you. It's the lives of all these people who've worked with you. You've got to go on and you've got to give, and give and give! They've got to like you, got to! You understand? You can't fall down, you can't. Because, your future's in it, my future, and everything all of us have is staked on you. All right now, I'm through. But you keep your feet on the ground and your head on those shoulders of yours, and, Sawyer, you're going out a youngster but you've got to come back a star!"*

Having been previously drilled by Marsh to the point of exhaustion poor little Peggy has no choice but to come back a star. But what makes her a star, of course, is the fantastic showcase in which she appears at the closing of *42nd Street* — Berkeley's dazzling version of the night life in mid-Manhattan, greatly aided by Harry Warren's pulsating melody and Al Dubin's lyrics: "Come and meet / those dancing

feet / on the avenue I'm taking you to / 42nd Street." The effectiveness of the number masks what the viewer might otherwise notice: that Peggy Sawyer is really not all that brilliant as a tap dancer and that most of the other sixty girls bouncing around on the stage could probably do as well. But whether they could get across the sweet, pleasing nature of Peggy is another matter. What makes the scene, and indeed the Keeler career, work is that Peggy is really Ruby.

The Ruby Keeler story is naive enough and bizarre enough to serve as the basis for an old-fashioned Hollywood musical. Born in Halifax, Nova Scotia, on August 25, 1909, she was only three when the family settled in New York, where her father became a driver for an ice company. She was one of five children in a folksy Catholic family. Her parents paid five cents a week in order that she could participate in her school's dance class. Helen Guest, the dance instructor, liked Ruby enough to give her further instruction in ballet. Recalls Ruby, "We were very poor and I think she gave me the lessons for nothing." At the age of eleven she enrolled in Jack Blue's Dance Studio on West 51st Street, where she met fellow student Patsy Kelly, who became a lifetime friend.

Ruby confined her dancing to school and church affairs until she was fourteen, when a fellow student at the Blue Studio advised her about openings in the chorus line of George M. Cohan's *The Rise of Rosie O'Grady*. She added two years to her age and was signed with Cohan for a wage of forty-five dollars a week, which pleased her struggling family. On the other hand, her mother was not about to let her daughter be sucked into what she considered the spicy life of the theater crowd, so she accompanied Ruby to and from the theater every night. Not long after her début in this new way of life, Ruby entered a dance contest conducted by Broadway impresario Nils Thor Granlund—he staged these contests as a means of finding women dancers for nightclubs—and she won. Granlund placed her with the El Fey Club on West 45th Street, where the reigning star was the lusty Texas Guinan, known as the Incendiary Blonde.

The year was 1923, when night life in New York roared with fun and crime, and yet the fourteen-year-old Ruby breezed through it like a child walking unharmed through a battlefield. The shady, boozy, smoky saloons of the prohibition era left no apparent marks on her. "Dancing in speakeasies was a job and none of us knew for sure who were gangsters. No one told us, so how could we know? Mother used to come and take me home." Ruby danced in the chorus at the El Fey Club for three years and then transferred to the nearby Silver Slipper. There she was spotted and offered a chorus job in the Broadway musical *Bye, Bye,*

In *Footlight Parade* (Warners, 1933) with her ideal screen lover, Dick Powell. Opposite: This may look simply like a swarm of Rubies, but — thanks to the bizarre choreography of Busby Berkeley — behind each poster-size face is a dancing girl, moving in time to "I Only Have Eyes for You" in *Dames* (Warners, 1934).

Bonnie. She even got a number of her own, "Tampico Tap," which brought her some good comment in the papers after the show opened in January 1927. "I wasn't ambitious, then or now, and the newspaper attention surprised me." She was further surprised when the prominent producer Charles Dillingham paid attention to her, resulting in a spot in his *The Sidewalks of New York,* the musical in which Bob Hope made his first Broadway appearance. A lot of attention now came her way, mostly in the form of two men who were busy turning their names into legends — the prestigious producer Florenz Ziegfeld and Al Jolson, who delighted in being known as "The World's Greatest Entertainer."

Ziegfeld signed Ruby for a spot in his Eddie Cantor musical *Whoopee,* which opened in December 1928. With some time on her hands before rehearsals began, she accepted an agent's offer to appear in theater prologues in Los Angeles. (Prologues, short stage presentations that preceded the showing of movies in the major houses, would be the subject of one of her movies a few years later, *Footlight Parade.*) Fanny Brice was on the train that brought Ruby to Los Angeles and among the people who met her was Al Jolson. Jolson then spotted Ruby, whom he had seen onstage in New York, and asked to be introduced to her. By this time he had already married and divorced two showgirls; he here met one who was destined to become the next Mrs. Jolson.

It was also at this point in her life that Ruby came into contact with the film community. While doing her prologues she took time to appear in a Fox short about dancing, which was made mainly to find out how tap-dancing could be recorded and photographed. Nothing came of this venture, and she returned to her commitment in New York. But Jolson followed her and conducted a whirlwind courtship. To the shock of her family she married him in a civil ceremony in Port Chester, New York, on September 21, she having just passed her nineteenth birthday and he twenty-five years her senior. After a European honeymoon Ruby joined the Ziegfeld show but left it during the out-of-town tryouts because Jolson wanted her with him in Hollywood.

Jolson's renown put Ruby in the spotlight, only he was so particular as to what she should or should not do that a year passed before he agreed to an offer. This came from Ziegfeld, who offered her a starring role in the Gershwin musical *Show Girl.* She had two numbers, "Liza" and "Harlem Nocturne," and received good notices. She also received a lot of publicity the night Jolson got up from his seat in the theater and took over singing "Liza" to her. The incident figured in the film *The Jolson Story,* in which he seemed to be coming to her aid. According to Ruby, he did it simply because, "He liked to sing. When he felt like singing, he sang." She adds, perhaps unnecessarily, "He had a lot of nerve." Despite the acclaim, she pulled out of the show after four weeks, giving strained health as the reason, and went to California to play the role of wife to a man in love with success.

Ruby lived as quietly as possible for the next two years, but fame came after her again in the form of Darryl F. Zanuck, then head of production at Warners. He wanted her for the ingenue lead in *42nd Street,* feeling that she alone was the girl to play sweet Peggy Sawyer. Her experience as a dancer in New York was just right and so was her own rather demure personality. While the success of the film flowed from a blending of all its elements, her tapping of the title song and her soft-shoe dancing to "Shuffle Off to Buffalo" charmed everyone. *New York Herald Tribune* critic Richard Watts, Jr., who had commented on her before now, called her "one of the best of all tap dancers." Like it or not, the diffident Ruby now stood in the star spotlight.

Her success in *42nd Street* can be partially attributed to her casting opposite Dick Powell, then twenty-eight and at the beginning of a lengthy film career. These two "nice kids" looked perfectly matched, so obviously so that of the nine pictures she made at Warners, Powell is in seven. The first four also involved her with Busby Berkeley, who devised routines in which she would become forever identified. Later, as a star fixture of the Berkeley nostalgia wave, she looked back on him with affection: "He was wonderful to work with. He always knew what he wanted and he always got it. All the girls loved him and some of them wouldn't take a job after a Berkeley picture for fear they might miss out on the next one."

The impact of *42nd Street* was so immediate that Warners quickly lined up several movies for Berkeley and his amazing choreography, with spotlight treatment to be given Keeler and Powell. The first of these, *Gold Diggers of 1933,* again concerned backstage show biz, with Dick as a rich boy pretending to be poor in order to make a name for himself as a composer of musicals and Ruby as a struggling dancer, Polly Parker. The very name reveals the character: dewy-eyed and trusting, remarkably so in view of the fact that all her colleagues are flinty, wisecracking chorines. This film limited her dancing to fleeting moments in the amorous "Pettin' in the Park" and waltzing, albeit charmingly, with a platoon of white-wigged, violin-playing girls in "The Shadow Waltz."

Better dance opportunities came with the next picture, *Footlight Parade,* which took her back to the days when she was involved in movie house prologues. An opportunity also came the way of James Cagney, finally given a chance to show on film the rather odd but appealing dance style that had brought him attention on Broadway a few years

earlier. As the director who has to go on because his leading dancer is drunk, Cagney joins Ruby in the saga of "Shanghai Lil," using both his fists and his tap shoes to find the girl for whom he has been searching high and low. The really gargantuan number in this film is the aquatic ballet "By a Waterfall," in which Ruby performs the kind of watery feats — diving, sliding down chutes, underwater antics — that Esther Williams would make her specialty a decade later.

In *Footlight Parade* Ruby also had a little more to work with in the way of a character. She first appears as the prim, bespectacled, sensibly dressed secretary to a producer. When she gets a chance to be a dancer, though, she discards the glasses, rumples her hair, lifts her skirt, and launches into a swift little tap routine. Everybody instantly agrees she should become a member of the production team. The scene, like most in these Warner musicals, is at the same time faintly ridiculous and strangely appealing. With another performer the scene might not work, but with Keeler — it's as if she had a special license to appear in front of the cameras. The rules apply to others, not to her.

In her fourth Berkeley musical Ruby glowed in a lovely routine built entirely around her. *Dames* (1934) called for Powell, again as a struggling songwriter, to come up with a gem of a song, "I Only Have Eyes for You," courtesy of Warren and Dubin. He sings the song to her on the New York subway and becomes so infused with his own lyrics that he sees her face in every picture he looks at. He falls asleep, and in his dream every girl looks just like her, which was sufficient to give Berkeley cause to drift into another flight of fancy. Berkeley equipped a horde of girls with Benda masks of Ruby and directed them through numerous formations. At the end the girls, carrying cards on their backs, bend over to form a giant jigsaw of Ruby's face. After this long number, the lovers wake from their snooze. She looks adoringly at him and says, "That was swell, Jimmy." Heard today the line is invariably greeted with a yell of disbelief—and, whenever she views the picture, a groan from Ruby.

Even at the height of her popularity in these years, Ruby did not find the idea of being a movie star very enticing. "I couldn't have cared less about having a career. I had no ambition and being a movie star truly didn't interest me. I remember watching Ginger Rogers at the time we made *Gold Diggers of 1933* and thinking she would make it all the way to the top, because that is what she wanted. You've got to have the drive. I never did. I always felt there was more to life than show biz. The idea of an early retirement appealed to me no end."

Be that as it may, Warners in 1934 was in no frame of mind to let Ruby slip quietly away; the formula was work-

In *Flirtation Walk* (Warners, 1934), Ruby's only dancing was the waltz down the wedding aisle—metaphorically speaking—with Dick Powell. An irresistible photo, nonetheless. Below: *Go into Your Dance* (Warners, 1935). With real-life husband Al Jolson dominating the picture, Ruby was noticeable only when she went into her dance.

ing too well for that. Next came *Flirtation Walk,* with Powell as a West Point cadet and Ruby as a general's daughter. Romance, not dancing, was the keynote, with a script that allowed the lovers a lot of misunderstanding and verbal scraps before finally falling into each other's arms. While the numbers of dance director Bobby Connolly have none of Berkeley's wild invention, they smoothly fit the picture. Warners was clearly trying to see if the Powell-Keeler casting could be moved beyond the visually gigantic. All signs pointed to a negative response.

Warners finally bowed to the obvious: a film co-starring Mr. and Mrs. Al Jolson. *Go into Your Dance* (1935) was yet another backstage musical, with songs by Warren and Dubin, two of which gave the Jolsons some solid stuff for their singing and dancing, "About a Quarter to Nine" and "She's a Latin from Manhattan." The film, a good piece of entertainment, presented Jolson at the crest of his appeal and gave Ruby a good vehicle for her dancing, under the direction of Bobby Connolly. Their roles called for nothing in the way of acting, since Jolson was once more the happy-go-lucky, strutting entertainer and Ruby his devoted, loving girlfriend. Seeing them together on the screen pleased the public.

Those who knew the Jolsons personally knew that the disparate personalities they portrayed in *Go into Your Dance* accurately reflected their private lives. Watching the film today causes wonder that any man so loudly brash and

any girl so quietly demure could really have been man and wife. It was a ludicrous marriage; ironically, the success of *Go into Your Dance* did nothing to help it. Warners offered them another picture together but Jolson turned it down. Although a man who needed success the way a diabetic needs insulin, he felt—and in this his instinct was correct—that the public had come to like Ruby more than it liked him. He could not share a spotlight, even with his wife. His popularity at this point quickly declined; ten years later, it shot to the top again when his story was made into a movie.

Since Warners had earned money casting Dick Powell as a West Point cadet in *Flirtation Walk,* the studio now moved him and Ruby to the United States Naval Academy at Annapolis for *Shipmates Forever* (1935). This time Powell is a nightclub singer who is more or less shamed into joining the academy because his father is an admiral. Ruby is the girlfriend who sees him through, while teaching dancing to children as a livelihood. Bobby Connolly, again the dance director, had less to do than before. Ruby taps prettily in a nightclub sequence as Powell croons, and she leads a talented group of children in some routines. (The children were actually a Los Angeles group known as the Meglin Kiddies.)

Despite some critical comments about the Powell-Keeler combination wearing a little thin, Warners decided on another picture for them. *Colleen* tells the story of an eccentric millionaire (Hugh Herbert, a mainstay of so many

Go into Your Dance (Warners, 1935). After having turned back the carpet and done a few steps, Ruby gets approval from Jolson, who presumably liked to play only on the high end of a piano.

In *Go into Your Dance* (Warners, 1935) Ruby had one of her best numbers: "She's a Latin from Manhattan."

Warner musicals of these years) who adopts a floozy (Joan Blondell) and puts her in charge of his dress shop. The sensible nephew (Powell) hires Ruby and puts her in charge. Eventually the family buys the eccentric out and everyone ends up on a liner going to Europe.

The stalwart team of Warren and Dubin failed to come up with any hits for *Colleen*—possibly, they too were getting tired of all this nonsense—but the dance number devised by Bobby Connolly at the end, "You Gotta Know How to Dance," is worthy of more attention than it has received. Ruby, while dancing with Paul Draper (the only legitimate dancer with whom she appeared on film), tries to persuade Powell that he, too, should be a dancer. Warren came up with a skillfully constructed staccato melody, beautifully suited to tapping, and Dubin added the lyrics:

> *If you want to win my heart,*
> *Don't be too intelligent or smart,*
> *Don't go in for lit'rature or art,*
> *But you gotta know how to dance.*

But nothing could save *Colleen*. The dismal response to the film ended the Powell-Keeler teaming, and Paul Draper's movie debut got lost in the general dullness. Draper had been trained in ballet but turned to tap-dancing and elevated it to concert proportions, devising a style that became known as ballet-tap. Some of that style is visible in the

Colleen finale. He returned to a considerable career on the stage.

Years later, in discussing Ruby, Harry Warren said, "She was a very nice woman but a reluctant movie star and very honest about her talent. She never discussed Jolson but we all thought life with him must have been a strain for her, and I think by the time she did this picture she was getting tired of the business." By late 1936 Ruby's contract with Warners called for three more films. By mutual agreement they decided to change the contract and make one final picture. *Ready, Willing and Able,* released in March 1937, was yet another backstage musical. Perhaps to make it sound a little different, they handed the job to Johnny Mercer and Richard Whiting, rather than Warren and Dubin. The pair flooded the picture with eight songs, only one of which became a lasting hit, "Too Marvelous for Words."

In this film, Ruby is mistakenly hired by a Broadway producer because she has the same name as the English star he has signed. "Handy with Your Feet" gave Ruby a nice little number, but Bobby Connolly's staging of "Too Marvelous for Words" is the only reason *Ready, Willing and Able* deserves discussion. Paired with dancer Lee Dixon, Ruby dances across the keys of a giant typewriter, tapping out the letters of the song's lyrics. Ruby claims it as the movie dance routine she most enjoyed doing. Sadly, it also proved to be the last one of any consequence.

Free of her Warner Bros. contract, Ruby accepted an offer to make two pictures a year for RKO. Only one was made, a feeble comedy called *Mother Carey's Chickens* (1938), and

In *Shipmates Forever* (Warners, 1935) Dick Powell was again the boyfriend, and the kind who gladly invited her to share his singer's spotlight. As she taps he sings "I'd Rather Listen to Your Eyes."

that contract also came to an end. The marriage with Jolson, long faltering, publicly creaked when she walked out of a stage show she was doing with him in Chicago, *Hold On to Your Hats*, after he started making comments to the cast about their marital problems. His flippancy strengthened her decision to ask for a divorce, despite her Catholic vows, and it became final in December 1940. Jolson told the press he was sorry if he had given her an inferiority complex and that he hoped they would be reconciled.

Through the years, Ruby had refused to discuss the marriage other than to say, "It was a mistake—a long mistake." Her friends could tell that she was particularly bitter about the boy they had adopted in 1935 and named Al, Jr. According to Ruby, Jolson paid the boy little attention and totally ignored him after the divorce. Junior made his own comment some years later by changing his name to Peter.

Possibly because of all the publicity, Ruby was offered a film by Columbia, *Sweetheart of the Campus* (1941), which made the mistake of casting her as the kind of cynical show-girl Joan Blondell and Ginger Rogers had played in the early Warner musicals. Ruby had a bright spot with "Tap Happy," but the picture soon faded into oblivion—a fate that she eagerly sought for herself. The opportunity presented itself when she met a successful real estate broker named John Homer Lowe. They were married in October 1941, and Ruby finally settled down to the family life she wanted, with no thought of ever again being involved in show business. Four children helped to make that thought a reality.

Hollywood did, however, call upon her in 1946—for permission to use her name in *The Jolson Story*. She told producer Sidney Skolsky that he could not, so Skolsky invented the name Julie Benson for Evelyn Keyes to play. The highly romanticized film did not amuse Ruby, who claimed that her years with Jolson made little sense as depicted in the movie: "It had nothing to do with our lives."

As the children passed their teen-age years, Ruby

Stepping with the elegant Paul Draper in *Colleen* (Warners, 1936). Below: The only memorable number in *Ready, Willing and Able* (Warners, 1937): the fine song "Too Marvelous for Words," pounded out by Ruby and Lee Dixon on an outsize typewriter.

In the last of Ruby's movie musicals, *Sweetheart of the Campus* (Columbia, 1941), she performs "Tap Happy" with Ozzie Nelson and his Orchestra.

accepted offers to appear as a guest on television talk shows. Her name did not cause much attention until the Busby Berkeley tribute at the Museum of Modern Art in New York in 1965, which she attended as a guest. This kicked off the Berkeley nostalgia cult, and she was asked to make other appearances with him from time to time. She began to refer to herself as a queen of camp and she seemed genuinely embarrassed by some of the moments in her old movie musicals. When her husband died of a heart attack in 1969 her friends encouraged her to do more of these appearances.

Ruby was, however, totally unprepared for an offer that came her way in 1970. Harry Rigby called from New York to say that he and his associates intended to revive the 1925 Vincent Youmans musical *No, No, Nanette*, and would she be interested in the part of Sue? She assumed that it would be a modernized, probably spicy sendup of the old musical and declined. Besides, she said, she was now sixty and who cared about Ruby Keeler?

Ruby next received two more telephone calls, one from her chum Patsy Kelly, who had signed with *Nanette* for a comedy role, and the other from Busby Berkeley, who told her he had been hired as dance supervisor and that he believed the company would do an affectionate and legitimate version of the show. With this encouragement she agreed to become a part of it. *No, No, Nanette* opened at the 46th Street Theatre on January 19, 1971, and enjoyed a first night such as producers imagine only in their fondest dreams. Despite Berkeley's position as dance supervisor, the dances were actually staged and directed by Donald Saddler, with two numbers tailored around Ruby, "I Want to Be Happy" and "Take a Little One-step." The slight plot of the original was kept intact, with Ruby as the wife of a Bible publisher who becomes upset about her husband's innocent involvement with young girls. The plot barely mattered; the producers concentrated their efforts on the décor and the dancing, and when Ruby went into her numbers there was instant, heavy applause. Audiences were delighted to find the sixty-year-old could still belt out a tap routine, seemingly with as much energy as in the Warner pictures of a generation ago. Moreover, she seemed to be truly enjoying herself. Everybody loves a comeback, as goes the old show-biz saying, and hers was called the comeback of the century.

After two years of *No, No, Nanette* Ruby decided to return to retirement. The comeback had been fun but there was no point in pushing things. Back to her nice home in Newport, California, back to the golfing she had always enjoyed, and back to being a grandmother. And back to wondering how such a shy, unambitious, and not greatly talented girl such as Ruby Keeler could have made such a name for herself.

GENE KELLY

Gene Kelly began his movie career ten years after Fred Astaire, which put him at a disadvantage historically. Those ten years were rich and vital in the history of movie musicals, and it is a pity that Kelly had to miss them. Even more of a pity is the fact that by the time Kelly stepped in front of the cameras to make his début in *For Me and My Gal* there were only a dozen or so years left in Hollywood's musical heyday. Be that as it may, Kelly's impact on film, both in terms of style and influence, has been equally as important as Astaire's, and in some areas even more important. While no dancer has ever worked harder, longer, or more meticulously to arrive at perfection — and in his mind perfection always eluded him — Astaire has never been much interested in dance as an art form. In that sense he is rather like a composer who has only a passing interest in the music of other composers. This is not true of Kelly, who has a passion for dance as an art and is supportive of what is going on in the dance world.

Du Barry Was a Lady (MGM, 1943). Taking center stage as a nightclub performer. Page 174: Gene Kelly dances lyrically in *Brigadoon* (MGM, 1954).

It has been Kelly's lot to be continually compared with Astaire. The main reason for this is that Hollywood has produced only two major male movie star dancers, and the human need to put everything on comparative terms leads to matching the one with the other. Stylistically they have little in common. It might be said that Astaire's movements find their roots in the ballroom, while Kelly's seem inspired by the sports arena. As a schoolboy he excelled at ice hockey, and he has said that the movements of this sport have strongly influenced his dancing. Kelly's style is the more *macho*, but one cannot draw from this the inference that Astaire's style is in the least feminine. It clearly is not.

If a comparison must be made, then it should come from someone who has danced with both of them, Cyd Charisse:

other hand, is the stronger of the two. When he lifts you, he lifts you! Fred could never do the lifts Gene did, and never wanted to. After a session with Gene Kelly, a dancer could go home and be black and blue."

Some of the most important things Kelly has done for dance have not been in the movies. In 1958 he devised and produced a television special for the NBC series *Omnibus* and deliberately titled it "Dancing — A Man's Game." Here, well aware of the stigma attached to male dancers, he stated the case for his art in a no-nonsense manner. His appeal to the public has always rested on his image as a muscular, likable workingman, in no way highbrow or effete. "I think dancing is a man's game, and if a man does it well he does it better than a woman. Unfortunately, in the Western world dancing is treated as a woman's game. This isn't so in the East. In Russia the dancer is a hero, and they can't understand why we make heroes of crooners. I don't want this to sound as if I'm against women dancing — we just have to remember that each sex is capable of doing things the other can't. Also, dancing *does* attract effeminate young men. I don't object to this as long as they don't dance effeminately. If they do then they are dancing badly — just as if a woman comes out on stage and sings bass. It's wrong. As for the personal sexual tendencies, and their bearings on a dancer, I think this has been overemphasized. This stigma on dancing is tragic because a great many boys would benefit from dancing lessons. It's the finest kind of exercise and it teaches poise. Unfortunately, people confuse gracefulness with softness. John Wayne was a graceful man and so are many of the great ballplayers. A quarterback making a forward pass can be as beautiful as a ballet movement, and a double play in baseball, if it's done well, has a choreographic feeling. Boxers, from James J. Corbett to Sugar Ray Robinson, use dancing as part of their art but, of course, they don't run any risk of being called sissies. The main problem is that we badly need male dancers and so many young men who have talent are put off by the belief that it is an effeminate business."

From television, Kelly went to the ballet world. The Paris Opéra and Opéra Comique invited him to choose material of his liking and invent a modern ballet for them — a highlight of Kelly's career. The result was *Pas de Dieux,* combining a telling of Greek mythology with the music of Gershwin's Piano Concerto in F. Long a Francophile, Kelly had been a hero to the French since his *American in Paris,* and his idea to do a ballet using another Gershwin work found immediate response.

Pas de Dieux relates how Zeus comes down to earth to win back Aphrodite, who has taken up with the low life on the Left Bank. He manages to do this after the usual amount

"Kelly is the more inventive choreographer of the two. Astaire, with Hermes Pan's help, creates fabulous numbers — for himself and his partner. But Kelly can create an entire number for somebody else, as he did for me in *It's Always Fair Weather.* I think, however, that Astaire's coordination is better than Kelly's. He can do anything — he is a fantastic drummer. His sense of rhythm is uncanny. Kelly, on the

of misunderstandings. Kelly found that his chief problem was teaching the rigidly, classically trained corps de ballet how to relax and move in different ways to accommodate the jazz aspects of the Gershwin music. "It was like an athlete learning how to ski after having spent years training to be a boxer. The jazz dancing required the use of different muscles—but they were willing subjects." *Pas de Dieux* was a great success, and it later influenced Kelly's election as a Chevalier of the Legion of Honor by the French government.

During Kelly's first year in Hollywood he was also compared with James Cagney, who had amazed and delighted moviegoers with his dancing as George M. Cohan in *Yankee Doodle Dandy*. What Kelly and Cagney actually had in common was, in fact, the Cohan influence. "Cohan set the style for the American song-and-dance man—a tough, cheeky, Irish style. Cohan wasn't a great dancer but he had wonderful timing and a winning personality. He influenced a whole breed of American actors, including Cagney, Spencer Tracy, and Pat O'Brien—and when Cagney did George M. Cohan in *Yankee Doodle Dandy* he was an improvement on the original. Cohan *was* the American theater up until the impact of Eugene O'Neill, and I have a lot of Cohan in me. It's an Irish quality, a jaw-jutting, up-on-the-toes cockiness—which is a good quality for a dancer to have."

Kelly comes by his Irishness honestly. Both sets of grandparents came from Ireland. He was born in Pittsburgh, the

Cover Girl (Columbia, 1944). Kelly, Rita Hayworth, and Phil Silvers "Make Way for Tomorrow."

third in a family of five children, on August 23, 1912. Kelly's father, a Canadian, passed on to his sons the Canadian passion for ice hockey. Gene, although proficient enough to play with a semiprofessional team, the Pittsburgh Yellow Jackets, decided against taking up the sport professionally. The background in dancing came from his mother, who sent her sons to dancing school against their wishes. This elicited taunts of "Sissy!" from the local boys, and the Kelly boys got into fistfights in order to defend themselves. Kelly's own interest in dancing did not really gel until he was fifteen and became interested in girls, whom he noticed favored boys who could dance. By that time a noted participator in ball games and gymnastics, he had no need to deal with taunts.

Kelly appeared in school plays in his final years at Peabody High in Pittsburgh. In 1929 he enrolled in Pennsylvania State College to study journalism. But the economic crash caused him to leave in order to help the family finances, and he found a job as a YMCA gymnastics instructor. At the same time, he and his brother Fred worked up dancing routines and entered talent contests to pick up extra money. A year later Kelly entered the University of Pittsburgh, studying law, and graduated in 1933 with a Bachelor of Arts degree. During the years of study, performing the traditional American ritual of working his way through college, he took jobs as a stage and dance coach at YMCA summer camps. In his senior year he became well known for his performances in the university's *Cap and Gown* productions.

Whatever plans Kelly had for making a living in anything other than entertainment were soon dropped after graduation, as he joined his mother in running a dancing school for children. "I found I had a penchant for teaching, that I liked it and that I was good with children. This eventually led to choreography—and to be a good choreographer you must first be a good teacher, because you have to show people what to do and convince them they can do it." As the family enterprise prospered, they decided to hire a hall and name it the Gene Kelly Studio of the Dance. This did so well that a second studio was opened in Johnstown. In order to keep at least one step ahead of his pupils, Kelly also had to study, and from that study came a growing interest in ballet.

In the summer of 1937 Kelly went to New York to get work as a choreographer—the career he had finally settled on. It took a year before a job came his way, and this was not in New York but in Pittsburgh, where he was still running his school. He was hired to help stage *Hold Your Hats* at the Pittsburgh Playhouse. He also appeared in it, doing well with the number "La Cumparsita," a piece that formed the basis for his elaborate Spanish dance in *Anchors Aweigh*

eight years later. Things now began to happen. One of the people who had been impressed by Kelly was dance director Robert Alton, and when Alton was hired for the Cole Porter musical *Leave It to Me,* which opened in November 1938 at the Imperial Theatre on Broadway, Kelly was in the cast.

In *Leave It to Me* Mary Martin sang "My Heart Belongs to Daddy," which became a highlight of musical theater. She performed the number with a group of five young men, Kelly among them. Kelly was noticed, and from this point on his career moved quite rapidly. Next came a spot as an actor-dancer-singer in the John Murray Anderson revue *One for the Money,* then a job as a summer-stock choreographer in 1939, leading to an audition for the part of Harry, the hopeful hoofer in William Saroyan's *The Time of Your Life.* It opened at the Booth Theatre on November 13, 1939; it ran twenty-two weeks; it won a Pulitzer Prize; and it established Gene Kelly as an actor-dancer.

Kelly got his first job as a Broadway choreographer on *Billy Rose's Diamond Horseshoe,* which did much to give his name value in the New York theatrical community. The next step would be the big one. John O'Hara had written an unusual musical with Rodgers and Hart called *Pal Joey,* and Kelly's friend Robert Alton was brought in as dance director. The actor who played the lead would have to be a top dancer as well as enough of an actor to make Joey an ingratiating kind of cad—a man who uses people, especially women, in his unscrupulous pursuit of success, but who does so with some humor and charm.

Says Kelly, "It was a case of being in the right place at the right time, and also a case of tremendous luck to have a part like that to play—to have a script by John O'Hara and songs by Rodgers and Hart, and a director like George Abbott. I think I did well in it because it gave me a chance to use my own style of dancing to create a character. I wanted to dance to American music and at that time nobody else was doing it. And Joey was a meaty character to play. He was completely amoral. After some scenes I could feel the waves of hate coming from the audience. Then I'd smile at them and dance and it would relax them. It was interesting to be able to use the character to manipulate the audience."

In reviewing *Pal Joey* for the *New York Times,* John Martin made some pertinent points about the substance of Kelly as an actor-dancer: "If Kelly were to be judged exclusively by his actual performance of the dance routines that fall to him, he would still be a good dancer, but when his dancing is seen in this fuller light he becomes an exceptional one. A tap dancer who can characterize his routines and turn them into an integral element of an imaginative theatrical whole would seem to be pretty close, indeed, to unique...he is not only glib-footed but he has a feeling for comment and

content that both gives his dancing personal distinction and raises it several notches as a theatre art."

With the tremendous success of *Pal Joey*, Kelly was sought after by interviewers, who asked him to verbalize about his concept of dancing. He explained that he did not believe in conformity to any school of dancing; rather, the dancing should be shaped by the drama and the music. Ballet technique is basic, but technique should never get in the way of the mood or the continuity. This concept would be the basis for his work in films—and that phase of his career was about to begin. Offers began to arrive soon after the opening of *Pal Joey*. Since he was contracted for the run of the play—which turned out to be 270 performances—he had plenty of time to ponder his choices.

Kelly finally signed with David O. Selznick. He went to Hollywood in October 1941, but he and Selznick could not agree on a suitable vehicle and Selznick sold the contract to MGM. Producer Arthur Freed had seen Kelly as *Pal Joey* and felt he would be perfect for Harry Palmer, a vaudevillian hoofer a little like Joey but eventually nicer, in *For Me and My Gal*. The role called for a lot of nifty, if not exceptional, dancing.

Having George Murphy, an experienced movie dancer, as a partner helped him in his first exposure to the chaotic world of movie-making, but Kelly credits Judy Garland as the one who really pulled him through: "She had a lot to do with persuading MGM to use me in the picture and she was even more helpful than she realized because I watched her to find out what I had to do. I was amazed at her skill—she could hit every mark and every move. All I could do for her then was to help with the dancing. She wasn't a dancer but she could pick up a step instantly. I learned a great deal about making movies doing this first one and much of it was due to Judy Garland."

MGM now had the task of finding vehicles for Kelly, who did not fit the then-conventional concept of a leading man. However, it saw an obvious role for him in the Cole Porter musical *Du Barry Was a Lady* (1943), which the studio had bought: the nightclub dancer who becomes involved in a dream sequence, which transforms him into a French revolutionary swashbuckler. While pleasing, the part placed no strain on him as a dancer. For *Thousands Cheer* (1943) Kelly had a dance written especially for him, giving him the chance to show his individual style. In this wartime all-star musical, Kelly portrayed an army private, who at one point is confined to barracks and given clean-up duties. He lightens the job by imagining the mop to be a girl, and he glides around the floor with it to the tune of "Let Me Call You Sweetheart." The dance gradually grows more complex as he dramatizes the situation. With this routine, "The Mop Dance," it now became apparent that Hollywood had someone of Astaire's inventiveness on hand—someone to watch.

Gene Kelly's first original movie musical, *Cover Girl*, was also his first important film. By 1944 MGM had used Kelly in a variety of pictures, including a couple of straight dramas, but it was Columbia that provided the real chance for him to shine. The veteran Broadway composer Arthur Schwartz stepped into a new career by accepting the job of producer on *Cover Girl*, and the esteemed Jerome Kern and Ira Gershwin wrote the songs. For the first time, Kelly had a genuinely talented dancer as a partner, Rita Hayworth.

To insure his own position in the production Kelly brought in Stanley Donen as his dance assistant. Both worked in collaboration with dance director Seymour Felix. Kelly and Donen had become friends when Donen was a chorus boy in *Pal Joey*. Just before coming to Hollywood Kelly had choreographed the Broadway musical *Best Foot Forward*, with Donen as his assistant. When *Best Foot For-*

ward was made into a movie musical by MGM they hired Donen as part of the package. Now that they were both in Hollywood, Kelly and Donen could begin what would become an important partnership in film choreography.

It was with *Cover Girl* that Kelly proved he had choreographic ability of a purely cinematic kind, and that he also had the skill to perform the highly complex and athletic dancing it called for. The most important and impressive part of the film is Kelly's "Alter Ego" dance, which used double-exposure to show Kelly dancing in conflict with himself. He claims it was the most difficult thing he has ever done on film, a technical torture to make, and something he would not want to tackle again. The dance, set in a deserted street at night, begins with Kelly spotting his reflection in a shop window. The character is a man depressed over the loss of his girl, his psyche split between regret over the loss and a feeling that it is for the best.

Explains Kelly, "I wanted to do something that couldn't be done in a theater. In the theater I could have done the scene with a few contortions and a fall to the floor, but I'd found out by now that what worked in a theater didn't always work on the screen. For example, on the stage I would hoof around for a minute or two and wink at the audience, and they'd love it. But in a film that falls flat—the personality is missing and you have to replace it with something that has meaning for the camera. With this situation I had to invent two dances that could be synchronized, and the main problem was rehearsing the cameraman. We had to use a fixed-head camera in order to get the precision

An American in Paris (MGM, 1951). A moment from the ballet with Leslie Caron (opposite), and "Love Is Here to Stay" (left).

181

and Stanley—without whom the piece couldn't have been done—would call out the timings for the cameraman, like 'one-two-three-stop.' We worked for about a month on that dance, then shot it in four days, with a lot more time spent editing all this double-printed footage. Having been told it couldn't be done, I was delighted to bring it off.'

With the success of *Cover Girl*, MGM now had to come up with opportunities for Kelly to use his expertise as a cinematic choreographer. *Anchors Aweigh* (1945) proved to be a breakthrough. Aside from being a lavish and entertaining musical, it provided him with two elaborate routines. The first is a sequence in a film studio as sailor Kelly is shown around as a guest. He slips into fantasy as he imagines what it would be like to court his girlfriend in a costume picture. He dances around a courtyard, scales the walls of a castle, leaps from parapet to balcony to reach his princess, and leaves by making a huge swing on a hanging drapery from one building to another—all to the tune of "La Cumparsita."

However, the highlight of *Anchors Aweigh* is "The King Who Couldn't Dance," in which Kelly combined, for the first time, live action with cartoon animation. The King was MGM's lovable Jerry the Mouse, playing the ruler of a country where dancing is forbidden. Kelly, in the guise of a sailor, changes all that. The idea for the four-minute sequence came from Stanley Donen. After he and Kelly devised a meticulous story board, they first filmed Kelly's dance and then added the mouse frame by frame—ending up with ten thousand frames to synchronize with the live action.

Kelly was next seen in a segment of the gargantuan *Ziegfeld Follies*. MGM well realized it would draw attention, because it paired Kelly with Fred Astaire. Everyone who had been comparing them now had the chance to see them together. "The Babbitt and the Bromide," about a pair of glib gentlemen who meet from time to time throughout their lives and trade the same clichés of greeting, had elements of vaudeville. The routine proved little other than that both dancers were superb. Kelly displayed a slight edge in tap-dancing, but Astaire remained the man with a style beyond comparison. They rehearsed the number for a week and then shot it in two days in May 1944. It was a full two years before *Ziegfeld Follies* was shown, by which time Kelly had been in and out of the United States Navy.

When Kelly returned to MGM after his war service the best the studio could offer was a thin script called *Living in a Big Way* (1947), a story about the problems of wartime marriage. Kelly was asked to devise several dance routines in order to perk it up. In one of these, "Fido and Me," Kelly dances with an amazingly well-trained dog. The major number is Kelly's dance with children at a housing project.

Anchors Aweigh (MGM, 1945). Kelly and Frank Sinatra protest "We Hate to Leave" (opposite), and, with Tom and Jerry, Kelly tells the story of "The King Who Couldn't Dance" (above).

Brigadoon (MGM, 1954). Kelly and Cyd Charisse dance among "The Heather on the Hill" (opposite), and the villagers dance it up (above).

Built around children's games, it develops into athletic leaping all over a half-completed apartment house. Kelly believes it to be one of his best routines; unfortunately, it is largely lost in this dud picture.

Things picked up in 1948 with *The Pirate*, which happily paired him with Judy Garland. Other plusses were a Cole Porter score and the direction of the highly artistic Vincente Minnelli. The Fairbanksian flair Kelly had exhibited in *Anchors Aweigh* was given full expression in the role of a carnival actor on tour in the Caribbean who assumes the identity of an infamous pirate in order to impress a girl. At one point, the romantically inclined girl, fantasizing about her hero, imagines herself joining him in his exploits. In this, "The Pirate Ballet," Kelly leads his ferocious men as they fight off enemies. In the course of the number, he swings through the rigging of his ship, taunts danger in a fire dance, and celebrates his capture of booty with a fearful spear dance. It is an exhaustingly acrobatic sequence. But only a little less so is the finale, "Be a Clown." Kelly chose the Nicholas Brothers as his partners in this frantic, knockabout routine. MGM warned Kelly that the sight of a white man dancing with blacks would cost them some bookings in Southern states, which turned out to be true. Looking at this brilliant piece of comic dancing today, it seems incredible that such thinking ever existed.

The Pirate, although a critical success, turned out to be rather too sophisticated for the masses. Still, it demonstrated the Kelly-Garland appeal, and to cash in on it MGM immediately assigned them to *Easter Parade*, a big but conventional musical with a sure-fire score by Irving Berlin. However, Kelly broke his ankle during the rehearsals. He suggested to the studio that it offer the part to Astaire, who

by this time had been off the screen for two years. The end results were all that MGM could have hoped for. Says Kelly, "I was pleased to be responsible for getting Fred back, but every time I see him and Judy doing 'A Couple of Swells', I do get a twinge of regret."

In the lavish *The Three Musketeers* (1948) Kelly played a very dashing D'Artagnan. Although it was not a musical, his fencing scenes betrayed the earmark of choreography, with much leaping, jumping, and flourishing. It was followed by his staging of "Slaughter on Tenth Avenue" for MGM's *Words and Music*, a facile account of the careers of Rodgers and Hart. As the centerpiece of *On Your Toes*, the ballet,

Avenue" had broken new theatrical ground as the first instance of serious modern ballet in a musical. It performed a similar function in the movies, and it was a perfect showcase for Kelly's muscular, masculine style of dancing. He wisely chose Vera-Ellen as his partner, whom he still regards as among the very best women dancers in film. And she looked upon this mixture of characterization, gymnastics, and drama as the best work of her career.

Take Me Out to the Ball Game (1949) brought Busby Berkeley back as a movie director after several years of bad luck and tragedy, but it was Kelly and Stanley Donen who invented all the dance material, making it easy for Berkeley

Words and Music (MGM, 1948). In "Slaughter on Tenth Avenue" with Vera-Ellen. Opposite: With that other dancer in *Ziegfeld Follies* (MGM, 1946).

choreographed by George Balanchine, had been presented on Broadway in 1936. In the original version, Ray Bolger, lending his comic flair to the material, danced himself into a state of exhaustion in his attempt to elude capture by a group of gangsters.

Kelly shortened the ballet from eleven to seven minutes. In the process, he truncated some of the lyrical passages, played up the dramatic substance, and invented a new story. In the film version, Kelly plays a tough guy in a low-life section of New York. He falls for a pretty street girl but loses her when a former boyfriend, a jealous hood, shoots and kills her. He and the hood then engage in a savage fight, which leaves them both dead. On Broadway, "Slaughter on Tenth

to manage the rest of the picture. This was, for the most part, a gesture of gratitude for what Berkeley had done for film choreography. Kelly says, "I learned a lot from Buzz, not the least of which was to keep my eyes open at all times in making films and to look for new ways to do things."

Take Me Out to the Ball Game is important in that it paved the way for *On the Town*. The dances that Kelly and Donen had devised for the former film, especially those with Kelly and Frank Sinatra, had delighted both the studio and the public. Arthur Freed gave the signal to proceed with *On the Town*, a Broadway hit in 1944 with music by Leonard Bernstein and script by Comden and Green. As directed by Kelly and Stanley Donen, it now became an important film musical—the first to be filmed with extended sequences on location. Others may have had the idea before him, but Kelly managed to do it, setting a precedent for opening up the movie musical.

As three sailors on leave in New York, Kelly, Sinatra, and Jules Munshin make a whirlwind tour of the sights—they visit the Statue of Liberty, prance around Rockefeller Center, and scamper around Central Park, all the while singing and dancing. And they go after girls. Since two of the girls turn out to be Vera-Ellen and Ann Miller, the *On the Town* audiences had every reason to look for exceptional dances. However, the MGM brass was disappointed with the results, believing the movie to be too different to be successful. Like film executives both before and since, they were proven wrong.

On the Town was a project born of the greatest kind of enthusiasm on the part of the people involved. Says Stanley Donen, "We had a five-week rehearsal period, and after four weeks we were ready to shoot…we were so excited about the whole production we could have shot it backwards."

It is Kelly's point of pride among his films. "I agree it may not be as good as *Singin' in the Rain* or as much of an achievement as *An American in Paris*, but I think it meant more to the movies at that time. It's dated now, of course, because the techniques gradually became more common and the theme of sailors on a spree has been done to death, but in 1949 the idea of believable sailors dancing and singing in the streets of New York—using the city as a set—was new, and it paved the way for musicals like *West Side Story*. After *On the Town* musicals opened up."

Kelly next danced in the far less impressive *Summer Stock* (1950), for which MGM slipped back into the conventional backstage musical pattern. It reunited Kelly with Judy Garland, but not under happy conditions. Her failing health

On the Town (MGM, 1949). Dancing with Vera-Ellen, and in the ballet fantasy (opposite), in which dancers Alex Romero and Lee Sneddon substituted for Frank Sinatra and Jules Munshin.

led the studio to sever her contract after this picture. Nick Castle was the dance director, but Kelly invented a dance sequence for himself. Set in a barn that has been converted into a summer theater, it opens with Kelly quietly dancing alone on the bare stage to the tune of Harry Warren's "You, Wonderful You." He discovers a stage board that squeaks and exploits it rhythmically. Next he spreads a piece of newspaper on the stage and uses it in somewhat the same way soft-shoe dancers use sand. With these modest devices he built up an engaging dance, proving that dances for film can be drawn from small devices as well as big ones. It is, indeed, a film dance, utilizing the intimacy of the camera and the introspection of the character. On the stage, it would not have worked nearly as effectively.

The idea for *An American in Paris* (1951) came from Arthur Freed, who, in the company of Ira Gershwin, had attended a Gershwin concert at which the famous piece was played. Freed mused that the title was fine for a film and asked Ira if he could develop the idea of a musical based around it, using a score of Gershwin songs. Ira agreed not only with the concept but with the idea that the only logical man to cast in the lead was Kelly. Alan Jay Lerner invented the story, about a GI who stays on in Europe after the war and studies painting in Paris. He is for a while supported by a wealthy American lady, but he falls in love with a modest young girl.

Kelly himself hired Leslie Caron to play the girl. He had seen her as a dancer with the Ballet des Champs-Elysées in Paris, and he convinced MGM that she was perfect for the part. Their teaming resulted in some indelible moments in film history, particularly their duet dancing of "Love Is Here to Stay" alongside the Seine and "Embraceable You," in which Caron appears in a montage of different dances as the enamored hero imagines what kind of a girl she might be. But the triumph of *An American in Paris* is the ballet finale.

The ballet was filmed after the rest of the picture had been completed. The original idea to shorten it was dropped when it became apparent to the studio that it had a potential hit on its hands. Vincente Minnelli worked with Kelly on the libretto of the seventeen-minute production and then left him alone for five weeks to rehearse his dancers. Art director Preston Ames, who himself had been a student in Paris from 1927 to 1932, was brought in to design the set that would bring him and his co-workers an Oscar. He assigned painters to create various backdrops in the style of some of the great French artists, such as Renoir, Dufy, Rousseau, Toulouse-Lautrec, and Utrillo, and Kelly designed his choreography to match the visual styles.

The libretto calls for the art student hero to continually meet and court and lose his girl, as she moves through vari-

ous Parisian locations, all in the style of the painters who have influenced him. The ballet is a summation of Kelly's work as a film dancer and choreographer, and it allowed him a full range of styles—classical ballet, modern ballet, Cohanesque hoofing, tapping, jitterbugging, and sheer athletic expression. He refers to it as "a synthesis of old forms and new rhythms." *An American in Paris* won seven Oscars, including best picture, and Kelly was awarded a special Oscar for his work in motion picture choreography.

In terms of artistry, *An American in Paris* is the highpoint of Kelly's film career. In terms of sheer enjoyment and popularity, it is exceeded by *Singin' in the Rain* (1952), which some connoisseurs regard as the best of all movie musicals. It was certainly a joyous experience for producer Arthur Freed, for the score was a compilation of songs that he, as a lyricist, had written with Nacio Herb Brown through the years for MGM musicals. It is also one of the best films Hollywood has ever made about itself, good-naturedly spoofing the years of transition from silents to sound. Kelly says, "All we began with was a skit about a movie star becoming a sound star, and we all of us dashed around the studio asking the veterans what it was like in the old days,

and the script was built around the information we picked up. So what happened in the framework of the story was true, this is what it was like around MGM in 1928—with a little comedic exaggeration, of course."

Kelly designed two major routines for himself in *Singin' in the Rain*, the title number and an extensive ballet built around two Freed-Brown songs, "Broadway Melody" and "Broadway Rhythm." In this last, Kelly did the little bit of business that is almost his trademark: the exuberant chanting in staccato style, "Got-ta dance! Got-ta dance!" The routine is built around the adventures of an eager young hoofer who comes to the Big Time to carve a career for himself. By the time he makes it he sees another equally eager youngster arriving with the same ambition. "The Broadway Ballet" took a month to rehearse and two weeks to shoot. Despite its impressiveness, it is the far simpler title dance that almost everyone remembers about this film. It is associated with Gene Kelly in the lasting and affectionate way that Rhett Butler is associated with Clark Gable and Robin Hood with Errol Flynn.

The sight of a happy man skipping along the sidewalk, climbing a lamppost, letting a drainpipe of rainwater cascade on his face, and splashing around in puddles is indeed a marvelous sight to behold. And yet for Kelly it was comparatively easy, requiring little of the labor that went into *On the Town* or *An American in Paris*. "The concept was so simple I shied away from explaining it to the brass at the stu-

Above: Could this be the one about the happy fellow singing and dancing in the rain? *An American in Paris* (MGM, 1951). Kelly and Leslie Caron in the ballet. Opposite: *Brigadoon* (MGM, 1954). The hefty fellow trying to do a Scottish reel is Van Johnson.

dio in case I couldn't make it sound worth doing. The real work for this one was done by the technicians who had to pipe two city blocks on the backlot with overhead sprays, and the poor cameraman who had to shoot through all that water. All I had to do was dance."

Singin' in the Rain has gradually gained the status of a classic film, not simply because of its music and its dances but because of its fine construction, its story, and its characters. It does not date. On the other hand, it gave Gene Kelly the problem of finding a vehicle as good for the rest of his career. Two years went by before he tackled another musical, and then he chose one completely different in character.

By the time *Brigadoon*, which began its life on Broadway in 1947, was filmed in 1954, it had assumed almost classic proportions. Also by this time, the movie musical as a genre had passed its box-office peak, and MGM refused to invest the money that Kelly and Vincente Minnelli felt the film needed to do it justice. Their idea to shoot it in Scotland was quashed as too expensive, as was the secondary concept of shooting it on rugged Californian locations. It ended up being filmed entirely on MGM sound stages, and to make Minnelli even more disgruntled he was forced to use for the first time in his experience CinemaScope, whose long rectangular shape forced both him and Kelly to rethink their staging concepts. They were not the only filmmakers to shudder at the thought of having to employ CinemaScope.

Brigadoon was a disappointment for Kelly, as it was for many other people, but there remains much to admire, including the superb set built by art director Preston Ames. It filled MGM's largest sound stage, constructed in such a manner that Minnelli could shoot a full 360 degrees and give the illusion of great distance. This was also of great advantage to Kelly in planning his choreography. The Scottish group-dancing he directed sparkles with vitality, and his dancing with Cyd Charisse, which accents the theme of idyllic love in relatively simple balletic style, gives the film its best moments.

The experience with *Brigadoon* made it abundantly clear that, for the movie musical, the handwriting was on the wall. Kelly refused to limit himself to musicals. Even before *Brigadoon*, he had appeared in dramatic pictures between musicals. Now he looked for assignments as director as well as actor. In 1957 he directed *The Happy Road*, followed by *The Tunnel of Love* in 1958.

For MGM's all-star tribute to composer Sigmund Romberg, *Deep in My Heart*, Kelly teamed up with his brother Fred to do a vaudevillian routine called "I Love to Go Swimmin' with Wimmen," an obscure item that Romberg had contributed to a 1917 Broadway musical. This

pleasing romp of a dance brought Fred Kelly on the screen for the first and last time; he went back to being a dance director for television and for the stage. Stanley Donen directed the Romberg picture and then joined Kelly as a co-director on *It's Always Fair Weather* (1955), an original musical scripted by Betty Comden and Adolph Green, with music by André Previn. As co-directors Kelly and Donen could never again reach the heights they had enjoyed with *On the Town* and *Singin' in the Rain*, but *Fair Weather* has some fair moments.

Again Kelly partnered himself with Cyd Charisse. Perhaps more interestingly, he partnered himself as well with two superb dancers, Dan Dailey and Michael Kidd. For this story of three wartime buddies who meet for a reunion ten years after leaving the army, Kelly's original concept had been to bring together the *On the Town* trio. Frank Sinatra, now a superstar, proved difficult to deal with; Jules Munshin was not enough of a name to be accepted by the MGM chieftains. Ultimately this turned out for the better, because the really worthwhile moments of *Fair Weather* are the dances done by Kelly, Dailey, and Kidd in unison.

Kidd's esteem at MGM was high because of the choreography he did for *The Band Wagon* and *Seven Brides for Seven Brothers*, and Dailey had long been well regarded as an engaging hoofer. The film's first dance is particularly impressive, as the three soldiers return to New York and go out on a merry binge. They leap from one saloon to the

next, dance under the Third Avenue El, spring in and out of taxis, and then attach garbage-can lids to their left feet and thump-dance all over the street. This is one of the select moments in film choreography.

Kelly had another dancing highpoint in *Fair Weather*, and it brought him a lot of attention from those who wondered how it could be done. The scene begins when he makes his escape from a troublesome situation at a gymnasium; later, at a skating rink, he puts on roller skates, and his mood picks up as he sails out onto the streets. He starts to sing "I Like Myself," all the while gliding along the sidewalks on the skates, giving him a feeling of release that finds an outlet in some nifty skating figures and tap-dancing. His dexterity while tapping with roller skates is amazing, but Kelly had mastered skating as an ice hockey player, and he claims that the tapping is not as difficult as it looks. Nonskater-dancers find that hard to believe.

For some years Kelly had been dreaming about a film that would be seriously devoted to the art of dancing, one that would take full advantage of cinematic choreography. The idealistic concept did not much interest MGM, but it finally came into being through the support of Arthur Freed, on the understanding that it would be filmed in England. *Invitation to the Dance* is the apotheosis of Gene Kelly's career,

even though it proved, as the MGM brass suspected, not to be a crowd-pleaser.

It consists of three ballets: "Circus," with music by Jacques Ibert; "Ring Around the Rosy," with music by André Previn; and "Sinbad the Sailor," with music from Rimsky-Korsakov's *Scheherazade* adapted by Roger Edens. A fourth part was planned but dropped as the production turned out to be longer and more difficult than realized. Production began at MGM's Elstree studio, taking advantage of its frozen British funds, in October of 1952. Four years would pass before the public had a chance to view the results. During the long, drawn-out production, Kelly made a dramatic film in England, *Crest of the Wave*, and *Brigadoon* at home base.

The artistry of *Invitation to the Dance* apart, the fact that it was made at all reveals much about the character of Kelly. As music director John Green explains, "Gene is not simply a persuasive man — he's a slugging persuader. There's very little velvet glove when he sets his sights on something, and so *Invitation to the Dance* came to be. Freed was the nominal producer but it was Gene who determined the road map of the entire film — he sought out the talent, hired it, commissioned the music, devised the choreography, directed it, and danced in each of the stories. It is *his* picture."

"Circus" was the episode that most impressed dance

critics. Here Kelly plays a clown à la Pagliacci, vainly in love with the circus's leading lady (Claire Sombert), who is also loved by a high-wire walker (Igor Youskevitch). It is the most serious dancing Kelly has ever done in a film. "Ring Around the Rosy" is a modern ballet, with Kelly as a Marine involved with a chain of people as a bracelet passes in possession among them. The dancing includes tap and modern movements as well as classic steps. "Sinbad the Sailor" brought Kelly back to the art of animation and the painstaking business of matching live dancing with drawn frames. The complicated sequence tied up the MGM cartoon department for a year, as it turned out a quarter of a million sketches and 57,000 frames to accommodate Kelly's account of a sailor who finds a magic lamp in old Baghdad.

Kelly did not want to appear in all three episodes but MGM insisted. "They were investing a million dollars and wanted some protection for their money. My name was about all they could gamble on. As a producer myself I could see their point of view. And I tend to agree with those who find the whole thing a bit much — each piece is enjoyable by itself but three in a row is probably more than most people can take." Be that as it may, no other entertainer has devoted as much time and effort to trying to interest the mass public in a film about the skill and joy of dancing.

In 1957 Kelly made *The Happy Road* for MGM in France, although the studio insisted that he play the lead in this genial little comedy as well as direct it. This was followed by his final MGM musical, *Les Girls* (1957), with a score by Cole Porter. As an American nightclub entertainer who tours with a trio of girls, Kelly got to dance with Mitzi Gaynor, Kay Kendall, and Taina Elg. Elg had been a ballet dancer in her native Finland, and in *Les Girls* she appears to advantage with Kelly in "The Rope Dance," a sensuous duet in a strange, geometric setting. While Kelly performed agreeably with the three girls, his highpoint is a satire on the Marlon Brando motorcycle thug of *The Wild One*. Dancing in black leather jacket, he belts out "Why Am I So Gone about That Gal."

Although *Les Girls* pleased audiences, it was considered a comedown from the heyday of the previous few years. With time it has gained in stature, but in 1957 moviegoers had their fill of dancing from television variety shows; they sought other forms of entertainment in films. At the same time, higher costs led the studios to limit their musical investments to filmings of Broadway smash hits — and even that entailed risk. Another factor — which is harder to understand than the others — was that there seemed to be no replacements for the likes of Kelly, Astaire, and the other giants of the movie musical. The times had definitely changed.

Opposite: *Deep in My Heart* (MGM, 1954). With brother Fred, doing "I Love to Go Swimmin' with Wimmen." Below: *It's Always Fair Weather* (MGM, 1955). Skating to the tune of "I Like Myself."

The rip-roaring "Broadway Ballet" in *Singin' in the Rain* (MGM, 1952).

The successful *Marjorie Morningstar,* in which Kelly co-starred with Natalie Wood, allowed him, as a performer-director of resort shows on the borscht circuit, a little dancing. After that, Kelly sought assignments as a director and as an actor. He directed *The Tunnel of Love* for MGM, although by now he was off contract and a free-lancer, and then appeared in *Inherit the Wind.* His career opened up in other directions; he was hired by Rodgers and Hammerstein to direct their *Flower Drum Song* on Broadway, and there were always things being offered by television.

In 1960, 20th Century-Fox hired him to appear as himself in *Let's Make Love,* teaching Yves Montand how to dance in order to win Marilyn Monroe. Four years later Fox hired him to spoof himself as one of the guest stars in *What a Way to Go,* pairing him with Shirley MacLaine. Together they strutted through a deliberately overblown routine called "Musical Extravaganza," dancing all over the deck of a luxury liner. Shades of Busby Berkeley — and that other dancing couple in *Follow the Fleet.*

When Jacques Demy, who had had such a hit with *The Umbrellas of Cherbourg,* decided to make *The Young Girls of Rochefort* in 1967, he aimed at a tribute to the Hollywood musical form. But he was not a choreographer, and his efforts failed to make much of an impression, even though he brought in Kelly to dance with his stars, Catherine Deneuve and Françoise Dorleac. Kelly staged his own dances, but the other dances reveal little understanding of groupings and movements. "I think Demy made a mistake in hiring Catherine and Françoise; the parts needed girls of exceptional dancing and singing ability but neither of them could sing and they had had no dancing experience. Almost everyone in the picture had to be dubbed and this puts a great strain on a musical. And they all made the mistake of assuming that it's easy to learn to dance for a film, because it looks so easy. It isn't."

It also is not easy to continue dancing beyond the age of fifty, no matter how much experience a man has had. The demands on Kelly as a guest star in films and on television were continual; with time, however, he became economical about such appearances. He preferred to direct films, and he did well with *A Guide for the Married Man, Hello, Dolly!,* and *The Cheyenne Social Club.* He was well in evidence when *That's Entertainment* was released in 1974, both as a host and as one of the stars whose material made up the happy compilation.

Two years later Kelly was hired to direct *That's Entertainment, Part II,* which included devising a new set of dances for the title sequences and dancing them in tandem with Fred Astaire. Those who had been curious about

whether seventy-seven-year-old Astaire and sixty-four-year-old Kelly could still dance had their curiosity satisfied. In 1980 Kelly supplied more evidence of his youthful agility by dancing with Olivia Newton-John in *Xanadu*.

While it is remarkable that Hollywood has produced only two major male star dancers, it is also remarkable that both have enjoyed long careers. That there have not been more performers of this caliber is due mostly to the fact that dancers need years of study to qualify for their work, which leaves little time for any other kind of study. Kelly says, "This concentration on perfecting dancing to the exclusion of other areas of being an entertainer is strange to anyone who isn't involved. The point is simply that nature is against you—by the time you've learned your craft your anatomy is starting to run down. The older you get as a dancer the harder it is to grind up the physical forces. A writer can still pound a typewriter at fifty; an actor is usually better at fifty than he was at thirty; but it's the reverse with a dancer. Just when he is experienced and mature he starts running out of steam. The dancer's life is probably the shortest artistic life in the world, and you have to face that fact when you get into it. You have to love being in this business otherwise you couldn't stand it, because it's so hard. It's almost masochistic and you couldn't do it if you didn't enjoy it. And you have to be born with a love of movement. As a boy I loved to run and jump—to move through the air and against the ground. You can't dance without that love."

Of the many awards that Gene Kelly has garnered, one of the most significant was presented at the Kennedy Center in Washington, D.C., on the evening of December 5, 1983, when he was made an honoree of the center, along with George Abbott, Lillian Gish, Benny Goodman, and Eugene Ormandy. The annual televised gala honors those who have made important, lifetime contributions to American art and entertainment. Yves Montand, chosen to begin the tribute to Kelly, made the point of how highly he is regarded by the French: "Gene will always be our American in Paris — and much more. He put dance on the street. For the first time we saw a classical dancer, in trousers, a short shirt, and loafers — but still elegant, dancing in the street and making us feel we can dance just like him. He is in the people's hearts everywhere — an American for the whole world."

Above: *Invitation to the Dance* (MGM, 1956). With Tamara Toumanova in "Ring Around the Rosy." Left: With Kay Kendall, one of the most delightful of *Les Girls* (MGM, 1957). Opposite: The "Musical Extravaganza" with Shirley MacLaine in *What a Way to Go* (Fox, 1964).

ANN MILLER

All I know is that some people are born to dance and I was one of them. I'm mad for dancing, not only on screen but off. I've never got my fill of it. 'I Could Have Danced All Night' might have been written just for me." To doubt these words from the mouth of Ann Miller would be like doubting that the North Pole is cold in winter. Not only is she a lover of dancing but her track record is almost unbelievable. She was fourteen when RKO chose her as one of its *New Faces of 1937*. In covering the first showing in Hollywood, *Variety* noted, "Ann Miller doing taps drew a salvo of applause at this screening." A few days later the *New York Herald Tribune* critic Howard Barnes wrote, "The plot is all about the familiar difficulties of putting on a Broadway show and it is the audition for this that brings on the new personalities that the entertainment boasts. The best of them, to my mind, are Ann Miller, a rather good tap dancer, and the Three Chocolateers, who strut exuberantly." No one has heard of the Three Chocolateers since then, whereas no one has ceased to hear about Ann Miller.

In *You Can't Take It with You* (Columbia, 1938), with Mischa Auer as the mad ballet master. Page 198: *The Thrill of Brazil* (Columbia, 1946). Ann does a samba titled "The Custom House."

In 1983 Ann Miller reached the age of sixty, an amazingly youthful sixty and an age, as Gene Kelly points out, at which most dancers have long since hung up their shoes. Veteran dancers, Kelly included, may occasionally take the shoes down to make a hopefully brief guest appearance, but in the case of Ann Miller the shoes seem to be seldom off. By 1983 she had already put in four years co-starring with Mickey Rooney in the vaudeville extravaganza *Sugar Babies*, and the end of its run is not yet in sight. In covering the New

York opening at the Mark Hellinger Theatre the esteemed Walter Kerr of the *New York Times* noted that she was in stunning shape, "ready to leap from a baggage cart, whip off gloves and overskirt, and tap as though there'd been no yesterday. She strides through sketches, split-skirt put to good advantage, with a hammer-and-tongs authority."

The Miller story is a Cinderella story. It might have served as the plot for one of the many minor-league musicals she made at Columbia in the early forties. She was born in Houston, Texas, on April 12, 1923, a date about which she has become very sensitive because as a fourteen-year-old she lied in order to pass herself off as an eighteen-year-old and get into the movies. The only child of an unhappy marriage, Ann owes her success largely to her mother, who transferred all of her own hopes onto her daughter.

In her autobiography, *Miller's High Life*, Ann tells of a meeting with a bedraggled gypsy fortune-teller at a Houston bus station when she was a child. The gypsy told her that her future was filled with music, dance, lights, and money. As a scene in a Columbia musical this would play rather feebly but truth is, of course, more absurd than fiction. After they saw Eleanor Powell in *Broadway Melody of 1936* mother said to daughter, "Someday you're going to be a big star like that." Not even a Columbia musical would have used a line like that.

Because her father hoped for a boy, Ann was named Johnny Lucille Collier, although she never used the first name. Because she showed signs of having rickets she was enrolled in dancing classes to strengthen her long legs, but they were lessons in ballet and she never took to them. Not until Bill Robinson came to play at the Majestic Theatre in Houston did little Lucille become enthused about dancing. There was, she says, "something in the way he danced that turned me on. After the show my mother took me backstage to meet him and she insisted, much to my embarrassment, that I do a little step for him. She wanted him to tell her if I was doing my steps properly . . . he watched my little ballet number. Then he did a few taps for me and asked me to tap along with him. He sang 'Bye, Bye, Blues' and clapped out the rhythm with his hands, and there I was doing my first tap dance with Mr. Bojangles in his dressing room. I took to tap dancing like a duck to water. I seemed to have a natural rhythm . . . but I knew that I would never be a ballerina or an acrobatic dancer. There was too much rhythm in me—which is probably why I never took to ballet. But tap dancing was something else . . . it was as though that little girl Lucille who loathed ballet had suddenly and magically sprouted wings on her feet . . . now I didn't mind rehearsing . . . because the wings on my feet seemed to lift me up and fly me away on some magic carpet. It is still like that with me to this day, a wondrous, exhilarating kind of magic when I'm dancing that simply flies me out of the here-and-now of reality."

Once indoctrinated with tap-dance fever, there was no stopping little Lucille Collier. Nor could her teachers stop her from going off on her own bat, whirling and jumping and making up her own steps. "I had an affinity for drums. I loved drums. Just dancing to drumbeats without any music at all was exciting to me." Such a passion inevitably led to appearances in local amateur shows and charity events, and as an eight-year-old she caused a few gasps when she did a sensuous belly dance as an Egyptian at the Big Brothers Club. Years later at Columbia, in a 1944 picture called *Hey, Rookie*, she did a more refined and even more passionate version of that dance and called it "Streamlined Sheik."

In the summer of 1934 Lucille and her mother went to Hollywood for an extended vacation. Mother registered

Lucille with Central Casting and put her in the Fanchon and Marco Dancing School, the best of its kind. It was there that she met sixteen-year-old Marguerite Cansino and her father, Spanish dancer Jose Cansino, who did a dancing act together. Jose was also a teacher at the school. His daughter later became known as Rita Hayworth. Another student at that time, Frances Gumm, afterward changed her name to Judy Garland — and it was Mrs. Gumm who played the piano for the children's programs at the school. While studying, Lucille picked up jobs as an extra in several movies. In the late summer she joined the cast of a stage revue, *All Abroad*, telling the producers she was fifteen instead of eleven. When summer ended it was back to Houston and back to school.

The return to Houston was a family calamity. Mr. Collier was discovered with another lady in his bedroom and the long-ailing marriage came to a quick end. Mrs. Collier and

Too Many Girls (RKO, 1940). Ann does "The Pottawatomie" with a young Cuban drummer named Desi Arnaz.

The title number from *Time Out for Rhythm* (Columbia, 1941), with Glen Gray and the Casa Loma Orchestra. Below: Doing "I Wish I Could Be a Singing Cowboy" with Allen Jenkins in *Go West, Young Lady* (Columbia, 1941), Ann dances with spurs — carefully.

her daughter soon went back to Hollywood, where they lived in a small apartment under meager circumstances. There was no alimony, and Mrs. Collier was almost totally deaf, which made her chances for employment slim. Her desire to promote her daughter in a career was practical as much as idealistic. No longer able to afford lessons with Fanchon and Marco, she found a more modest studio belonging to William Morgan, who gradually managed to get Lucille jobs at Elks, Rotary, and Lions Club luncheons. Morgan assigned a pianist named Harry Fields to accompany her; it was Fields who came up with the name Ann Miller.

Mother and daughter struggled through the next two years. The only way Ann could get work was to lie about her age. Her first major job was in San Francisco, at the Bal Tabarin, where she was hired for three weeks but stayed on for sixteen. Her tap-dancing, with its machine gun-like precision, now reached a more important audience. One evening RKO starlet Lucille Ball dropped in, in company with studio talent scout Benny Rubin. She reportedly said to Rubin, "That girl's a marvelous dancer. You ought to get her a screen test — she could give Eleanor Powell a run for her money." Rubin apparently needed little persuasion. When he asked Mrs. Collier the age of her daughter, she instantly replied, "Eighteen." Rubin looked skeptical and said he would need to see a birth certificate.

Ann's father became a party to a forged certificate of birth, something that was relatively easy for him to arrange since he happened to be a criminal lawyer. It invented a new name, Lucy Ann Collier; a new date, April 12, 1919; and a new birthplace, Chireno, Texas. Now there was no stopping the suddenly four-year-older Ann Miller. In early 1937 her mother took her to RKO Radio Studios for her test. She was a full five-foot-seven, with stunning legs, although her bust was aided by pads.

Out of that test came *New Faces of 1937*. "We rehearsed my number in the morning and shot it in the afternoon. It took only two hours to do it. They had three cameras on me, and again as with my singing and dancing, I seemed to know instinctively, with no previous training, how to pose for the cameras, how to angle my tap-dancing routines so that my body would look right from certain camera angles. I did it all by instinct. It was as though an invisible force was guiding my every move. And I did it right. Everyone seemed pleased." RKO was so pleased that it straightaway put her into *Life of the Party*, with eighth billing and two dances. Ann Miller was on her way.

For its filming of the important Edna Ferber-George S. Kaufman play *Stage Door*, RKO invented a small part for Ann, the friend of the character played by Ginger Rogers. In this tale of fledgling actresses living at a theatrical boardinghouse, Ann and Ginger do a number together in a nightclub, "Put Your Heart into Your Feet and Dance." Fourteen-year-old Ann Miller barely needed the persuasion of the lyrics to do just that.

RKO gave Ann the female lead in her next film, *Radio City Revels*, released at the start of 1938. The studio paired her with tenor Kenny Baker, who gave her her first screen kiss — which she claims was her first kiss ever. Although many people at the studio suspected she was not as old as she claimed to be, she was now a valuable property, and one to be protected. She was enrolled at the Hollywood Professional School, doing her schoolwork in the evenings and by mail. *Radio City Revels* brought her into contact with dance director Hermes Pan for the first time; it would become a long and friendly association throughout her film career.

The career enjoyed another step forward when Columbia borrowed her for Frank Capra's production of *You Can't Take It with You*, which won an Oscar as the best film of 1938. Her role as the lightheaded ballet dancer Elsie Carmichael was small but highly visible. She found it easy to draw upon her own ballet experiences to play a girl unable to cope with the movements. Her scenes were greatly aided by Mischa Auer as her mad Russian ballet teacher, whose comment on her dancing was, "Confidentially, she stinks." But that was also the teacher's assessment of everything else.

Back at RKO Ann was given what might have been an interesting part, a nonmusical role in the Marx Brothers' *Room Service*. Unfortunately, it turned out to be their least funny picture. This was followed by the even worse *Tarnished Angel*. Something was going wrong with her career, and for reasons that she had no way of understanding until they were explained to her. MGM had been making noises about the fact that her dance routines were obviously similar to those of its Eleanor Powell. Ann now learned that Eleanor, like herself, was represented by the William Morris Agency, and that it was Eleanor's impressive contract that had enabled the agency to set up shop in Hollywood. Obviously, it didn't want any competition with its prize earner. It advised Ann to give up her RKO contract and go to New York, where it would find her a part in a musical. Ann was reluctant to give up her budding movie career but the agency talked her mother into the move. It turned out to be a very good one—more by luck than by any honest endeavor on the part of the agents.

Ann was signed for *The George White Scandals of 1939*. White had been doing these musical revues since 1925, but his star was on the wane and this would be the last of them. The levels of both quality and taste had dropped, and in the Boston tryouts Ann found herself in a show some critics

Reveille with Beverly (Columbia, 1943). "Thumbs Up and V for Victory."

regarded as sleazy. It was cleaned up somewhat by the time it made its Broadway opening at the Alvin Theatre, where it ran for four months. It then went on the road for half a year, and everywhere it went the performer who drew the most raves was Ann Miller, dazzling audiences with a flashing number called "The Mexiconga." One New York critic described her as an eye tonic, a personality that whirls with hurricane force across the footlights. And practically every critic made some reference to her as the best tapper since Eleanor Powell deserted the stage for the movies.

The Hollywood studios in 1940 started bidding to get Ann Miller back on the screen. The best offer came from her old bosses at RKO, who gave her third billing in the Rodgers and Hart musical *Too Many Girls*. George Abbott had produced it on Broadway and he was brought to Hollywood to make it into a film. Lucille Ball had the lead, and it was in making this picture that she met a young Cuban drummer and dancer named Desi Arnaz. With LeRoy Prinz as dance director, Ann had excellent material in the frantic college dance "The Pottawatomie," the name of the school where the story takes place, and "Spic 'n' Spanish," a conga done in company with bongo-beating Desi. *Too Many Girls* drew good notices; for Ann, it was a good return to the movies.

Republic, a studio profitably devoted to making B pictures, attempted to widen its market by making *Hit Parade of 1941*, with radio stars Kenny Baker and Frances Langford in the leads, and a part for Ann Miller as the dancing star of a major radio show. Since this was a film it mattered little that the device of dancing on radio was hardly arresting. What

mattered were her two big numbers, "Pan America Conga" and "Swing Low, Sweet Rhythm," which caused *The Hollywood Reporter* to say, "There should be a law against Ann Miller's ever taking time off from dancing." To cash in on this reaction, Republic immediately gave her the lead in *Melody Ranch*, a Gene Autry Western. Hoping to make Autry more palatable to a larger than usual audience, the studio conferred on the film a slightly higher than usual budget. It did not work.

The next offer came from Columbia, to co-star with Rudy Vallee in *Time Out for Rhythm* — with the rhythm of the dancing its only virtue. That it proved a boon to Ann was due entirely to Bosley Crowther, then America's foremost film critic, who described it in the *New York Times* as hopelessly heavy and labored, but added, "Except for the lovely and lively Miss Miller, who simply won't be suppressed, it is one of the dullest diversions in months. Miss Miller, when she sings or dances, does so charmingly and with ease." Harry Cohn, the czar of Columbia, was so impressed with this comment from Crowther that on the basis of it he signed her to a long-term contract.

Cohn had Rita Hayworth under contract as his major musical star, but he needed a singer-dancer to head up his profitable program pictures, the double-bill items that hovered somewhere between an A and a B. Ann Miller was exactly what he needed, and for the next five years he kept her busy, and he did very well by the arrangement. Her musicals at Columbia were a vital part of film programming during the years of World War II. Unfortunately, their lightweight material and nonmemorable songs soon dated these movies, now totally forgotten. The pity is that her dances from these movies are now seldom seen.

Go West, Young Lady (1941) was a good start to the series. It gave young Glenn Ford a boost in his budding career and it gave Ann the kind of role Marlene Dietrich had played in *Destry Rides Again*, that of a brassy dance-hall hostess. It even included Ann brawling with Penny Singleton, much as Dietrich had tangled with Una Merkel in *Destry*. One of the picture's merrier moments was Ann's song and dance with the veteran character actor Allen Jenkins, "I Wish I Could Be a Singing Cowboy." Cohn then loaned Ann to Paramount—it did not hurt Cohn to let some other studio help build up her image—for two of its minor musicals, *True to the Army* and *Priorities on Parade*. When she returned to Columbia, she got her first starring vehicle, *Reveille with Beverly*.

Reveille with Beverly is a good example of a typical wartime musical. Released in February 1943, it was based on the career of broadcaster Jean Ruth, whose disc jockey show was aimed at the armed forces. The film used the simple

Above: While filming *The Thrill of Brazil* (Columbia, 1946), Ann engaged in a contest with expert typist Ruth Myers to see who could tap faster. The typist was clocked at 584 taps to the minute; Ann beat her with 627. Opposite: *What's Buzzin' Cousin* (Columbia, 1943). The title of the number is "$18.75." Honestly. Right: *Jam Session* (Columbia, 1944). Doing "The Victory Polka" with Bill Shawn.

205

device of the spinning records evolving into visuals of the artists concerned, such as the bands of Bob Crosby, Freddie Slack, Duke Ellington, Count Basie, and an appearance by skinny, youthful Frank Sinatra. Its finale was a camp show, with disc spinner Ann giving out with the spirited "Thumbs Up and V for Victory."

Made at a cost of about three hundred thousand dollars, it turned out to be a sleeper for Columbia, bringing in three million dollars. Legend has it that the besieged garrison at Corregidor had only one film on hand, *Reveille with Beverly*, and that they ran it over and over to keep up their spirits. When General Douglas MacArthur met Ann years later he said, "I'd know you anywhere. You did quite a dance. I must have seen that film a hundred times."

Next came *What's Buzzin' Cousin*, with a big production finale titled "$18.75," which happened to be the price of a war bond at that time. It looked like something Eleanor Powell might have done had she been under contract to Columbia and working on small-budget pictures. The film's release in the summer of 1943 coincided with Eleanor's decision to retire from the screen, which now left the tap-dance field with Ann as its principal star. In point of fact, there simply were no others even close to that particular spotlight.

In *Hey, Rookie* Ann did the lively "There Goes Taps" with

Bill Shawn. The real pleasure in this picture for her was doing "Streamlined Sheik," in which she perfected the belly dance little Lucille Collier had done not so many years previously in Houston. At least Ann was now twenty-one years of age, although still stuck with the fib of being four years older. By now, however, her age was not a factor; she was simply a beautiful young girl doing a job she obviously loved doing, and she became a pin-up favorite of the troops while doing it. In *Jam Session* she danced "No Name Jive" and "The Victory Polka," again with Bill Shawn. Then Kay Kyser came to Columbia to star in *Carolina Blues*, bringing not only his band but his beautiful bride, model-singer Georgia Carroll. Kyser insisted that Mrs. Kyser get the lion's share of the spotlight, which meant Ann received less than usual.

Carolina Blues was well titled as far as Ann was concerned, but *Eadie Was a Lady* helped her to forget it. Eadie was a Boston socialite who behaved very properly by day; by night, she danced up a storm in a burlesque show. Ann sang the title song with Mae West flourishes but came into her own with the dance finale "The Greeks Never Mentioned It." If the choreography appears better than the average in these Columbia musicals the credit goes to Jack Cole, a student of the famed Ruth St. Denis in New York. Cole finally settled in Hollywood after years as a choreographer-dancer for stage shows and nightclubs. A specialist in Oriental and Hindu dancing, he became one of the most original of film dance directors. It is interesting to watch his early work with Ann Miller in *Eadie Was a Lady*.

As World War II drew to a close, so did Ann Miller's reign as a star of wartime musicals. *Eadie Was a Lady* was the last one to deal with servicemen, although even here they were seen only as members of an audience. Trying for a change of image, Columbia starred her in *Eve Knew Her Apples*, but made the mistake of giving her five songs to sing and no dancing. It was released to poor reviews in April 1945, and a year and a half drifted by before Ann appeared in her next film, *The Thrill of Brazil*. By this time there had been not only a change in her screen image but a change in her personal life. She married Reese Milner, an heir to a steel corporation, who demanded that she give up her career. Twenty-three years old and, by her own admission, more gullible than she should have been, Ann advised Harry Cohn that she would leave the studio after completing the *Brazil* film. He reminded her that she had a contract to fulfill and that the best he could do was to give her two weeks off for a honeymoon. He also advised her against marrying Milner, saying she would regret it.

Cohn was right, and the wealthy Milner made things difficult by demanding that he be allowed to buy up her contract. Cohn sued Milner for keeping Ann out of the planned

The Petty Girl. Ann was going through a difficult pregnancy and the plans would have had to have been delayed anyway. But the forceful, powerful Cohn was not a man to tolerate the interruption of his operation, especially by the husband of a star. By the end of 1946 Ann had lost not only her contract but also the baby at birth and her husband. This was the first of three marriages, all with millionaires and all ending in divorce. Sadly, Ann was never able to carry over the happy romances of her movies into her private life.

The Thrill of Brazil, set in Rio de Janeiro, was a good Miller vehicle. Presenting her as a nightclub star, it gave Ann several well-staged Latin dances. Had her personal troubles not interfered, the success of this film might have persuaded Columbia to build her image. After leaving the studio she was in need of a long rest to recover her health. This unhappy period happily led to an even finer level of her career. After the RKO level and the Columbia level, now came the MGM level. Louis B. Mayer was an Ann Miller fan, and, having lost Eleanor Powell, he needed another such spectacular tapper. There was only one other. When Cyd Charisse injured a leg while rehearsing *Easter Parade* her role went to Ann, giving her an MGM début that proved magnificent. She was seen for the first time in Technicolor, and the addition of color to her image was magical—MGM magical. Finally she was riding with the Rolls Royce of movie-musical makers.

Easter Parade (1948) needed a little reshaping in order to accommodate a tapper rather than a ballet dancer. The Irving Berlin score was a collection of old and new songs, and for Miller the composer suggested a song he had written for *The Ziegfeld Follies of 1927*, "Shakin' the Blues Away." It could hardly have been a better choice. Ex-choreographer Charles Walters was the director, Robert Alton was the dance director, the orchestrations were by the brilliant Conrad Salinger, and John Green conducted the superb MGM orchestra. "Shakin' the Blues Away" was razzmatazz in motion, in contrast to her graceful gliding with Fred Astaire to the beguiling tune of Berlin's "It Only Happens When I Dance with You." Said the *Hollywood Reporter:* "She looks beautiful, her wardrobe is terrific, and since there has never been any argument about the quality of her hoofing, it is a certainty that she is now in the big league."

Having danced with Astaire, Ann was next chosen by Gene Kelly for his *On the Town*, for the part of the glamorous New York anthropologist who thinks that sailor Jules Munshin is the personification of the prehistoric man she is studying. For the museum sequence composer Roger Edens and lyricists Betty Comden and Adolph Green wrote "Prehistoric Man" especially for Ann, a dance that leads to the

Top: *On the Town* (MGM, 1949). Dancing, with Gene Kelly, Frank Sinatra, Jules Munshin, and Betty Garrett, to the "Prehistoric Man." Above: *Lovely to Look At* (MGM, 1952). Ann is wolf bait in "I'll Be Hard to Handle." Opposite: Metro at last! In *Easter Parade* (MGM, 1948), dancing with Fred Astaire to the aptly titled "It Only Happens When I Dance with You."

Lovely to Look At, MGM's 1952 remake of RKO's 1935 filming of the 1933 Jerome Kern musical *Roberta*, told more or less the same story, that of an unsuccessful Broadway producer — this time Red Skelton — who inherits a Parisian fashion salon and ends up combining fashion with music. Hermes Pan was again the choreographer, and Ann did well by his setting of "I'll Be Hard to Handle," backed up by a group of male dancers wearing wolf masks. Looking back on those days Ann says, "I loved working at MGM. Sometimes I pinched myself to see if it was all true."

MGM hired Busby Berkeley to devise something interesting for what was obviously a lackluster musical, *Small Town Girl* (1953), set in a hamlet called Duck Creek and featuring Farley Granger as a playboy in love with a Broadway star in the shape of Ann Miller. Berkeley quickly came up with the idea for the flamenco-like tapper, "My Gaucho," surrounding Ann with a squad of guitar-thumping admirers, but he was stuck for something worthy of his reputation. He asked lyricist Leo Robin if he had any ideas. Robin came back a day or so later with the lyrics of "I've Gotta Hear That Beat," and Berkeley mulled them over until a concept started to take shape. Then he explained to producer Joe Pasternak what he wanted.

Berkeley said, "I asked them to build me a stage five feet high that would cover one end of a studio floor, with a small platform in the rear and steps coming down either side. My idea was to place eighty-six musicians under this stage and drill holes for their arms. From the top you would see all these arms with musical instruments sticking up through the floor as Ann danced around them. As she sang 'I've

collapse of a dinosaur skeleton in the dignified museum, which in turn leads to her leaving her place of study and joining the three sailors and their girlfriends as they all go out on the town. With Vera-Ellen and Betty Garrett as the two other girls, both trained dancers, it was a group in which *joie de vivre* was beautifully expressed in the form of dance.

To add some sparkle to the Frank Sinatra-Kathryn Grayson musical romance *The Kissing Bandit*, which Sinatra freely admits was his worst film, MGM brought in Ann, Cyd Charisse, and Ricardo Montalban to do "Dance of Fury," choreographed by Robert Alton. It is the only possible reason for seeing *The Kissing Bandit*. To broaden Ann's public appeal MGM next used her in the Red Skelton picture *Watch the Birdie*. With only a few songs and no dances, it wasted Ann's talents. Skelton's next picture with Ann was better because it was a musical. *Texas Carnival* gave her the role of an oil millionairess who takes a shine to carnival pitchman Skelton and puts her amorous feelings into a frantic floor-tapping, table-hopping, bongo-banging dance aptly titled "It's Dynamite." Hermes Pan did the choreography, and it was a happy reunion with a man who had helped her in those early days at RKO.

And it was to RKO she next went, on loan-out, to do a picture with the fabled Busby Berkeley as dance director, *Two Tickets to Broadway* (1951). The film had little to offer either Berkeley or Miller, her major spot being a television studio production titled "Let the Worry Bird Worry for You," calling for brisk tapping and broad smiles, both easily within her range.

Gotta Hear That Beat,' she would get it from the various disembodied instruments. I explained this to Pasternak, who went pale and said, 'I hope to hell you know what you're doing because I don't.' Word spread around the studio that I had probably flipped out this time, but I'd heard that before. We started filming it the next day and it worked like a charm." It did indeed.

But the real triumph of Ann Miller's movie career was about to come her way, MGM's version of Cole Porter's own career triumph, *Kiss Me Kate* (1953). The craze for 3-D was still strong when MGM began production in early 1953 but it had died off by the time the film was released in late November. After several showings in 3-D the film was afterward released in the conventional print, which was some-

thing of a pity because the dancing (again courtesy of Hermes Pan) was a major asset of the film, and in 3-D it was astonishingly effective.

While Howard Keel and Kathryn Grayson did well with the leading roles in *Kiss Me Kate*, Ann made the secondary role of Lois Lane more eye-catching than Porter had planned. Porter was on hand for the filming and he agreed to an additional number for her, suggesting "From This Moment On," which had been dropped from *Out of This World* in 1950, two years after the original Broadway presentation of *Kiss Me Kate*. The number was highly mobile and rapidly paced, and Ann was backed by Tommy Rall, Bobby Van, Bob Fosse, Carol Haney, and Jeanne Coyne. Haney was also Pan's assistant on the film, and Coyne had

Opposite, left: *Small Town Girl* (MGM, 1953). A flamenco dance for "My Gaucho." Opposite, right: *Kiss Me Kate* (MGM, 1953). A highlight in anybody's book of choreography: "From This Moment On." Hermes Pan devised and directed it. To the left of Ann are Jeanne Coyne and Carol Haney, and the boys leaping out of the woodwork are Bobby Van, Bob Fosse, and Tommy Rall. Right: The shortest title of any Sigmund Romberg song—"It," a flapper highlight of *Deep in My Heart* (MGM, 1954).

long been Gene Kelly's assistant, and later his wife. If their dancing of "From This Moment On" is not the finest piece of ensemble dancing ever done on film, then it at least qualifies for consideration.

But this is also the movie in which Ann did a sizzling version of "Too Darn Hot"; and a jazzy duet with Tommy Rall on a rooftop, "Always True to You in My Fashion," in which Rall performed some stunning leaps and spins; *and* a show-stopping "Tom, Dick and Harry," with Rall, Fosse, and Van as the swinging boys. Delightful as the rest of this version of *Kiss Me Kate* is, these four dances with Ann Miller stand out, a virtual textbook for dancers.

In previous and more productive times MGM would probably have rushed Ann into another big musical, but things were slowly and sadly changing in this particular genre of film. A year went by before she was seen as one of the many names in the studio's tribute to composer Sigmund Romberg, *Deep in My Heart*, for which it assigned her a Roaring Twenties flapper number titled "It," which Romberg had written for *The Desert Song* in 1926 but usually dropped from subsequent productions. "It" in twenties vernacular was sex appeal and vitality, and both qualities were apparent in the Miller version of the dance. She switches from "shimmy" and "black bottom" to "buck-and-wing," all the while wearing a short, orange satin dress and long earrings. Set against a huge mural painted by John Held, Jr., famous for his cartoons of the twenties, it was peopled by frantic groups of boys and girls in flashy garb. It

took three hours to film the dance and it was worth every exhausting second.

Things looked up for the Miller career with MGM's remake of the Vincent Youmans musical *Hit the Deck*, a constant favorite since it was first seen on Broadway in 1927 (it became one of the earliest movie musicals when RKO filmed it three years later). MGM acquired the rights and did it with Ann, Debbie Reynolds, Vic Damone, Jane Powell, and Tony Martin in 1955. To accommodate Ann, the role of Loo-Loo, the shop owner who chases her sailor boyfriend Bilge all over the world to get him to marry her, was changed to a San Francisco nightclub dancer named Ginger, who waits for years to hear Bilge, here played by Tony Martin, pop the question. The musical numbers were directed by Hermes Pan, with Ann doing a slinky "Keepin' Myself for You" as one of the nightclub numbers, and seen front-and-center in the lavish finale, "Hallelujah!," performed on the deck of a battleship with plentiful naval support.

As with *Kiss Me Kate*, MGM considered Ann good for an additional number. Finally someone remembered that Youmans had left a trunkful of paper on which he had noted ideas for songs. One of them was picked out and given to lyricist Leo Robin, who shortly afterward handed in "Lady from the Bayou," possibly the sexiest dance Ann ever did in the movies. Writing about it in *The Hollywood Reporter* Jack Moffitt noted, "I liked her sultry and tropical 'Lady from the Bayou' even better because it lets her reveal a new and interesting personality and a dance routine that is, for her, something different."

Obviously, *Hit the Deck* should have led to more of the same, but it did not. Incredibly, it would be Ann's last movie musical. Ironically, she retired from film dancing at the same age Eleanor Powell had decided to stop—thirty-two. MGM next came up with a role in *The Opposite Sex* (1956), its musical version of *The Women*, with most of the songs going to June Allyson and Joan Collins, and nothing musical for Ann Miller. She played the part of Gloria, which Paulette Goddard had done in the celebrated George Cukor film of 1939. Then came the mild little comedy *The Great American Pastime*, released in December 1956, then nothing. Ann waited. Finally she asked for, and received, her release from MGM in 1958. The day of the Hollywood musical had set.

Like many another musical star, Ann Miller had to look for other outlets, the obvious ones being television and the stage. In time she appeared on virtually every major TV show. Her career as a stage star opened up when she performed in her hometown of Houston in Cole Porter's *Can-Can*. The applause and the reviews gave her the boost to aim for Broadway. In May 1969 she became *Mame* at the

Hit the Deck (MGM, 1955). The sultry "Lady from the Bayou" (opposite), and Ann's final production number on the screen, "Hallelujah!" (above). If it had to end, then what a way to go!

Winter Garden Theatre. There had been six Auntie Mames by this time, and to give some inducement to theatergoers to see this one, composer-lyricist Jerry Herman and choreographer Oona White came up with a new number for the second act, "That's How Young I Feel," and it was a showstopper. Ann was *Mame* for a year at the Winter Garden, until illness forced her to take time off. Afterward she picked it up and did it in stock companies in other cities, notably in Los Angeles, giving her film community friends a chance to find out that the reviews from the East were not exaggerated. In the following years Ann also starred in touring productions of *Anything Goes, Panama Hattie, Hello, Dolly!,* and a television presentation of the spoof musical *Dames at Sea.* In 1971 she amused a vast TV audience as the star of a Heinz Soups commercial, written and directed by humorist Stan Freberg and choreographed by Hermes Pan, which clearly evoked the spirit of Busby Berkeley.

After touring for fifty weeks in the comedy *Cactus Flower,* in which a tap number was inserted for her benefit, in the 1978–79 season, Ann was approached by Broadway producer Harry Rigby. He had had great success reviving *No, No, Nanette* and he now had the even grander notion of reviving vaudeville. He put together a series of twenty-five skits based on traditional material and using tried-and-true songs and dances and called it *Sugar Babies.* Rigby also had the inspired idea of bringing in Mickey Rooney as top banana. After tryouts in various cities *Sugar Babies* opened at the Mark Hellinger Theatre in Manhattan on October 9, 1979, and settled in for a long run, with subsequent productions in other places. As this book goes to press in early 1984, Mickey Rooney and Ann Miller are still regaling audiences with their *Sugar Babies.* No grass has yet to grow under either set of feet.

The choreographer most associated with her, her friend Hermes Pan, says, "Ann Miller, to my mind, is possibly one of the best tap dancers of all time, male or female. She has a sense of timing and rhythm that borders on the fantastic. She always reminds me of a spirited race horse at the post who couldn't wait to take off with a sure foot. There's only one Ann Miller!"

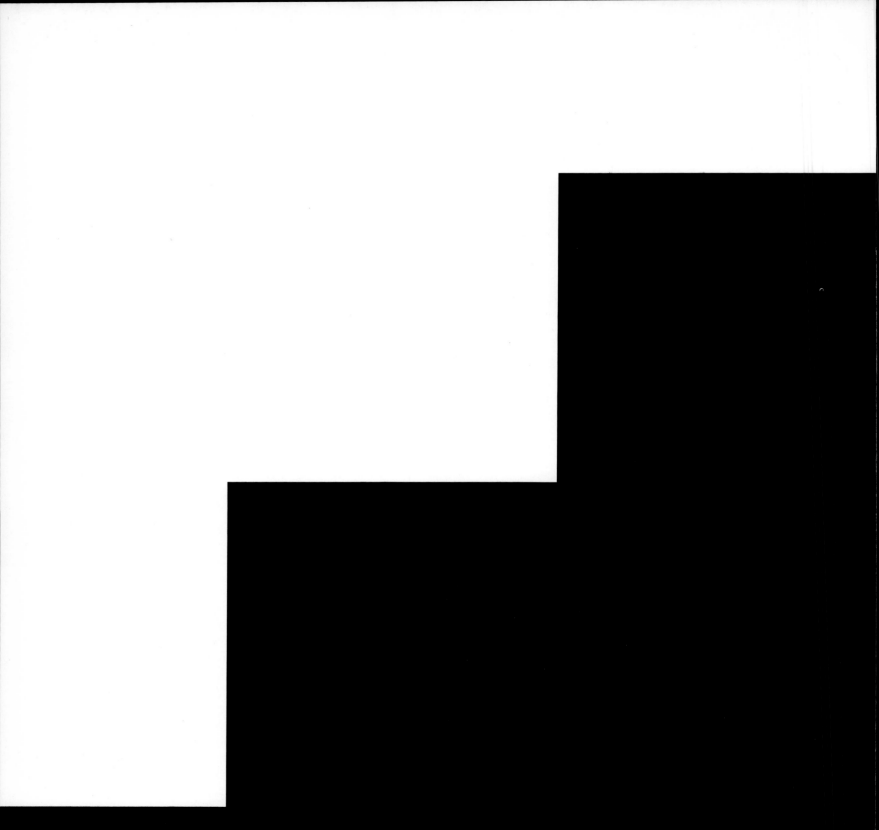

GENE NELSON

Of the dozen musicals in which
Gene Nelson danced, only one rates as a classic, and that
was the last one, *Oklahoma!* And by the time *Oklahoma!*
came out, the heyday of the Hollywood musical was over.
His was a short career as a dancing movie star, which is a
pity. Had he entered films in the thirties or the early forties
he would have had a far more spectacular career, especially if
he had had the good fortune to work at MGM in the years
when that studio was making the best musicals in Hollywood history. But in those years another Gene resided at
Metro — Kelly — and Gene Nelson came under contract to
Warners, which was then trying to compete with MGM in
the musical league and coming in second.

If Gene Nelson can be compared with any other dancer it can only be Gene Kelly, and the basis for that comparison is their athleticism — except that Nelson was even more of an athlete. Nelson's father, a Swede named Berg, had come to America as a young man, where he made a living as a machinist in the fishing canneries of the northwest. Nelson was born in March 1920 in Seattle; three years later, the family moved to Los Angeles. "My father was really a frustrated performer, and whenever an opera company came to town he would volunteer as a supernumerary, an extra as they're called in the movies, and he would carry spears or whatever. Mother was a fine singer but she limited her singing to the church. My father was greatly interested in anything athletic or acrobatic, and he taught me swimming, diving, jumping, and tumbling. He also loved to dance, and I understand he was considered a local expert with the tango. So when I became interested in dancing myself, I had a very supportive father."

As a boy, Nelson was highly active, always running and jumping, or climbing trees like a monkey. "I loved being in the air. For me the trampoline was a marvelous thing, jumping up and flipping. I became quite a showoff." The interest in dancing hit him at the age of twelve, when he went to the Wilshire Theatre in Santa Monica and saw Fred Astaire in *Flying Down to Rio*. "It stoned me. I came out of that theater flying, and dancing all the way home. I was so impressed with Astaire I could hardly put it into words. I told my family I had to be a dancer. We were living in Santa Monica by that time and at the Miramar Hotel a man named Roy Randolph had a dancing school. And my father put a linoleum floor in our garage for me to practice on. But I got tired of the lessons, all the tippy-tappy stuff bored me, and I dropped out after about six months. It started to seem like school lessons, and I was never very good in school. But mostly it was interfering with my play time and I wanted to be out playing with the kids."

At the age of fourteen Nelson took up dancing lessons again, greatly influenced by New York dance teacher Steve Granger. "Steve knew all of Bill Robinson's routines and he gave me private lessons. It was fun to dance like the great 'Bojangles'; this was different from those dance classes at the hotel. I teamed up with my friend Ted Hanson and we did school shows together, and we went out to the Soldier's Home to do benefits, and market openings — anything to be able to dance. By this time I was in Santa Monica High School. I wanted to play football but my father said that I

I Wonder Who's Kissing Her Now (Fox, 1947). With June Haver. Preceding page: *Lullaby of Broadway* (Warners, 1951). "Zing Went the Strings of My Heart."

couldn't if I wanted to be a dancer, so I had to accept that."

Nelson became a pupil of the top dancing school in Los Angeles at the time, Fanchon and Marco. At the age of fifteen he made his first paid appearance, as a member of the Fanchon and Marco Juvenile Revue, a dance team made up of the top pupils, who performed in short acts or prologues, before the showing of movies in first-run theaters. (These prologues were the subject of the Busby Berkeley film *Footlight Parade*.) "We appeared at Christmas and Easter and in the summertime, and they paid us fifteen dollars a week. For a kid in 1935 that was heaven."

Nelson graduated high school at the age of eighteen with only a vague ambition to do something in show business. But then came another discovery in Nelson's young life—ice skating. "I went one evening with some friends to the Polar Palace, then the top ice rink in Hollywood, and fell in love with skating. I hadn't done it before, so it was a new experience. I loved it—I was enamored with it—the sense of movement, the leaps and spins. I had a ball. I got a job in a cafeteria, working from five until eight, and then went straight to the Polar Palace to skate. The manager was Bert Clark, who also happened to be Sonja Henie's technical advisor and the man she looked to for young men to make up her teams in her touring ice show and her movies. I noticed he watched me and after three months he asked me if I'd like to audition for Sonja. I did and got the job, and did a three months tour all over the country. When we got back Sonja had a film to do at Fox, *Second Fiddle*, and I was kept on to appear in it as one of the team backing her up in the production numbers."

Gene Nelson was kept on for a second season with Henie's touring company and this time given some solo bits to do, in addition to understudying her dancing partner. After the tour there was another picture at Fox, *Everything Happens at Night* (1939), and then an engagement at the Center Theatre at Rockefeller Plaza in New York, in a show called *It Happens on Ice*. In the course of his run at this theater, which had been converted into one specializing in ice shows, Nelson gradually enlarged some of the routines he had learned with the Henie company, such as modern dance on ice, jitterbugging, and doing Arabian cartwheels. This is the cartwheel done without hands, and Nelson was the first person to do it on ice. Eventually he set a record by doing thirteen of them in succession.

By this time it was late 1941. With America's entry into

the war, Nelson tried for the Air Corps, in hopes of being a pilot. Instead he found himself in the Signal Corps. He was stationed at Fort Monmouth, New Jersey, in March 1942, and given duties as a clerk. Like many another wartime soldier he felt misplaced and misused, but there was a brighter side to his life at this point because he had just married a dancer, Miriam Franklin. Years later, as Miriam Nelson, she became a choreographer; today, she remains one of the most active of Hollywood's dance directors.

Looking back on those early days at Fort Monmouth, Nelson says, "I was bored to death. It was an officer's candidate center and all I had to do was sit on my butt and shuffle papers. I had to do something to keep in shape and let off steam. I had a portable radio and in the evenings I went to the recreation hall and danced. One evening a short little fel-

Tea for Two (Warners, 1950). Doris Day and "Oh Me, Oh My!" Opposite: *The Daughter of Rosie O'Grady* (Warners, 1950). "A Farm Off Old Broadway."

Tea for Two (Warners, 1950). "Crazy Rhythm."

The West Point Story (Warners, 1950). Two scenes from the finale, with Virginia Mayo (above) and solo (below).

low came in, a private first class, and he said, 'Wanna be on the post show?' He was Irving Lazar, who later became a top Hollywood agent, but at that point he needed guys to entertain the troops. I was glad to do it, and one night he mentioned that Irving Berlin was coming out to see the show. That didn't mean anything to me at the time but a couple of days later I came across a transfer report and my name was on it. I had been transferred to Camp Upton and assigned to Special Services — this is how I found out about it. The next thing I found out was that I had been picked for *This Is the Army*."

Nelson was one of three hundred soldiers chosen as dancers, singers, and actors for Irving Berlin's celebrated wartime musical. They became a separate army unit, completely self-sufficient. After four months of training and rehearsing, they opened in *This Is the Army* at the Broadway Theatre in New York on July 4, 1942. The following year Nelson was with the company when they went to Warner Bros. studios for the filming, and then to England, where the show met with great success among the British public. In all, Nelson spent three and a half years of his army service with the Berlin show.

While her husband was overseas, Miriam had taken a job as an assistant dance director at Paramount. After leaving the service in late 1945, Nelson joined her in Hollywood. "I wasn't sure what I was going to do but I met an agent, John Darrow, who happened to represent Gene Kelly at MGM, and he told me that they were looking for someone at Fox. Their top female stars, Betty Grable and June Haver, were virtually partnerless as far as dancing was concerned. They liked me and signed me for two years."

At 20th Century-Fox, Nelson took advantage of the studio system of the time, which gave contractees training in all the performing arts — acting, singing, deportment, and so on. June Haver came by one day and watched him in the rehearsal hall. Afterward she went to producer George Jessel to tell him she wanted Nelson as her dancing partner. "Jessel called me into his office. June was there, and he said, 'Well, you've got a fan here.' June was a very lovely, kind girl and I'll always be grateful. So I was put into the production numbers of *I Wonder Who's Kissing Her Now*, with a couple of dances with June. The choreographer was Hermes Pan, and since he had worked so closely with my idol, Astaire, I felt as if things were really moving along for me."

I Wonder Who's Kissing Her Now (1947) was a turn-of-the-century musical about songwriter Joe Howard, with Mark Stevens as Howard, and it had plenty of songs and dances, three of which Gene performed with gusto. When the two-year contract was up, however, Fox let him go. "The problem was that although I was twenty-six I still looked like a nineteen-year-old. When *Mother Wore Tights* went into production they needed a song-and-dance man to play opposite Betty Grable. I went to producer Lamar Trotti and begged for a chance but he laughed and said, 'She looks like your mother.' They brought in Dan Dailey, and that picture started his musical career at Fox. I was just a boy dancer and they couldn't figure out what to do with me."

Nelson was considered for MGM's *Easter Parade* when Gene Kelly had to drop out because of a leg injury, but he lost it when Fred Astaire was persuaded to come out of retirement to do the film. He was beginning to wonder about the drift of his career when Gower Champion cast him in the Charlie Gaynor show *Lend an Ear* at the Las Palmas Theatre in Hollywood. It went to New York, where Nelson's solo number was such a show-stopper that *Life* magazine ran an article about it. The executives at Warners noticed it and called him in, and, again thanks to June Haver, offered him a part in her *Look for the Silver Lining* (1949), in which she played Marilyn Miller. It did well at the box office and Warners signed her for *The Daughter of Rosie O'Grady* (1950), another turn-of-the-century musical full of songs and dances. Since there was a part in it for a young dancer, Haver asked Warners to consider Gene Nelson. It did, and he was signed.

Nelson received sixth billing in *The Daughter of Rosie O'Grady*, in which Gordon MacRae was featured as Tony Pastor, a prominent figure in New York show business who had owned several vaudeville theaters and nightclubs. The film consisted mostly of a dozen songs and eight dances, with Haver and Nelson turning in some neat hoofing in "A Farm Off Old Broadway." His work, and the public response, resulted in Nelson being signed to a long-term contract and given third billing in the Doris Day-Gordon MacRae musical *Tea for Two* (1950).

With Doris as the principal star, Warners turned out a string of pleasing musicals in the early fifties without investing much money in the scripts. Most of them were remakes, or loosely based on musicals the studio had made in the thirties, and since Warners now owned a number of the top music publishing houses, it had an enormous catalogue of standard songs. *Tea for Two,* although a kind of spinoff of the Vincent Youmans musical *No, No, Nanette,* used songs from other sources; in this and its other musicals of the period, Warners leaned heavily on the songs written by Harry Warren and Al Dubin twenty years previously for the Busby Berkeley pictures.

In *Tea for Two,* Nelson appears as a Broadway dancer courting Doris in order to get her to invest in his show, in which she eventually stars. That was reason enough to show the two of them rehearsing "I Know That You Know"

and several scenes from *No, No, Nanette* done in the style of the original stage show. LeRoy Prinz, the head of Warners's dance department, had been the choreographer on the original. According to Nelson, he functioned as a dance administrator at Warners, expertly assigning the right assistants to create the dances in each film. Nelson largely devised his own, which in the case of *Tea for Two* included a lively dance on stairs to the tune of "Oh Me, Oh My!" and a sensuous African number, "Crazy Rhythm," done mostly atop a huge drum.

The West Point Story (1950) brought James Cagney back to the screen as a hoofer for the first time since *Yankee Doodle Dandy* but used an improbable plot to do it. Here he is a down-on-his-luck Broadway director who is somehow persuaded to go to the Military Academy at West Point to direct its annual show, which requires him to become a temporary cadet. Two of the show's principal stars, cadets Nelson and Gordon MacRae, get thrown into confinement for breaking rules. Cagney gets them out by inviting the French ambassador to the academy show, and the ambassador's diplomatic privilege allows him to ask for the two star cadets' release, upon which they take part in a spectacular finale with Doris Day and Virginia Mayo.

Although the dancing opportunities were limited, Nelson was delighted to be working with Cagney. "He loved dancing and in other pictures I did later he would frequently come over and watch me. By nature he was an eccentric dancer, that is, he was a hoofer who invented funny little bits of business for himself. All of it was an extension of his stance and his walk and his body mannerisms. There was nobody else like him — and we loved him."

Lullaby of Broadway (1951) gave Gene Nelson his first starring role, opposite Doris Day, and a finale based on the song that had won Warren and Dubin an Oscar in 1935. No attempt was made by LeRoy Prinz to duplicate the incredible number that Busby Berkeley had invented for the original presentation of the song. The plot had Doris as a musical comedy star who returns to Broadway after years in London. She discovers her mother, a former star, to be an alcoholic, doing sleazy nightclub jobs to survive. Reformation is called for, along with a lot of singing and dancing.

Warner Bros. always had a first-class musical department and by 1951 it was under the command of Ray Heindorf. "He was a superb musician, arranger and conductor, and he would get me, or any other performer, whatever arrangement or group of musicians we needed to do a number. In this one I wanted to do 'Zing Went the Strings of My Heart' in an upbeat, jazzy fashion, and so he brought in the Page Cavanaugh Trio, who were the best."

In this routine, Nelson did some remarkable leaps from

Lullaby of Broadway (Warners, 1951). The title number, with Doris Day. Below: *Painting the Clouds with Sunshine* (Warners, 1951). Gene is flanked by Virginia Gibson and Virginia Mayo.

atop a piano, as well as some incredibly fast tapping. In *Lullaby of Broadway* he also performed "Somebody Loves Me" with Doris, who needed help in getting it right. "She was, of course, a musician by nature, so there was no problem with her timing, and she picked up the steps quite quickly. What she had to discover was the thing all non-dancers find out when they do a routine like this — that it's hard work and that it takes days of constant practice to be able to do it. But she did it — beautifully."

Painting the Clouds with Sunshine (1951) not only used as its title a song Warners had featured in *Gold Diggers of Broadway* (1929), it also dug up the basic plot of *Gold Diggers of 1933,* about three showgirls trying to find success. This time they were Virginia Mayo, Lucille Norman, and Virginia Gibson, looking for rich husbands as well as success in Las Vegas. It was up to Gene Nelson, Dennis Morgan, and Tom Conway to persuade them that love was what most mattered. What most mattered, of course, were the songs and dances. For Nelson this centered particularly upon a dance with trumpet to "The Birth of the Blues," with the eminent Ziggy Elman doing the actual trumpeting. Aside from the bouncy title song, there was also "Tip Toe Through the Tulips" and the sultry "Mambo Man." It was a busy picture for a dancer.

As a certified Warner Bros. star, Nelson was required to be one of the name guests in its all-star tribute to the entertainment industry's continuing role in entertaining the armed forces, *Starlift,* in 1951 — although this film made it look rather as if Warners was the only studio involved in that mission. James Cagney, Gary Cooper, and Doris Day also took part. Nelson did a couple of numbers in the show staged at Travis Air Force Base in northern California. The main one featured him as a military policeman who dreams while on duty; with the aid of photographic magic, he pieces together a lovely girl (Janice Rule) with whom to dance. It doubtless left a lot of servicemen wishing they had access to the same magic.

Warners continued its own magic act, that of remaking movies, by turning its 1942 version of the James Thurber-Elliott Nugent play *The Male Animal* into a musical. Called *She's Working Her Way Through College* (1952), it starred Ronald Reagan in the part originally played by Henry Fonda, that of a mild-mannered college teacher who runs into amorous problems on campus. This version was altered to accommodate Virginia Mayo as a burlesque queen who enrolls in academe to improve her mind and make things complicated for her professor, who also happens to direct the annual college show. Nelson played the college football star who becomes enamored of the lady and takes part in the musical she has written, which is finally accepted by the college as its show after multiple complications.

She's Working Her Way Through College is an agreeable picture. It is important in the Gene Nelson catalogue because it contains his most extensive and impressive dance routine. It occurs when he needs to express his love for the lady (Mayo) with whom he has fallen in love, and as an athlete he does it in the most physical manner — in a gymnasium, employing all the equipment it offers. The idea came to Nelson after reading the script and noting the spot for an unspecified dance. He outlined the routine to producer William Jacobs, who agreed on the condition that it be shot after the rest of the film was completed. He did not want the dancer injuring himself and holding up production.

The gymnasium dance, which lasts for five minutes or so, begins as Nelson sings and taps to a song he had picked out from the Warner catalogue, "Am I in Love," which Harry Warren and Al Dubin had written in 1937 for *Mr. Dodds Takes the Air*. Warren claimed it as one of his own favorites but it had never become popular. Nelson chose it because of its rhythm; he worked with Frank Perkins to get an arrangement that would allow for all the things he wanted to do in it. This included swinging on bars, swinging on rings from one end of the gymnasium to the other, high jumps and flips on the trampoline, running jumps and flips on the mats, and a section at the punch ball, using fists and elbows in a quick rhythmic pattern. For this sequence he was coached by Mushy Callahan, a prizefighter Warners kept on salary. (Callahan had coached Errol Flynn in his nimble footwork in *Gentleman Jim*.) Nelson's footwork in this routine is more than nimble, it is fantastic. By the time he filmed it — which took four days — he had been rehearsing for almost three months. It was worth the effort. In fact, it is the most impressive thing of its kind ever done by a dancer in a film

The success of *She's Working Her Way Through College* encouraged Warners to do a sequel, titled *She's Back on Broadway* (1953), except that it bore little relationship to the previous picture. It was designed as a Virginia Mayo vehicle, featuring her as a slipping Hollywood star who hopes to revive her career with a Broadway hit. Nelson was given co-billing, but the role was really a supporting one and he objected to being put into it. Steve Cochran, as a Broadway producer, got the girl. "They really didn't have a part for me, so they just invented one in order to fit me in to do the dances. I thought I deserved a little better but in those times things were already getting a little hard for the movie business and it was best not to object too strongly."

None of the new songs written by Bob Hilliard and Carl Sigman was memorable. "I'll Take You as You Are" was used

twice, first as a rehearsal between Mayo and Nelson, and then as a production number. Nelson is also seen doing a solo to "Breakfast in Bed" and paired again with Mayo for "Behind the Mask." The best song in the picture is an oldie, "I May Be Wrong, but I Think You're Wonderful," used by Nelson in a dance tryout sequence.

Nelson's final film for Warners, *Three Sailors and a Girl* (1953), was much better. Jane Powell, on leave from MGM, was the girl. The sailors were Nelson, Gordon MacRea, and comedian Jack E. Leonard. Lyricist Sammy Cahn served as

Opposite, above: *Starlift* (Warners, 1951). With Janis Rule, Gene proves "It's Magic." Opposite, below: *She's Working Her Way Through College* (Warners, 1952). Gene and Virginia Mayo show how it's done. Below: *She's Back on Broadway* (Warners, 1953). With Virginia Mayo.

Three Sailors and a Girl (Warners, 1953). The girl is Jane Powell. *So This Is Paris* (Universal, 1955). "Three Bon Vivants," the other two being Paul Gilbert (not shown) and Tony Curtis (below), and "Looking for Someone to Love"—the hard way (opposite).

the producer—the only time he ever produced a film—and Sammy Fain supplied the music. The plot, which dated back to *The Butter and Egg Man* in 1928, came from the Warner Bros. archives (it had already been done four times). Somehow, after months on a submarine, three sailors become involved with a showgirl and sink the money their buddies expect them to invest in Wall Street stock into a stage show.

The film allowed Nelson a dance in the confines of a submarine; a more spectacular one in a large car garage, in which trampolines obviously had been placed in the service pits; and a more traditional dance as the finale of the show that the sailors miraculously save, this being the best thing in the Cahn-Fain score, "The Lately Song." Sadly, it rang down the curtain on Nelson's career at Warners. "By this time they had dumped all their big stars—Flynn, Cagney, Davis, Bogart had all gone—and they decided not to pick up my option. Whether we liked it or not we were all now freelancers. The times had changed."

Free-lancer Nelson's next picture came from Universal, which offered him *So This Is Paris* (1955). Anyone confusing this film with *Three Sailors and a Girl* can be forgiven— it too was about three sailors, the other two being Tony Curtis and Paul Gilbert. Actually, it was even more like *On the Town*, set in Paris. The three gobs set the tone by singing "Wait Till Paris Sees Us." Having been exposed to the city's charms, they pose as "Three Bon Vivants" as part of their efforts to help stage a show and raise funds for French orphans. Gloria De Haven played an American showgirl romanced by Curtis, and Nelson wound up in the arms of an heiress, slinkily portrayed by Corinne Calvet. As with several of his previous films, the only factor worth discussion is the dancing, and for the first time Nelson was given screen credit as a choreographer. His big number is "Looking for Someone to Love," a sentiment that he vigorously projected by dancing on a cobblestone street and leapfrogging over taxis and bicycles, among other things.

Nelson had been lucky in avoiding any really painful injuries, aside from the minor sprains and bruises common to all dancers—until the last week of working on *So This Is Paris*, when he landed badly from a leap and twisted his back. He suffered a herniated disc and got through the filming by taking painkilling pills. "I went to a surgeon who advised an operation, but I wanted to avoid that and so I went to another doctor. He suggested therapy, and the first part of that was to get me off of codeine, on which I was becoming hooked. I switched to about twelve bufferins a day and being taped up, and a lot of rest."

While he was recuperating from this injury, Nelson learned that Agnes de Mille wanted him for the part of Will Parker in the filming of Rodgers and Hammerstein's *Oklahoma!* (1955). It was an offer no dancer could refuse, whether in pain or not. De Mille had choreographed the original *Oklahoma!*, which opened on Broadway in 1943, and the dancing had contributed to taking the show an important step forward in the American musical theater. Just prior to *Oklahoma!* she had choreographed Aaron Copland's *Rodeo*, and she brought much of the same quality of modern and peculiarly American style to the Rodgers and Hammerstein play.

When they finally agreed to a filming of their work, they specified to producer Arthur Hornblow, Jr., that the choreography would have to be done by De Mille, and with her choice of dancers. The man she wanted to play Will Parker, the cowboy who courts Ado Annie and who regales his buddies with his account of a trip to Kansas City, was Gene Nelson. "I was in agony but I didn't tell her or anybody else. I did an audition for her and got the part, and I went through all the rehearsals taped up. Every moment I wasn't working I was in my dressing room, either sitting or lying down. I finally took the tape off the day we started to shoot 'Kansas City' on location in Arizona."

Because of Nelson's dancing ability, De Mille extended the original choreography of "Kansas City," giving him the opportunity to twirl a lariat as part of the fun and to leap all over the train station. He ends the number by jumping on a moving train. "Agnes invented a lot of the choreography on the spot. She didn't know much about tap dancing and we would discuss bits of business and she'd say, 'Show me some steps.' I would and then she'd say, 'That's good, let's do that.' The basis of her choreography was character—the dances evolved from the character the dancer was playing. She had analyzed Will Parker and figured out what the man would do to express himself. That was her technique with all her ballets and musicals. She built the number around me."

"Kansas City" took four weeks to rehearse and one to shoot, amid the scenic splendors of southern Arizona—the producers considered Oklahoma itself too plain—and the film met with as much enthusiasm as had the original stage production. Nelson's performance was greeted as exactly right for the part. In any logical, rational industry such success would have led to another such opportunity, but the movie business is a peculiar one. And in 1955, when television had drained away the mass audience and so many of the top programs were hiring Hollywood's musical talent, it was a difficult business for musical stars. *Oklahoma!* turned out to be Nelson's swan song as a film dancer. But there was no lack of work in the other medium; he appeared on *The Ed Sullivan Show, The Colgate Comedy Hour, Shower of Stars,* and *Your Show of Shows,* in addition to working as a dramatic actor in films, starting with *20,000 Eyes*.

Nelson's career change in the late fifties was also brought about by a severe injury. While making a Western on location in Tennessee, he jumped a horse in a chase sequence. The horse reared up and fell back on him, breaking Nelson's pelvis. He was hospitalized for eight weeks, with another eight weeks in bed at home. "I now had to figure out what

to do. I couldn't dance, even if there had been pictures to dance in. I liked writing, so I adapted three books into script form, and since I had been a choreographer I knew I could direct. The man who turned the tide for me was Albert J. McCleary, an old friend who came to see me in the hospital. He was the producer of a daily NBC series called *Matinee Theatre* and he invited me to come and see him when I could walk. He gave me a show to direct, the Bret Harte story 'Prosper's Old Mother,' and that started me off as a director."

To date, Gene Nelson has directed something like three hundred television films and shows, and he has hired a vast amount of talent, including the services of his ex-wife Miriam as a choreographer. With Miriam he had a son, Christopher, and with his second wife, Marilyn, another

ers hired Alexis Smith and Yvonne De Carlo. The survival song "I'm Still Here," sung by De Carlo, spoke for all aging entertainers. Nelson's big number was "I'll See You Later Blues." It took him a while to get into shape, and he had to stay in shape, because the show ran for fourteen months. He had thought his days as a dancer long over before he tackled *Follies,* and once the final curtain came down, that was it. No more dancing.

Nelson's dozen movies as a hoofer place him among the most important of the limited number of film star dancers. Had he come along a little earlier in film history and had he appeared in more prominent pictures, he undoubtedly would have been even higher up on the list. "I'm not complaining. Anyone who can enjoy any kind of success doing what they love doing is ahead of the game. I loved dancing."

Oklahoma! (Magna, 1955). "Everything's up to date in Kansas City."

son, Douglas, and a daughter, Victoria. His career as a film director began with a low-budget melodrama for Robert Lippert, *Hand of Death* in 1964. Then he was hired to do *Kissin' Cousins,* starring Elvis Presley, which Nelson also co-wrote. This led to a job directing *Your Cheatin' Heart,* a successful account of the career of country singer Hank Williams, with George Hamilton in the lead. Then another film with Presley, *Harum Scarum.* Gene Nelson's work as a director, while not as spectacular as his dancing, has been solid and constant.

In 1971 Nelson received an unexpected call. He was invited to New York and offered a role as a song-and-dance man in Stephen Sondheim's musical *Follies,* which concerned a number of veteran entertainers who had survived the rigors of show business. Aside from Nelson, the produc-

He also loves the work of other dancers and film choreographers. "It's a marvelous medium for dancing. The sky's the limit. You can do wonderfully imaginative things with film—it's like being a magician. You can do anything. Look at what Bob Fosse did with *All That Jazz,* especially that opening sequence, where he has six dancers spinning, and cutting from one to the other. Brilliant. In my heyday I could only do about four pirouettes without starting to fall, but with film I could do a dozen by cutting and editing. The magic of film is that you can create anything you want. Imagination. Think of the illusions created by Gene Kelly in the finale of *An American in Paris,* with those sets and color and lighting. It was all created cinematically. Magic. I wish that whole era would come back—I'd like to have another crack at it."

226

He's back on Broadway, dancing and singing "The Right Girl" in *Follies*.

When *Ragtime* was filmed in 1981, it received a great deal of attention for bringing James Cagney back to the screen after twenty years of retirement. Less was made of the fact that it also brought back Donald O'Connor, after a similarly long movie absence. His presence was all the more striking by contrast — whereas the elderly Cagney obviously moved with painful difficulty, O'Connor, on hand in his old guise of song-and-dance man, appeared quite limber. In the early part of *Ragtime* he is seen in a 1906 New York setting, singing and dancing a cheeky vaudeville number, "I Could Love a Million Girls." He returns later as the dancing master of heroine Evelyn Nesbitt (Elizabeth McGovern).

DONALD O'CONNOR

O'Connor was well qualified to play the role of a dancing master. Fifty-six at the time of doing *Ragtime*, he had been dancing since the age of three. And, unlike Cagney, he had not come out of retirement. While his days of movie stardom ended in the mid-sixties, he segued right into the better nightclubs, particularly those of Las Vegas, and into the theater. In 1984 O'Connor was still playing Captain Andy in touring companies of *Show Boat*.

One of O'Connor's most important films was *The Buster Keaton Story* in 1957. He was well qualified for that role, too. Keaton had been born into a theatrical family and had become a knockabout performer while still an infant. He toured all over America as a child and survived hard experiences. O'Connor's story is much the same. He was born Donald David Dixon Ronald O'Connor, the seventh child of an Irish dancer-comedian, who was also a circus strong man, on August 28, 1925. His mother was also a dancer, in addition to being a circus tightrope walker and bareback rider. When Donald joined them they were living in Chicago. Both parents had been circus performers but they afterward formed their family into a vaudeville act, known simply as the O'Connor Family. O'Connor senior died when Donald was less than a year old and his mother kept the family act going, with the aid of the two eldest sons, Jack and Billy. Donald was brought onstage while still a baby; he was taught to sing and dance at the age of three.

The O'Connor family did fairly well until the economic crash of 1929. Recalls O'Connor, "I was five years old and washed up. In 1929 we were knocking 'em in the aisles at the Capitol in New York; a year later we were performing in the aisles in a tiny, smelly, stageless theater on a side street. A two-day booking, four shows a day, the whole family — Mother, Billie, Jack, and me, Jack's wife Millie and their daughter Patsy, dressing in the entrance — and at the end of the run we picked up a check for twelve dollars. For all five of us. A year after that we were scratching for nightclub dates to pick up five dollars to eat on. But it didn't occur to any of the family to get into another racket. We were living at the Plymouth Hotel and the old man in the drugstore downstairs would always let us win a dollar or two on the pinball machines — and then I could always get together with some of the other guys who were laying off and go out to Coney Island. We knew all the rides men, of course, and could get a free spin on the Dodge-ems and the Roller Coasters. If we got hungry all we had to do was drop into one of the clubs and do a routine, and they'd give us supper. But it was rough on Mother. For her — for me, too — not working was failure.

On Your Toes (Warners, 1939). In his début as a film dancer, O'Connor plays a teen-age vaudevillian, with Queenie Smith and James Gleason as his parents. Page 228: *There's No Business Like Show Business* (Fox, 1954). "A Man Chases a Girl."

No matter what your bookings were, or how big or small your check, you had to get bookings or lose your self-respect."

The Depression gradually passed and things slowly picked up for the O'Connors. In 1938 the tide turned when they played a benefit show at the Biltmore Hotel in Los Angeles. A talent scout spotted Donald there and afterward brought him to the attention of Paramount. At the time, Paramount was lining up a production of *Sing You Sinners*. It needed a boy who could sing and dance to play the kid brother of Bing Crosby. Thirteen-year-old Donald was highly qualified for the part. Paramount signed him for a year at a weekly two hundred and fifty dollars and used him in a number of films, noticeably in *Beau Geste,* playing Beau as a boy. When Warners sent out a call for a fourteen-year-old who could dance well to play the son of vaudevillians in *On Your Toes,* the studio loaned him out. Again, Donald was eminently qualified. But by the end of the year, he had grown a foot taller and his voice had broken; the contract was not renewed.

O'Connor now rejoined his family to get together a new act. Brother Bill had died and the mother wanted to retire. That left three, with Donald as the star. They traveled a great deal and did fairly well. Then, in December 1941, agent Arthur Jacobson called to say he had arranged a contract for Donald with Universal Pictures. It paid two hundred dollars a week to start. Happily, it was the start of a contract that would last for twelve years. America had just entered the war, and the studios were losing a lot of young talent to the armed forces. O'Connor was then sixteen, and the studio knew it could get at least two years out of him before he had to answer the call of Uncle Sam.

At the time, Universal made its way by producing program pictures, the kind that catered to the taste of the general public. It lagged far behind MGM, Warners, Paramount, and 20th Century-Fox in terms of prestige films, but it nonetheless did well with the slickly made, run-of-the-mill movie product. In the war years it turned out dozens of minor musicals—Deanna Durbin was its major musical star—and Donald O'Connor found that working for Universal was a very full-time job—almost like being a wartime defense-plant worker, clocking in and clocking out. Universal was in the *business* of producing lightweight, escapist entertainment.

O'Connor began 1942 playing a few bit parts, and then supporting roles in such pictures as *Get Hep to Love, What's Cookin'* (as one of a group of kids bound on breaking into show business), and two of the films in which Universal featured the Andrews Sisters, *Private Buckaroo* and *Give Out Sisters*. He ended the year with a lead opposite

Opposite: *Mr. Big* (Universal, 1943). With Peggy Ryan and Gloria Jean, doing the "Jimmy's Backyard" number. Below: *Patrick the Great* (Universal, 1945). With Peggy Ryan.

Gloria Jean in a B musical, *It Comes Up Love.*

Nineteen forty-three proved better for Donald O'Connor. He had a bigger role in *When Johnny Comes Marching Home* and a number called "Say It with Dancing." Now he was ready for leading roles, starting with *Mr. Big,* which teamed him with Gloria Jean and Peggy Ryan, both of whom had appeared with Donald in most of his 1942 pictures. All three were being groomed by Universal as young stars. Gloria, because of her pretty soprano voice, was signed by Universal as insurance in case Deanna Durbin ever became difficult—which did not happen—and Peggy Ryan proved to be an all-purpose comedienne, perfect for playing the slightly daffy "best friend." The more they played together, the more it seemed that Ryan and O'Connor made an agreeable pair. In point of fact, they were a second-rung Mickey Rooney and Judy Garland, although given nothing like the material or the backing provided by MGM. Their films were also cast in the "putting on a show" mold made popular by Mickey and Judy. *Mr. Big* takes place in a drama school and has a bunch of the livelier kids deciding to turn

the annual show into a musical. Louis Da Pron was the choreographer. Universal kept him, like O'Connor, busy during these highly productive years.

Top Man gave O'Connor, for the first time, top billing in a movie, pairing him with soprano Susanna Foster (another Durbin threat). Peggy Ryan had her usual supporting part, as the funny girl who never gets the boy. Ryan shared with O'Connor a vaudevillian background; she, too, had been dancing since a child. She also shared his birthday (August 28), although she was a year older. In *Top Man* O'Connor takes over as head of his family when his father leaves for war service and does his bit by organizing a show in an airplane factory. Soon after the film came out a fan magazine voted him 1943's "Star of Tomorrow," an encouragement quickly realized by Universal, which stepped up his workload and starred him in four vehicles in 1944.

For *Chip Off the Old Block* Peggy Ryan graduated to female lead. In most of their previous films she and Donald played characters identified as Don and Peggy, and this film was no exception. Here Don is a naval cadet who falls in

Opposite: *Something in the Wind* (Universal, 1947). And something is amiss in Donald's ballet routine. Below: *Anything Goes* (Paramount, 1956). With Jeanmaire.

love with the beautiful daughter (Ann Blyth in her movie début) of show business parents and ends up an entertainer rather than a naval officer. Peggy was once again the game loser, always pretending to make light of it. One of the numbers was titled "I Gotta Give My Feet a Break," but before O'Connor's feet could actually get a break they were tapping again in *This Is the Life*. This time Peggy lost him to Susanna Foster, once Susanna got over her crush on an older man. The film ran eighty-seven minutes, which at least made it weightier than the other Universal musicals in which he had so far appeared.

The Merry Monahans was O'Connor's first musical of sufficient substance to be compared with the product being turned out by MGM and Fox. It took him back to the days of vaudeville, again pairing him with Peggy Ryan, this time as brother and sister. They played the children of song-and-dance man Jack Oakie, who headed a family act. The story was conventional backstage stuff, but it allowed for some twenty musical numbers, such as "When You Wore a Tulip," "In My Merry Oldsmobile," "Swanee River," and other old standards. At about the same time as *The Merry Monahans* made the rounds, O'Connor and Ryan fleetingly popped up as themselves in Universal's all-star morale booster, *Follow the Boys*. Nineteen forty-four had been a busy year for them.

Donald O'Connor and Peggy Ryan now had enough identity as stars to be used by Universal as guest stars in their biggest-yet musical, *Bowery to Broadway*, yet another foray into the heyday of vaudeville. In this they stepped up and did a pleasing bit of song-and-dance nonsense called "He Took Her for a Sleighride in the Good Old Summertime." They were next given the leads in *Patrick the Great,* another backstage musical, this one with O'Connor running into problems when he competes for a role with his actor father. The situation is resolved when the widower father finds romance and the son, whose talent is of the kind that cannot be suppressed, goes on to lead the life for which he was born. It was not a role that called for much study on the part of O'Connor; as before, most of his efforts went into the numbers Louis Da Pron had devised for him and Peggy.

Patrick the Great was the final picture for O'Connor and Ryan. By the time it was released in April 1945, O'Connor had been in the army for a year, and by the time he got back from the service Peggy Ryan had left Universal. Her film career faltered not long afterward, and she performed in nightclubs before retiring into a happy marriage. She and O'Connor were good friends, and he says, "She was a very patient, hard-working girl and she could master a dance routine in half an hour, whereas I could be hard at it all day

Singin' in the Rain (MGM, 1952). Debbie Reynolds, Gene Kelly, and Donald say "Good Morning," and Donald and Gene demonstrate "Moses Supposes" (opposite).

Singin' in the Rain (MGM, 1952).
"Fit as a Fiddle" with Gene Kelly.

I Love Melvin (MGM, 1953). A couple of nifty solos (above and below). Opposite: *Call Me Madam* (Fox, 1953). Vera-Ellen kicks up her heels.

long, and still not get it completely right. She was very talented." Many years later, when she was visiting Los Angeles in 1966, she got up with him at the Greek Theatre in Hollywood and they did a dance together.

Donald O'Connor was just one of many talents whose blossoming careers were interrupted by wartime service. He was only nineteen when he went into the army. Leaving Universal at this point could not have been easy. His most recent pictures had brought him appreciative comments from the top film reviewers, who referred to him as "fresh and delightful" and "the funniest young man around right now." In reviewing *This Is the Life, Variety* noted, "O'Connor continues to demonstrate his versatility as a screen entertainer in singing, dancing and acting."

During the two years and five months he was in the service, O'Connor was held on contract by Universal. When he returned, however, the studio had trouble finding a vehicle for him, so he spent some time doing stage shows. While in the army he was attached to Special Services and he frequently performed in productions designed to entertain the troops. Shortly before going into the service O'Connor married Gwendolyn Carter, who later joined him as a dancer in his stage acts. They had a daughter, Donna. The marriage ended in divorce in 1954.

Every film O'Connor had done at Universal prior to his military service had been a musical. Although only twenty-two when he resumed his life before the cameras in 1947, he felt the need to broaden his image. Since he was not a handsome leading-man type, the obvious choice was to turn to comedy. That this was a good choice became clear in his first postwar movie, *Something in the Wind,* in which he played in support of Deanna Durbin. Durbin's own image was in the process of change; she, too, had been a great success as a youngster and now needed a more mature type of film vehicle. In *Something in the Wind* O'Connor is the sympathetic brother of the stuffy hero (John Dall) who kidnaps Durbin when he thinks she is laying claim to the family fortune.

At one point during her imposed residence in the family manor, O'Connor entertains her with an extended slapstick comedy routine, "I Love a Mystery," in which he acts out all the parts in a frantic radio drama. Seeing this number today it is soon apparent as the birthplace of many of the comedic devices he was later to use in his acclaimed "Make 'Em Laugh" routine in *Singin' in the Rain.* For the Durbin piece he mugs, leaps up, down, and sideways, backflips, spins, falls behind couches, and makes a series of bizarre facial and body expressions. It is the highlight of an otherwise forgettable picture, although it is possibly the first Hollywood movie to deal with television. In its finale O'Connor per-

forms on a TV variety show and does a ballet that turns into a shambles because of the technical intricacies of performing for the new medium.

Something in the Wind made it clear that O'Connor's return to the screen was a healthy one, and Universal then gave him top billing in *Are You With It?* (1948), which allowed him one especially good tap routine in a restaurant. Most of the plot took place in a carnival, to which the young hero has been drawn after being fired from his work as a mathematician. The story was slim but Louis Da Pron, still Universal's main choreographer, could always be counted upon to come up with interesting ideas for O'Connor. Next came *Feudin' Fussin' and a-Fightin'*, which had been the title of a popular song in 1948 and therefore had a little preconditioning going for it. Although O'Connor played a gullible young traveling salesman in hillbilly country, he somehow managed to get in some fancy tap-dancing.

Yes Sir, That's My Baby (1949) was a step forward, although not a big one. For the first time, O'Connor appeared in Technicolor and teamed, with pleasant results, with Gloria De Haven—he as an ex-GI going to college and she as the wife who joins with the other wives to protest their husbands forming a football team instead of staying at home in their off-campus time. She sings "Men Are Little Children" and he sings "They've Never Figured Out a Woman." Fortunately, they both sing and dance the title song together. Unfortunately, it became clear to both O'Connor and Universal that the kind of musicals it was giving him were not strong enough to maintain his popularity. The studio could not offer him the kind of powerful musical vehicles in which MGM was showcasing its stars.

Another course for O'Connor was needed—and, in 1950, someone came up with the idea of *Francis*, the story of a young army lieutenant who finds a friend in a talking mule. The public took to it, so much so that there would be six other pictures with Francis, at the rate of about one a year. Eventually it got to be too much for O'Connor and he refused to do the seventh picture. Mickey Rooney did *Francis in the Haunted House,* but despite Rooney's talent it broke the mold. Looking back on the experience, O'Connor shakes his head, "When you've made six pictures and the mule still gets more mail than you do . . ."

Despite O'Connor's eventual discontent with the *Francis* pictures, the series did allow him the opportunity to enlarge his craft as a comic actor, to say nothing of the great exposure this kind of success gives a performer. In reviewing the first one, Alton Cook of the *New York World-Telegram*

Call Me Madam (Fox, 1953). An elegant dance with Vera-Ellen.

remarked that O'Connor's "precarious air of brashness and boyish ways are very funny, even though it did take the role of supporting actor to a mule to bring them out." Universal wisely spaced out the *Francis* films between others. The studio kept O'Connor very busy in 1950; aside from Francis there was *Curtain Call at Cactus Creek,* as a prop man with a traveling western show, *The Milkman,* with Jimmy Durante, and *Double Crossbones,* which somehow brought him into contact with all the infamous pirates of the Spanish Main.

O'Connor's films of 1950 were audience-pleasers but nothing more than that. Already he was thinking in terms of not limiting himself to the movies and returning to live

entertainment. In 1950 he did five weeks on tour in England at a salary of ten thousand dollars a week. While he was appearing at the Palladium in London, O'Connor received a phone call from MGM offering him a role in *Singin' in the Rain.* Louis B. Mayer had reached an agreement with Universal for O'Connor's services for fifty thousand dollars. "I got the call as I was lying in bed writing a short story. And although I was flattered, I said no, because in those days, under the terms of the contract, I wouldn't have seen a penny of that fifty thousand. Finally, Universal agreed to give me the money, so I said okay."

The character played by O'Connor in *Singin' in the Rain* — Cosmo Brown, the sidekick of the hero, Don Lockwood (Gene Kelly) — had originally been assigned by producer Arthur Freed to Oscar Levant. The acerbically witty pianist had long been a friend of Freed and he had done well in two outstanding Freed productions, *An American in Paris* and

The Barkleys of Broadway. But as *Singin' in the Rain* moved into production and its style began to emerge, it seemed to co-directors Gene Kelly and Stanley Donen that Levant's slightly bitter tone was out of keeping with the lightness of their genial spoof. In this view they were supported by writers Betty Comden and Adolph Green.

All four of them hounded Freed until he changed his mind and agreed to the hiring of O'Connor. From Kelly's point of view it was not simply a matter of humor; he also wanted a male dancing partner in order to realize certain comedic dances. The teaming of Kelly and O'Connor turned out to be one of the primary reasons for the film's success. With Kelly as the ham-actor hero and O'Connor as his easygoing partner in their prefilm vaudeville days, the two of them were able to do some amusing, knockabout numbers.

When they were shooting "Fit as a Fiddle," O'Connor recalls that Kelly was in a bad mood; he smashed his fiddle on the floor and walked off the set. "I knocked on his dressing room door, and there he was with his feet up on the table, and smiling like a cat. 'I'm tired,' he said. 'Me too,' I said. Then we both started to laugh out loud. Neither of us had the guts to tell the other the fatigue we felt after doing the long session, and Gene used the thing with the fiddle as an excuse to rest for a while."

In spoofing Hollywood's crazy period of transition from the silent movies to the sound era, Kelly and Donen felt they needed a routine that would play with the business of speech instruction, elocution, which became important in those days. Freed's musical right-hand man, Roger Edens, came up with "Moses Supposes," and Kelly concocted a swiftly paced tap dance for himself and O'Connor. Later in the film, the two of them, in company with fledgling actress Debbie Reynolds, spend a restless night worrying about what to do with their flop picture. After it occurs to them to save it by turning it into a musical comedy, they cheerfully break into "Good Morning," yet another nifty bit of tapping and stylish leaping around. But, for Donald O'Connor, the highlight of *Singin' in the Rain* is "Make 'Em Laugh."

In the script, at the point when Cosmo is trying to cheer up the hero after he has lost his girlfriend, Comden and Green gave no indication for a comedy number. They left the choice of song up to the producer and the directors. However, nothing in the listing of songs that Arthur Freed had written with Nacio Herb Brown was suitable. Stanley Donen suggested to Freed that they needed something like the song Cole Porter had written for Kelly in *The Pirate,* "Be a Clown." Freed and Brown took the suggestion to heart, and came back with something that sounded amazingly close to "Be a Clown." No one had the nerve to point out the similarity of the song—and Porter himself never bothered to make an issue out of it — but it worked perfectly for what was needed for O'Connor at this point in the picture.

When O'Connor was asked how he wanted to perform the song and what he would need, he replied that first he would like to go through the MGM props department and pick up ideas. He came across a collection of dummies and picked one with no head. For *Film Comment,* O'Connor told John Mariani: "The dummy struck me as very funny, because although it had no head it had symmetry. And I used something that happened to me back in 1940. I was taking a subway to Brooklyn and was wearing dark glasses. Suddenly this guy who looks like an ex-fighter sits down next to me. I move away. He moves closer. He moves closer and puts his hand on my knee . . . that's where I got the bit where I put my hand on the dummy's knee and it smacks me."

O'Connor got lots of other bits by remembering all of the acts he had seen in vaudeville as a child. "I ad-libbed all sorts of stunts. I'd done the somersault off a wall before in two other pictures. Gene gave me the bit where I scrunch up my face after running into the door. We began to rehearse the number and I'd get very tired. I was smoking four packs of cigarettes a day then, and getting up those walls was murder. I'd roll around the floor and get carpet burns . . . finally we filmed it straight through, and I went home and couldn't get out of bed for three days." When O'Connor returned to work, Kelly greeted him with the news that the whole routine would have to be done again because the film had been ruined in the printing. "So I did it again and went to bed for three more days." But O'Connor admits it was better the second time because he was more relaxed and had a better plan of attack on his wild material.

There's No Business Like Show Business (Fox, 1954). The title of the number (opposite) is "Lazy." It might apply to Marilyn Monroe (center), but hardly to Donald or Mitzi Gaynor. In this film, Donald and Mitzi play the children of Dan Dailey and Ethel Merman (below). Ethel apparently disapproves of Donald's feelings for Marilyn.

I Love Melvin
(MGM, 1953).
With Debbie Reynolds.

In *American Film* (February, 1979), Gene Kelly recalled that the idea for the number sprang from the fact that O'Connor was always making the rest of them laugh. Once he decided to do "Make 'Em Laugh," though, it was difficult to plan the filming because O'Connor improvised everything and seldom did anything the same way twice. So Kelly and his two assistants, Carol Haney and Jeanne Coyne, sat and took notes to get a concept that would match the beats of the music, which they would afterward call out to him. "All of that number came right out of Donald. None of it was imposed on him, except for the finish. I wanted him to do the trick he had done as a little boy in vaudeville. So we got his brother over to rehearse him with a rope to get his confidence back and then break through the wall at the end. The rest was all his, and it was unbelievable."

O'Connor was supposed to perform with Kelly in "The Broadway Ballet," but filming went over schedule and he had to leave MGM to keep a television commitment, *The Colgate Comedy Hour,* a series that went on the air in October 1951 and that featured him for the following three years. *Singin' in the Rain* had started production in the middle of June, but the usual studio consternation about being over-schedule and over-budget was less than usual because it was obvious the picture would be a winner. O'Connor's departure, however, left a gap; Kelly decided to change the concept of the ballet, diminishing the comedy aspect and playing up the romantic-dramatic, and to this end he hired Cyd Charisse, resulting in a piece that made the film even more of a winner.

O'Connor's next musical took him to 20th Century-Fox. In filming Irving Berlin's *Call Me Madam,* the studio had the good sense to use the lady who had made it such a success on Broadway, Ethel Merman. In this story of an American woman ambassador to a tiny European country, O'Connor was her press attaché and Vera-Ellen was the princess with whom he falls in love. Since Robert Alton was the choreographer, the customers had the right to expect some exceptionally good dancing. One of the numbers was "Something to Dance About," and Alton's direction of O'Connor and Vera-Ellen lived up to the title. He also devised for them the spirited, lilting "It's a Lovely Day Today." In both numbers the pair was superbly matched, with O'Connor's ballroom dancing approaching ballet at times.

Nineteen fifty-three was O'Connor's best year as a film dancer. Because of the impact of his work in *Singin' in the Rain,* MGM designed a musical in which to star him with Debbie Reynolds, *I Love Melvin.* The script was thin, with O'Connor as an assistant to a *Look* magazine photographer and Reynolds as the would-be movie actress he tries to impress, but fortunately Robert Alton was again on hand to

Singin' in the Rain (MGM, 1952). A cheerful triumvirate—O'Connor, Debbie Reynolds, and Gene Kelly—in two moments (above and opposite) from the most cheerful of film musicals.

design some sparkling dance numbers. O'Connor did a solo called "I Wanna Wander," a comedic piece in which he plays multiple characters, and a charming routine with Reynolds, "Where Did You Learn to Dance?" But, as was true of so many other movie musicals, parts of *I Love Melvin* were better than the whole. Sadly, MGM was not encouraged to come up with anything else for O'Connor.

In addition to the annual *Francis* picture, Universal now came up with a musical for O'Connor, *Walking My Baby Back Home*, which was pleasant enough but far from memorable. Fortunately, Louis Da Pron was still the resident choreographer at Universal. He was glad to be able to devise some new things for an old friend. The plot had O'Connor as a socialite who, after coming out of the army, tries to make his way as a band leader with some ex-GI buddies and a WAC girlfriend (Janet Leigh). Eventually he finds success with Dixieland jazz, which allowed the film to come up with a number of old standards, including "South Rampart Street Parade" and "Honeysuckle Rose." Aside from a couple of solo dances and a minstrel routine done in blackface with Leigh, O'Connor took the old routine of pantomiming an operatic aria to an offstage recording and made it funny. It was all amusing material but not far removed from what O'Connor was already doing on television.

O'Connor was next scheduled to go to Paramount to join Bing Crosby in *White Christmas*. When he injured a leg he had to forego the film, and the part went to Danny Kaye. It was a pity, among other reasons, because Irving Berlin had

written a number called "Choreography," which O'Connor would probably have done even better than Kaye. But there was no escaping Berlin — after doing yet another *Francis* film at home base, O'Connor went back to 20th Century-Fox to play one of the children of Ethel Merman and Dan Dailey in *There's No Business Like Show Business*, whose title told the customers what to expect. Released for Christmas of 1954, it would be one of Hollywood's final big-time musicals, a full two hours of Irving Berlin songs and dances, both new and old. Mitzi Gaynor and Johnny Ray played the other children in this saga of a show-biz family, and Marilyn Monroe was the girl song-and-dance man O'Connor marries and brings into the family. "Alexander's Ragtime Band" was given a lavish treatment, with bits done in several languages; O'Connor did his bit as a Scotsman. He was also involved in the celebrated title song and "When the Midnight Choo-Choo Leaves for Alabam," as well as two dance spots. In a stage rehearsal scene with Monroe and Gaynor, "Lazy," he does some fancy leaping. The true O'Connor spot in *Show Business* is "A Man Chases a Girl," in which — inspired by a kiss from Monroe — he dances in and around fountains, statues, and trees and up walls. Choreographed by the brilliant Robert Alton, it is one of the highpoints of the O'Connor career.

By the mid-fifties, television occupied a great deal of O'Connor's time. After three years of *The Colgate Comedy Hour* he signed to co-star with Jimmy Durante in *The Texaco Star Theatre*, but he dropped out after a year because he wanted to do more films. He made the last of the *Francis* pictures in 1955, the one in which the talking mule joins the navy, and then went to Paramount to do *Anything Goes* with Bing Crosby. This picture finally reunited him with the star in whose *Sing You Sinners* he had made his movie début as a thirteen-year-old. Quite apart from all the work, O'Connor had a substantial family life. He married for the second time in 1956, not long after *Anything Goes* hit the screen, and raised a second family of three children with his wife, Gloria.

Anything Goes had first been made by Paramount with Crosby in 1936. This version had jettisoned most of the songs from the Cole Porter musical on which it was based. For the new version a number of Porter standards resurfaced, although they were augmented with three new numbers by Sammy Cahn and Jimmy Van Heusen. All three involved O'Connor. He was at his best with children and rubber balls, doing "You Can Bounce Right Back." In the others he joined Bing for a magic act, "A Second Hand Turban and a Crystal Ball," and a slapstick vaudeville piece, "Ya Gotta Give the People Hoke," which came perilously close to "Make 'Em Laugh." Happily, *Anything Goes* again brought him into contact with the delightful Mitzi Gaynor, most enjoyably so in their song and dance to "It's DeLovely." Unhappily, it proved to be O'Connor's last motion picture musical. Released in January 1956, *Anything Goes* was Bing Crosby's final film under a contract that had been signed in 1932. An era had, indeed, come to an end.

Paramount kept O'Connor on hand to star in *The Buster Keaton Story*, a long-overdue tribute to one of the greatest of all film clowns. It should have been a better film, and might have been had the studio taken a more serious attitude toward accuracy. Keaton was hired as technical advisor and he coached O'Connor in his routines. In discussing the picture, O'Connor makes no secret of his disappointment. "It wasn't Buster's life. They called him technical advisor but they never listened to him. I remember talking to him right after we'd shot a scene of him as a boy in the circus going on for his father who had just died. I asked Buster, 'What kind of circus was it?' He looked at me and said, 'I was never in a circus.' So I asked him, 'Well, how old were you when your father died?' 'Forty-five,' he said."

The Buster Keaton Story was an unhappy experience in more ways than one. Its failure to impress either the critics or the public caused O'Connor to turn back to television and to nightclubs, and he did not appear on the screen for the next four years. In 1961 he was seen in *Cry for Happy* and *The Wonders of Aladdin*, neither of which were impressive, and then there was another gap of four years before he reappeared, playing second fiddle to Sandra Dee and Bobby Darin in *That Funny Feeling*. The feeling of appearing in such poor material must have been anything but funny. But by now Donald O'Connor was well launched in a second career as a star of touring stage companies, in addition to working in the better nightclubs and on television. And what critic John Crosby said about him in 1954 still stands: "O'Connor is one of the greatest all around talents in show business — he can sing, dance, clown, act — anything."

ELEANOR POWELL

One of the stars most arrestingly brought back into focus by *That's Entertainment* in 1974 was Eleanor Powell. Thirty years had passed since her last starring role in a film, and the nine films in which she had starred between 1935 and 1943 had for a long time seen little television exposure. For the young moviegoers of 1974 she was a discovery; for the older ones, the clips from *Born to Dance*, *Rosalie*, and *Broadway Melody of 1940* made it obvious that no one had replaced her. In 1929 the Dance Masters of America had conferred on her the title "The World's Greatest Feminine Tap Dancer." So far in the history of Hollywood, the title still hangs on the memory of Eleanor Powell.

Broadway Melody of 1936
(MGM, 1935). Eleanor puts on
her top hat and tails.
Page 250: *Rosalie* (MGM,
1937). Pretending to be a West
Point cadet, Eleanor engages in
one of the academy's finest, and
most improbable, drills.

Her film career was the shortest of any of the major musical stars. A specialist, she did only one thing extraordinarily well — tap-dancing — and the remainder of her talent was modest, as she was the first to point out. When tap-dancing diminished in popularity in the mid-forties, so did Eleanor. On the other hand, what she did in those films of hers was so splendid that she is assured a place in the annals of entertainment. She moved with astonishing speed and grace, the choreography that she devised for herself was highly imaginative, and her tapping could not have been more precise had she been a computer. She was, in short, unique.

Eleanor did not rush to see *That's Entertainment*, fearing that her dancing might seem quaintly outdated, but after some six weeks of encouragement by friends she went to a Saturday matinee with a girlfriend. Said Eleanor, "There was a man sitting behind us and I heard him say to the lady he was with, 'I'm here for just one reason — to see Eleanor Powell. I had a crush on her when I was in the navy and I had her pictures all over my locker.' I was sinking lower and lower in my seat. When I came on in the picture he hooted and whistled, and when it was all over I heard him say, 'I'm still in love with her.' My friend was just about to turn around and reach out to him but I said, 'Don't you dare. Let him leave with his illusions. I don't want him to see this gray-haired old lady.'"

In 1974 Eleanor Powell was hardly a gray-haired old lady. She was sixty-two and in good spirits. Had the former sailor met her then, he would have found a woman somewhat different from her screen image. In her films Eleanor was invariably rather demure, whereas in person she was warmly outgoing and talkative. No one ever had reason to regard her as affected, egotistic, or difficult to approach. Whenever anyone suggested that MGM might have done better had they taken advantage of the more boisterous side of her personality she would laugh and refer to herself as the Janet Gaynor of musicals: "I was always the wide-eyed innocent, but because my dancing was solid and rather masculine everyone thought I was a very capable, dependable sort of girl. I wasn't. I barely knew how to order train tickets. I just lived to dance."

Eleanor often said that she loved dancing so much she would rather dance than eat. Actually, she did not discover dancing until she was eleven, when she was taken by her mother to dancing classes, at a dollar a lesson, in order to make her more sociable. The only child of divorced parents in Springfield, Massachusetts, Eleanor was pitifully shy, the kind of child who would hide when visitors came to the house. Once past the embarrassment of actually getting out on the floor at the Saturday morning dance class, she found a new world. "I went out of my mind. I wasn't conscious of anybody, I was gone with the music. This was where I belonged."

The following summer, while visiting her relatives in Atlantic City, she was doing acrobatic dancing on the beach to amuse herself when a man came up to her. He said he was a producer and wondered if she might be interested in performing in a show he was doing at the Ambassador Hotel. He turned out to be Gus Edwards, then the foremost producer of children's shows. "I did two nights a week, doing the little acrobatic number I had learned at the dancing school, to the tune of 'Japanese Sandman.' I was good in acrobatics because I had a limber back and I was good in ballet." And thus twelve-year-old Eleanor Powell made her début as a dancer, at seven dollars a show.

Eleanor vacationed in Atlantic City during the following two years and each time appeared in evening shows. By now the desire to be an entertainer had taken hold; she asked her mother for a trial period in New York. One of the celebrities who had told her to look him up if she ever came there was band leader Ben Bernie, who had his own nightclub. He hired her, which helped her find an agent. He helped her land her first part in a Broadway show, *The Optimists*, which closed after twenty-four performances in early 1928. After this, her life consisted mainly of auditions, and at each one she was asked if she could tap. Up to this point Eleanor Powell had taken a haughty view of tap-dancing, regarding it as rather obnoxious. But it became obvious that in order to get work as a dancer in New York she would have to learn tapping. She signed up for ten lessons at thirty-five dollars at a dancing school owned by Jack Donohue, than a famous dancer, particularly known as the partner of Marilyn Miller.

The sixteen-year-old girl who would soon be honored by the Dance Masters of America as the greatest tapper did not take easily to tapping. She quit after the first lesson because she felt awkward and unable to pick up the steps. Donohue telephoned to ask why she was not in the second class and then offered to help her. "My problem was that I was very aerial in my dancing, very turned out. The first thing he did was sit on the floor in front of me and hold my ankles, explaining that tapping is done with the feet and not the whole body. At the next lesson he turned up with some kind of army belt and two sandbags. He hung the bags on either side of the belt and I was riveted to the floor. I could barely move, which is why I later danced so close to the floor. That's how I got to learn to tap without raising my foot. I thought I would never learn but then suddenly, like an algebra lesson which baffles you until the light suddenly shines, I got it. After that I was up front of the class with Donohue showing the other kids how it was done."

George White's Scandals of 1935 (Fox, 1935). Eleanor dances with Ned Sparks in her movie début.

It had taken Eleanor Powell years to master ballet but only ten lessons to become expert at tapping. She said, "Yes, but I could never have done it if it hadn't been for the ballet, which is the foundation of all dancing, professional or amateur, and of all grace, whether you are a dancer or just a walker or a sitter. It is the ballet steps and the exercises that teach poise and grace and give the figure elasticity and beauty." She continued to study ballet all through the years of stardom on the stage and in the movies. "I have to, otherwise I couldn't keep my tapping up to scratch. If you want to get an idea of what ballet exercises can do for your body, just compare the tap dancers who have taken them with those who haven't. When you see a tap dancer who has never taken ballet exercises, he is almost sure to be a stiff tap dancer. A tapper needs that touch of limberness which is such an asset to a ballet-trained dancer like Fred Astaire."

Those ten lessons in tap were all Eleanor needed to launch her career, which began with *Follow Thru* in January 1929. Using exactly the same tap routine she had learned with Donohue, she performed "Button Up Your Overcoat" and quickly made a name for herself. *Follow Thru* ran for a year, and after that Eleanor had little trouble finding work. It came in the form of *Fine and Dandy*, *Crazy Quilt*, Ziegfeld's *Hot Cha!*, and *George White's Music Hall Varieties*. Once she learned to tap-dance, Eleanor became a tap dancer like no other. Between shows she appeared with big bands in New York. With Paul Whiteman's band, she gained the distinction of being the first tapper to do a special in Carnegie Hall.

Eleanor devised her own routines by dancing to phonograph records, particularly those of Fats Waller. "I often wondered if I had some colored blood in me because the kind of off-beat tapping I came up with was a colored sound. A tap dancer is really a frustrated drummer. You're a percussion instrument with your feet—you're a musician. You have to be."

In the early part of 1933 Eleanor made a number of appearances as a headliner at Radio City Music Hall and at the RKO Roxy. As a dancer she was already in a class of her own. In the spring of that year, she was again employed by George White and toured in his *Scandals*. White afterward went to Hollywood to make a film of the show *George White's Scandals of 1934* at the Fox studio, while Eleanor continued with other engagements.

The film was successful, and a year later Fox invited White back to do *George White's Scandals of 1935*. This time he invited Eleanor to come along. She had previously shown no interest in the movies, feeling that her kind of dancing needed the warmth of a live audience. Besides this, her ambition was to perform in Europe, where, she believed, dancing was more appreciated than in America. But White was the kind of man who usually got his way, and Eleanor finally agreed to take a part in the picture. All her fears about filming were justified by her experiences making *George White's Scandals of 1935*.

George White's methods of making a movie were far more relaxed than the norm, with shooting starting in the late morning hours and with a leading man, James Dunn, who was gradually ruining his career with drink. And he was not the only one drinking during the course of production. Eleanor was given the part of a dancer who tries to woo Dunn away from the leading lady, Alice Faye. Most of her footage in this picture centers on one dance number in a nightclub, in which she is introduced as the world's greatest tap-dancer. While her dancing is impressive, the filming of it is not, and Fox did not offer her anything else. Perhaps because she was unhappy the performance lacks the sparkle that would soon become her trademark. In this first film she also lacks glamour, putting one in mind of the kind of

Born to Dance (MGM, 1936)—on stairs, on anything (above). This film contains the grandest of finales (top).

255

Broadway Melody of 1938 (MGM, 1937). "I'm Feeling Like a Million" with George Murphy.
Opposite: In *Honolulu* (MGM, 1939), Eleanor upgrades the local standards of native dancing.

cleanly athletic girls who participate in the Olympics — admirable but not sexy.

By 1935 MGM, envious of the success RKO was enjoying with the Astaire-Rogers pictures, decided to invade the territory. Looking around for suitable musical talent, MGM rested its eyes on Eleanor Powell. The decision was made to offer her a part in the upcoming *Broadway Melody of 1936*. The idea held little appeal for Eleanor, whose somewhat puritanical nature had been offended by Hollywood's antic life style; in addition, she had been put off by the haphazard manner in which the George White picture had been made. She told her agent to refuse the offer of a dancing spot in the MGM film and insist that it would have to be a leading role, and at a high salary. Knowing she had no reputation as an actress, she felt sure the studio would back down, leaving

her free to return to New York. Instead, MGM met her demands, which went up and up as she tried to get out of making a movie. Finally, she had to agree. This is probably the only instance in film history of a woman trapping herself into a film career. Once under contract to MGM she was put through a "glamouring process," which included having her teeth capped, her eyebrows plucked, and a new hairdo.

Broadway Melody of 1936 was a major box-office winner. It starred Jack Benny as an odious gossip columnist, young Robert Taylor as a Broadway producer, and Eleanor in the traditional role of the hopeful who gets the big chance that turns her into a star. The role was not far removed from reality. With the release of the film Eleanor was offered a long-term contract, which she refused because she had a previous commitment in New York to star in the Shuberts' revue *At Home Abroad,* with songs by Schwartz and Dietz and co-starring Beatrice Lillie.

MGM offered to buy the Shubert contract but they declined. As for herself, still unsure about a film career, she had been looking forward to returning to Broadway. By late 1935 she had every reason to feel on top of the world—while getting rave notices for her work in *At Home Abroad* at the Winter Garden Theatre, she could look down the street and see the crowds lined up to get into *Broadway Melody of 1936* at the Capitol. She had also won a contract to appear in a weekly radio program, which brought the sound of her tapping and her singing into millions of homes. The end result was a collapse from physical exhaustion and a period of recuperation, during which she made the decision to accept the MGM long-term contract.

Broadway Melody of 1936 set the pattern for the Powell films, with musical routines that had little to do with the plot. These were almost always solo numbers backed up with hordes of male dancers. The pattern also called for quieter numbers, in which the viewers could enjoy a more intimate contact with the dancer. *Broadway Melody of 1936* offered a lovely example of the latter type, as Eleanor performs first an *a cappella* tap to "You Are My Lucky Star" and then a ballet version of it. The finale, however, of this

and other pictures was invariably a stunningly staged production number—in this case "Broadway Rhythm"—in which Eleanor would make a quick and brilliant entrance and then move through patterns of acrobatic tap steps, complete with her fluid back-bending movements, strong high kicks, splits, and spins.

Born to Dance seemed the only logical title for her following film. Cole Porter wrote the score, and James Stewart, cast as Eleanor's leading man, revealed an engagingly quaky voice as he croak-crooned "Easy to Love" in a park setting. Since it was now obvious that a Powell picture required at least one demonstration of pure tapping prowess, she got it in the form of a veritable tap blitz in "Rap Tap on Wood." It is, however, the finale of *Born to Dance* that stays in the mind. Dance director Dave Gould devised the setting, although Eleanor's actual routine was always thoroughly her own creation.

"Swingin' the Jinx Away" is set on a battleship, albeit one in an Art Deco navy, and Eleanor makes her entrance down the spiral stairs of the ship's superstructure and then slides down a pole. The lyrics clearly nose-thumbed the Depression that, in 1936, held so many Americans in its grip, and Eleanor's wonderfully cheerful dancing qualified as escapist entertainment of the best kind. She had mastered the art of playing to the camera, and her smile was one of genuine delight. There was no need to fake it—Eleanor Powell was on top of the world.

Broadway Melody of 1938 kept up the high level. MGM gave Eleanor two hoofers to help round out the dancing—George Murphy and Buddy Ebsen, with whom she trotted to "Follow in My Footsteps." Again, it was the grand finale everyone waited to see. "Your Broadway and My Broadway" gave her plenty of scope, with a New York skyline and masses of top hats, white ties, and tails. Eleanor managed to make the difficult look smoothly easy, a facility that came only from months of hard work.

In signing with MGM Eleanor had stipulated a clause that would give her twelve weeks a year for nothing but rehearsals and creating dances. Another understanding was that the actual sound of tapping would be dubbed in after the filming of the dances. When the music was recorded, she also danced for the conductor so that he could match the timings she wanted. A mattress would be placed on the floor of the recording studio and she went through the motions wearing ballet slippers. Since the success of her films depended on her dance numbers, everything was directed toward their realization. She even sat in on the editing of the dances.

The filming of the big Powell production numbers was always an event at MGM, with executives and stars sitting

Broadway Melody of 1938 (MGM, 1937). "Your Broadway and My Broadway." Opposite: *Broadway Melody of 1940* (MGM, 1940). Eleanor and Fred Astaire "Begin the Beguine."

on the sidelines. "Garbo and Joan Crawford used to come and watch me for hours. So did Jean Harlow. I would see Jeanette MacDonald and Nelson Eddy quite a bit. In fact, Nelson came over to watch me so much I think that's where they got the idea of putting the two of us in *Rosalie*."

Rosalie was gloriously preposterous, with Eleanor as a princess of some mythical European country and Nelson Eddy as a West Point cadet and football champion. They fall in love while she is a college student in America, and the blithe story ends with him saving her little country from political corruption. The plot could hardly have mattered less. Eddy's robust singing of Cole Porter songs and Eleanor's dancing transported viewers to a world of suspended belief. In one charmingly absurd plot device Eleanor becomes a cadet and leads a hundred others in Busby Berkeley-like drill formations to a medley of Sousa marches.

But it is the incredible "Drum Dance" that lingers in the mind of anyone who has ever seen *Rosalie*. MGM built a giant set on the backlot and brought in three thousand extras to play the citizens of Eleanor's little kingdom, including a few hundred elaborately costumed fellow dancers. The set called for an arc of drums, ranging from huge to small, providing her with a giant, bizarre series of stairs on

which to leap and tap. After having executed these gyrations she then slashes her way as she spins through a series of cellophane-covered hoops. It is safe to say that there is nothing else in the history of film musicals to compare with the "Drum Dance" in *Rosalie*.

MGM, realizing that overexposure of Eleanor's talent would puncture the balloon, wisely limited its Powell pictures. More than a year separated the release of *Rosalie* in December 1937 and *Honolulu* in early 1939. The title number of the latter was tapped on the deck of a liner sailing to Hawaii, in the company of Gracie Allen, and a distinct part of the routine was performed with a skipping rope. In the one big number, Eleanor demonstrated her version of a Hawaiian tribal dance, dancing barefoot for the first time on screen. In the second part of this number, "Hymn to the Sun," she returned wearing tap shoes to beat out a fast-paced rhythmic dance such as no Hawaiian tribe ever danced.

In *Honolulu* she also paid tribute to the tap dancer she most admired, Bill Robinson, in a number called "A Pair of New Shoes." Sadly, the racial prejudice of the times made it impossible for them to dance together in a film; while it was acceptable for Robinson to dance with the young Shirley

Temple, partnering a grown white lady was forbidden. She had, however, known him in New York and danced with him at parties, and she looked upon him as an inspiration.

The most memorable of Eleanor Powell's film dances are those in which she is the solo featured talent. It had been that way on the stage and it remained so in films—with one notable exception, her work with Fred Astaire in *Broadway Melody of 1940*. It was Astaire's first film after the long and beautiful partnership with Ginger Rogers had ended, and everyone wondered who his next partner would be. It was Louis B. Mayer's idea to pair him with his own prize dancer. This posed a problem for Astaire, since he had always before been dominant in his partnerships. It would not be easy for him to adjust to a dancer of equal rank, someone who was an inventor of her own choreography and fully as much a perfectionist as himself.

They approached each other with an almost paralyzing amount of respect. Said Eleanor, "For the first three weeks of rehearsal on that picture, it was 'Mr. Astaire' and 'Miss Powell.' You would think we were two scientists in a laboratory, we were so serious. People expected so much from us." She finally broke down the barrier by pretending not to know what to do with the middle part of a certain routine and asked his help. Soon they were on a "Fred" and "Ellie" basis, and the pace of work quickly picked up.

Broadway Melody of 1940, although a backstage musical, rose above the average. Eleanor played a famous Broadway dancer in need of a new partner. She is advised of Astaire's ability when he does an exhibition in a dance hall with his partner, George Murphy, but through a misunderstanding it is Murphy who gets the job. Eventually she realizes that all the dances done by Murphy are being taught to him by Astaire, and he winds up as her partner, as the customers for this film had every right to expect.

The respect Astaire and Powell had for each other is readily apparent in one of their dances, "The Jukebox Dance." He begins by questioning her about certain steps and both of them give illustrations, leading to a swift and jazzy tap session. It was clearly what the customers wanted to see. *Broadway Melody of 1940* also contains Eleanor's ballet version of Porter's "I Concentrate on You," and yet another naval chorus number, "I Am the Captain," with yet more uniformed men aiding her in getting through another elaborately acrobatic routine. But the *pièce de résistance* is— and always will be—"Begin the Beguine." Set on a sharply lit black-and-white stage, with a glistening mirror floor and a backdrop of a starry night, the dance is divided into two equally impressive parts. In the first the two dancers, dressed in embroidered evening clothes, dance the pulsating Porter melody in a near-flamenco style. Then, after a break

supplied by a quartet of singers, they reappear in more modern clothing—she in a flared dress and he in a white tuxedo—and they do a jazzier version of the song, involving a great amount of complicated tapping.

"Begin the Beguine" is a great moment in film dancing. Interestingly, it is not typical of anything else in the careers of Astaire and Powell. Neither performed before or after in such an extended choreographed tap routine with any other partner, although stylistically the dance is closer to Astaire than it is to Powell. The syncopation is intricate and their tapping is competitive—in the most agreeable manner—and some of their dance steps are in counterpoint. At one point the music drops out and the tapping is *a cappella*. Then they sweep into the finale, matching each other movement for movement, faster and faster, ending with a series of rapid tap turns around each other. Looking back on the dance Astaire says, "Her tap was individual. She 'put 'em down' like a man, no ricky-ticky sissy stuff with Ellie. She really knocked out a tap dance in a class of her own."

Although there was talk of them perhaps making another film together, it did not happen. Possibly, neither really wanted to. In their one film together, Astaire and Powell had said all they needed to say to each other in terms of dance partnership. Eleanor was too much of a soloist, and, even though he danced with many ladies, Astaire was really a soloist too. When ladies danced with Astaire there was no doubt about who was leading whom. And the dancing with Powell, no matter how admirable, lacked the charm and the amorous mystique of the dancing with Ginger Rogers.

Eleanor had top billing in *Lady Be Good,* released in the summer of 1941, but hers was really a secondary role, supporting Robert Young and Ann Sothern as a pair of songwriters, who, in one ludicrous scene, glibly toss off the Gershwin title song. The film has two remarkable but very different Powell dance numbers, the first of which is with a dog. After auditioning all kinds of dogs she finally borrowed a small fox terrier from a prop man at the studio. She took the dog home with her and kept it for three months, gradually training it to do the tricks around which to build her dance. The result was as charming as it was unusual, as the little terrier stood on its hind legs, wiggled its hips, made turns, and jumped in and out of her arms.

This number was as different as it could be from the film's finale, staged by Busby Berkeley. "Fascinatin' Rhythm" was arranged for eight pianos and orchestra, and called for a chorus of sixty-five men, complete with tuxedos and canes. In typically complex, fluid Berkeleyesque choreography, Eleanor moved through a maze of moving curtains, each of which pulled back to reveal a pianist. The huge curtains move in zigzag motions as Eleanor dances from one pianist to the other—an elaborate device that had to be done in one take in order to be effective. She then dances around a large circle made by her men, who use their canes to make Berkeley geometry. The routine ends with Eleanor being tossed head over heel—over and over—down a corridor made by the men.

Berkeley said about this number, "We rehearsed this trick over and over in order to get it right, and it was two in the morning by the time we finished. It was very hard on Eleanor physically; she was battered and bruised but she never complained. Not a whimper. She wouldn't give up until I had what I wanted on film. After the preview of the picture she thanked me. I've known very few women that talented and that gracious."

The Berkeley creation for *Lady Be Good* marked the end of Eleanor's association with the mammoth movie musical form. Next came *Ship Ahoy* (1942), co-starring her with Red Skelton in a comedy set on a ship in wartime. As a dancer traveling with a big band, that of Tommy Dorsey (with a young vocalist named Frank Sinatra), Eleanor is the unwitting dupe of some foreign agents. The film's most impressive number is a Spanish bullfight fantasy titled "La

Lady Be Good (MGM, 1941). At tap-dancing, no one was better (above); Eleanor demonstrates "Fascinatin' Rhythm" (opposite).

Torria," for which MGM supplied Eleanor with a genuine thirty-five-pound toreador cape—and a bullfight expert to show her how to use it. *Ship Ahoy* also gave her a chance to do another Hawaiian number, the famous "War Chant"; a spirited romp, involving acrobatics with young muscle men, around the deck swimming pool supported by the Dorsey band playing the jazzy "I'll Take Tallulah"; and, finally, a dance with drummer Buddy Rich, in which she pounds his drum and bounces his sticks. The plot also required her to tap out a message to government agents to the tune of "Moonlight Bay."

Eleanor's final film under her MGM contract was the limp *I Dood It* (1943), which again teamed her with Red Skelton, except that this time he received top billing. As if to make it even more obvious that she no longer rated major marketing the film used two clips from previous films. The customers were probably a little confused to see her in younger

guise doing dances from *Born to Dance* and *Honolulu.*

Be that as it may, *I Dood It* (the title is taken from a line constantly used by Skelton in his radio program of the time) does contain one impressive number, "So Long, Sarah Jane," of which Eleanor was especially proud. The number takes place at a rodeo in the West, and during the course of it Eleanor twirls a lariat. She spent sixteen weeks with rope expert Sam Garrett, who was so surprised by her eventual skill that he advised her to quit films and become a rodeo star.

It was an extremely difficult, and sometimes dangerous routine, because the lariats were heavy and thick and had iron clips (hondas) at the point that made the loop. "By the time I finished that number I had bulging muscles in my right arm. When you get that thing spinning it's going about fifty-five miles per hour and when you first jump through it the temptation is to cringe. The honda hit me in the head

several times and I was knocked out cold, so I had to practice wearing a football helmet and shoulder pads. I got so I could rope anything."

The seven-year contract with MGM had run its course, and neither party was greatly interested in a renewal. But before leaving the studio Eleanor agreed to do a guest appearance in the all-star wartime musical *Thousands Cheer*, which has as its finale a variety show given at an army camp. An ebullient Mickey Rooney, serving as the emcee, at one point beams and exclaims, "Here she is—the world's greatest tap dancer: Miss Eleanor Powell." The curtains part and there she is indeed — and making her first appearance in Technicolor. It is a relatively simple (for her) jazz dance done on a bare stage with a mere yellow curtain as a background, and it is of course perfect. But what a pity that Technicolor had to come so late in her film career.

Nineteen forty-three marked not only the end of the con-

Ship Ahoy (MGM, 1942). "I'll Take Tallulah" with drummer Buddy Rich (left), and a Hawaiian dance from the same film (below).

tract but a turning point in her private life. Single up to now, she finally met the man she wanted to marry, Glenn Ford, four years her junior and then in the early stages of his own career as a movie star. Shortly after their marriage Ford joined the Marine Corps for wartime service and Eleanor, possibly to help pass the time, agreed to star in a film for independent producer Andrew Stone. He titled it *Sensations of 1945*, but it is the least sensational of her films. It called for her to play a Broadway dancing star who also happens to have a talent for publicity. She is hired by a producer for her ideas, which include a fake assassination on her life, a circus nightclub, a movie of Cab Calloway in Times Square —which causes a jitterbug riot—and a tightrope walk across a gorge at one thousand feet. The only good things about *Sensations of 1945* are her dances, one of which is performed on the deck of a giant pinball machine. In the finale of this limp picture she actually dances with a horse, albeit one with an amazing sense of rhythm, adding this sensation to the earlier one of having danced with a dog in *Lady Be Good*. It is interesting to wonder which of God's other creatures she might have partnered had her film career lasted longer.

Eleanor was thirty-two as *Sensations of 1945* went into release. The lukewarm reception given the picture by the critics and the public confirmed her feeling that it was time

to hang up her dancing shoes. The interest in tap-dancing had fallen off and she felt there really was not much more for her to say on the subject. She also felt very strongly that she, and women in general, could not have a happy marriage with two star careers in the same family. After Glenn Ford returned from the service, his career gradually grew stronger, and Eleanor was pleased to be in support. In 1945 she gave birth to her son Peter and became a doting mother, with no interest in performing as a dancer. Five years later, however, MGM producer Joe Pasternak coaxed her into doing a spot as herself in his Esther Williams musical *The Duchess of Idaho*, the last film in which she would ever appear. Her short scene takes place in a nightclub as band leader Van Johnson virtually repeats Mickey Rooney's introduction in *Thousands Cheer*: "Here she is . . ." Up steps Eleanor, who whips off the skirt of her evening gown, hands it to Van, and then proceeds to dazzle the customers with yet another whirlwind tap routine.

Eleanor began a new career in 1953. Always a church-goer, she now started giving Sunday school lessons because she loved being with children. Out of this came a television series called *Faith of Our Children*, which she did in Los Angeles for three years and which brought her five Emmy Awards. She enjoyed referring to herself as the Dancing Preacher. Sadly, her marriage to Glenn Ford ended in divorce in 1959. She spent Christmas of that year in Las Vegas with her fourteen-year-old son. At a show starring Pearl Bailey, Pearl introduced her to a responsive audience and made her come up onstage and do a few steps. Pearl's comment that it was time she got back into show business brought a strong round of applause.

Eleanor said about this, "I was forty-seven and I had no great desire to be in the spotlight again, but I was out of shape and overweight, and that had bothered me for quite a while. For the first time in his life my son Peter showed some interest in show business and he was so full of enthusiasm for me to do something that I just had to do it. I worked for nine months to take off the weight and get an act together. Thank God the Sahara Hotel in Las Vegas was willing to give us a chance for a week, and after the first week they extended it to three. Then clubs across the country picked us up and we were a hit."

It was a remarkable comeback, especially for a woman in her late forties returning as a dancer. She played most of the better nightclubs throughout America in 1961, 1962, and 1963, and went to Monte Carlo to do a command performance for Prince Rainier and Princess Grace. But by 1964 she had had enough. "I couldn't see any reason to keep going just so that people could wonder how much longer I could hold up." This time there would be no taking down

The Duchess of Idaho (MGM, 1950). With Van Johnson. Below: *I Dood It* (MGM, 1943). Eleanor says "So Long, Sarah Jane" with a lariat.

the dancing shoes once they were hung up.

After that her life was spent doing social work, especially anything to do with children, and advising youngsters who came to her about their hopes as dancers. After the success of *That's Entertainment* she occasionally appeared at lectures for film groups and discussed clips from her movies. About this she said, "The kids I talk to are fantastic. Some of them have seen my numbers hundreds of times and even studied them in slow motion. They ask really difficult, technical questions. The lectures are very interesting, but then, everything I've done was interesting. I know I sound like Pollyanna, but I've really enjoyed everything I've done."

Eleanor's last public appearance was in October 1981, when she was a guest of the National Film Society at a ceremony in the Sheraton Hotel at Universal City. She was made a recipient of an award they had named in her honor, "The Ellie Award," to be given annually thereafter to outstanding contributors to the art of film musicals. She appeared to be her usual hale and hearty self, but her friends knew that she was stricken with cancer, and that there was not much time left. She died on February 11, 1982, in her home in Beverly Hills.

An unusual dancer, so too was Eleanor Powell an unusual woman. Although she worked tremendously hard at perfecting the dances she had devised for herself, she did not seem to be driven by ambition. Eleanor Powell had a genial nature and she was as much interested in the dancing of other people as in her own. To those who would tell her they would love to have been able to dance but had no talent for it, she would say, "Nonsense. If you can walk, you can dance. Dancing is even more natural than walking. If you want to see natural movements, watch children. Just remember how they move down a street — they seldom walk, they skip and jump and run. In short, they go dancing along." She also recommended dancing to those who were shy or inhibited, as she had been until the age of eleven. "Once a girl can forget herself enough to get onto a dance floor, she can master any social problem that exists. Dancing completely breaks down all of the funny little barriers we erect for ourselves as we get older."

The eulogies for Eleanor Powell were generous and plentiful, but no sentence summed it up better than one spoken by Frank Sinatra: "We'll never see her likes again."

Sensations of 1945 (United Artists, 1944). Eleanor performs inside a giant pinball machine, accompanied by Woody Herman's Band.

INDEX

Numbers in *italics* refer to page numbers on which illustrations appear.

Abbott, George 45, 59, 137, 179, 196, 204
"About a Quarter to Nine" 168
Adrian 118
Affairs of Dobie Gillis, The 57; *57*
"Alabamy Bound" 31; *31*
Alexander, Rod 14
"Alexander's Ragtime Band" 248
Allen, Gracie 258
"All of You" *102*
"All's Fair in Love and War" 116
All That Jazz 9, 226; *13, 14*
Allyson, June 45, 100, 210; *45*
"Alter Ego" 181–83
Alton, Robert 14, 98, 147, 179, 207, 208, 247–48
"Always True to You in My Fashion" 210
American in Paris, An 150, 177, 188, 189, 190, 226, 244; *180, 181, 190*
Ames, Preston 189, 191
"Am I in Love" 223
Amy, George 119
Anchors Aweigh 179, 183, 185; *182, 183*
Anderson, John Murray 179
Andrews Sisters 233
Annie Get Your Gun 121
Ann-Margret 63, 65; *63, 65*
Anything Goes (1936) 249
Anything Goes (1956) 249; *235*
Apple Blossoms 88
April in Paris 138–40; *140*
Are You With It? 242
Arlen, Harold 85, 96, 132
Arnaz, Desi 204; *201*
Astaire, Adele 85, 88–89, 95, 100–102, 103
Astaire, Fred 13, 15–16, 21, 40, 44, 80, 81, 83–103, 147, 153, 154, 158, 159, 175, 176–77, 183, 185–87, 193, 195–96, 207, 214, 219, 220, 254, 256, 259–60; *81, 82, 84–89, 91–99, 101–3, 144–45, 150, 152, 155, 186, 206, 259*
At Home Abroad 257
"At the Codfish Ball" 27; *27*
"Audition Dance" 96
Auer, Mischa 203; *200*
Autry, Gene 204

"Babbitt and the Bromide, The" 98, 183
Babes in Arms 37, 118
Babes in Toyland 140; *141*
Babes on Broadway 37, 118; *118*
"Baby, Take a Bow!" 24; 25
"Baby, You Knock Me Out" 155; *154*
Baker, Kenny 148, 203, 204
Balanchine, George 16–17, 43, 132, 187; *20*
Ball, Lucille 202, 204
Ballets Russes 16, 44, 145–47, 159
Band Wagon, The 14, 89, 100–102, 153–54, 191; *86–87, 150, 152*
"Bang-Bang" 62; *62*
Barkleys of Broadway, The 98–100, 244; *86, 96*
Barnes, Howard 198
Baum, L. Frank 134
Baxter, Warner 163
"Be a Clown" 185, 244
Beau Geste 233
"Begin the Beguine" 95, 259; *259*
"Behind the Mask" 223
Belcher, Ernest 48
Belle of New York, The 44, 100, 103
"Belly Up to the Bar, Boys" 47; *47*
Benny, Jack 256
Bergman, Ingrid *4*
Berkeley, Busby 13, 17, 33, 37, 46, 57, 74, 80, 104–22, 161, 163, 166, 168, 173, 187, 195, 208–9, 216, 220, 260; *104, 113, 119*
Berlin, Irving 84, 85, 92, 93, 96, 98, 185, 207, 219, 247, 248
Berman, Pandro S. 90
Bernie, Ben 254
Bernstein, Leonard 52, 61, 187

Berry Brothers 35; *35*
Best Foot Forward 45, 181; *45*
Billy Rose's Diamond Horseshoe 179
"Birth of the Blues, The" 222
Blackburn Twins 45; *45*
Black Tights 159; *158*
Blondell, Joan 116, 169; *162–63*
Bloodhounds of Broadway 59; *59*
"Blue Room" 148; *149*
Blue Skies 98; *96*
Blyth, Ann 236
"Bojangles of Harlem" 93
Bolger, Ray 21, 124–40, 187; *125–31, 133, 135–41*
Bolm, Adolph 145
"Boogie Barcarolle" 96
"Boogie Woogie Conga" 136
Born to Dance 14, 27, 250, 257, 261; *255*
Bowers, Kenny 45; *45*
Bowery to Broadway 236
Boy Friend, The 72–74; *72–74*
Brascia, John 156; *155*
"Breakfast in Bed" 223
Bremer, Lucille 96–98
Brigadoon 154, 191; *142, 174, 184–85, 191*
"Bring On the Beautiful Girls" 96, 147; *144–45*
"Broadway Ballet, The" 148–50, 190, 247; *149, 150–51, 194–95*
"Broadway Melody" 150, 190
Broadway Melody, The 10–13; *10–11*
Broadway Melody of 1936 27, 116, 200, 256, 257; *252–53*
Broadway Melody of 1938 257; *256, 258*
Broadway Melody of 1940 14, 95, 250, 259; *259*
"Broadway Rhythm" 150, 190, 257
Broadway Serenade 118
Broadway to Hollywood 37; *36*
Brown, Nacio Herb 13, 189, 244
Buchanan, Jack 100
Buster Keaton Story, The 231, 249
Butter and Egg Man, The 224
"By a Waterfall" 114, 121, 166; *110*
Bye Bye Birdie 63–64; *63, 64*
Bye, Bye, Bonnie 164–65
By Jupiter 136–37

Cabaret 9
Cagney, James 39, 114, 166, 178, 220, 222, 224, 228, 231; *38, 39, 162–63*
Cahn, Sammy 156, 223–24, 249
Call Me Madam 14, 44, 247; *241, 242–43*
Calvet, Corinne 225
Calvin, Henry 140
Can-Can 52, 210; *52*
Cantor, Eddie 110, 111, 165
Captain January 27; *27*
Carefree 93; *92*
"Carioca, The" 90
Carnival in Costa Rica 44
Carolina Blues 206
Caron, Leslie 102, 144, 189; *101, 180, 181, 190*

Carousel 14; *18–19*
Carpenter, Carleton 46
Carrie 74
Carroll, Georgia 206
Castle, Nick 100, 189
"Castle in Spain" 140
Chakiris, George 61; *60*
Chambers, Tommy 97
Champion, Gower 47, 48–51, 148, 220; *47, 48–51, 145*
Champion, Marge 48–51; *48–51*
"Change Partners" 93
Charisse, Cyd 100, 102, 142–59, 176–77, 191, 207, 208, 247; *102, 142, 144–47, 149–59, 184–85*
Charisse, Nico 145, 147, 148
Charley's Aunt 137
Chase, Barrie 103
"Chattanooga Choo-Choo" 31, 35; *30, 35*
Chevalier, Maurice *3*
Chip Off the Old Block 234–36
Cinderella Jones 119
Cochran, Steve 223
Cohan, George M. 39, 164, 178
Cohn, Harry 204, 206–7
Cole, Jack 14, 40, 51, 206; *41*
Colgate Comedy Hour, The 225, 247, 248
Colleen 168–69; *171*
Columbia Pictures 40, 51, 52, 63, 64, 96, 147, 170, 181, 200, 201, 203, 204, 206, 207; *3, 8, 40, 41, 51, 52, 63, 64, 92, 159, 172–73, 178, 198, 200, 202–5*
Comden, Betty 98, 100, 154, 155, 187, 191, 207, 244
Como, Perry 148; *149*
Condos Brothers 32; *32*
Connecticut Yankee, A 107, 109
Connolly, Bobby 14, 109, 136, 168, 169
Conrad, Con 90
"Continental, The" 90; *89*
Conway, Tom 222
Cook, Alton 242–44
Copland, Aaron 148, 225
"Couple of Song-and-Dance Men, A" 98; *96*
"Couple of Swells, A" 98, 187
Cover Girl 40, 181–83; *178*
Coyne, Jeanne 209–10, 247; *208*
Crawford, Joan 22, 24, 90, 258; *22–23, 24, 84*
Crazy Quilt 255
"Crazy Rhythm" 220; *218*
Cronjager, Edward 119
Crosby, Bing 48, 62, 96, 98, 233, 248, 249; *96*
Crosby, John 249
Crowther, Bosley 204
Cry for Happy 249
Cummings, Jack 15
Curtain Call at Cactus Creek 244
Curtis, Tony 224–25; *224*
"Custom House, The" 198

Daddy Long Legs 85, 102; *82, 101*

Dailey, Dan 35, 156, 191, 220, 248; *3, 34, 35, 245*
Dale, Virginia 96
Dall, John 240
Dames 166; *106–7, 165*
Damn Yankees 10, 59; *58*
Damone, Vic 210
Damsel in Distress, A 93
"Dance in the Gym, The" *1*
"Dance of Fury" 148, 208
"Dancing—A Man's Game" 177
"Dancing in the Dark" 154; *150*
Dancing Lady 24, 90; *84*
D'Andrea, Carole *1*
Dandridge, Dorothy 31; *30*
Da Pron, Louis 234, 236, 242, 248
Darin, Bobby 249
Darrow, John 219
Daughter of Rosie O'Grady, The 220; *216*
Davis, Jr., Sammy 21, 57, 62, 156; *21, 56, 62*
Day, Doris 138–40, 220, 222; *140, 217, 221*
Day, Richard 110
Days of Glory 44
"Dearly Beloved" 96
De Basil, Colonel W. 145–46
Dee, Sandra 249
Deep in My Heart 154, 191, 210; *153, 192, 209*
De Haven, Gloria 225, 242
Del Rio, Dolores 90, 116; *85*
De Mille, Agnes 225
Demy, Jacques 195
Deneuve, Catherine 195
Dietz, Howard 89, 100, 154, 257
Dillingham, Charles 88, 165
Dixon, Lee 169; *171*
Donen, Stanley 15, 47, 59, 102, 148, 155, 159, 181, 183, 187, 188, 191, 244
Donohue, Jack 138, 148, 254, 255
"Don't Say Goodnight" 114; *111*
Dorleac, Françoise 195
Dorsey, Tommy 260; *118*
"Do the Conga" 117
Double Crossbones 244
Down Argentine Way 31, 33; *30, 33*
Down to Earth 8
Draper, Paul 98, 169; *171*
"Drum Dance" 258
Du Barry Was a Lady 33, 180–81; *176–77*
Dubin, Al 113, 116, 163, 166, 169, 220, 223
Duchess of Idaho, The 263; *263*
Dunn, James 24, 255; *25*
Dunne, Irene 92
Durante, Jimmy 244, 248
Durbin, Deanna 233, 234, 240

Eadie Was a Lady 206
Earl Carroll Vanities of 1928, The 109
Easter Parade 98, 185–87, 207, 220; *206*
East Side, West Side 148
Easy to Love 121
"Easy to Love" 257
Ebsen, Buddy 27, 135, 257; *27*
Ebsen, Vilma 27
Eddy, Nelson 132, 134, 258
Edens, Roger 192, 207, 244
Edwards, Gus 132, 254
"$18.75" 206; *204*
Elg, Taina 193
Elman, Ziggy 222
"Embraceable You" 189
Eve Knew Her Apples 206
"Evening with Fred Astaire, An" 103
Everything I Have Is Yours 50; *50*
Everything Happens at Night 217
Fabray, Nanette 100
Fain, Sammy 224
"Fantasia Mexicana" 148
Farm Off Old Broadway, A 220; *216*
"Fascinatin' Rhythm" 118, 260; *119, 261*
"Fascinating Rhythm" 89

Fashions of 1934 114–16
"Fated to Be Mated" 158
Faye, Alice 32, 255
Felix, Seymour 14, 109, 132, 181
Ferguson, Constance 145
Feudin' Fussin' and a-Fightin' 242
Fields, Dorothy 93
Fiesta 46, 148; *146*
Fine and Dandy 255
Finian's Rainbow 15; *102*
"Fit as a Fiddle" 244; *238–39*
Five Golden Hours 159
"Flaming Flamenco, The" 148; *146*
Flirtation Walk 168; *167*
Flying Down to Rio 13, 14, 74, 89, 90, 214; *85*
Flynn, Errol 223, 224
"Foggy Day, A" 93
Fokine, Michel 146
Follies 226; *227*
"Follow in My Footsteps" 257
Follow the Boys 40, 236; *42, 43*
Follow the Fleet 85, 92–93, 195; *91*
Follow Thru 254–55
Fontaine, Joan 93
Footlight Parade 39, 114, 165, 166, 216; *39, 110, 162–63, 165*
Ford, Glenn 204, 262, 263
For Me and My Gal 118, 122, 175, 180
Forrest, Robert 134
42nd Street 13, 74, 113–14, 163, 166; *108, 160*
"42nd Street" 113–14, 163–64; *108*
Fosse, Bob 9–10, 52, 53, 64, 209, 210, 226; *12, 52, 208*
Foster, Susanna 234, 236
Four Jacks and a Jill 136, 138; *125*
Foy, Jr., Eddie 88
Francis series 242–44, 248, 249
Francis in the Haunted House 242
"Frankie and Johnny" 156; *155*
Freed, Arthur 13, 15, 95, 98, 121, 147, 148–50, 180, 187, 189, 192, 244
"From This Day On" 154
"From This Moment On" 209–10; *208*
Funicello, Annette 140
Funny Face 14, 89, 93, 98, 102

Gable, Christopher 72; *72*
"Gal with the Yaller Shoes, The" 156
Gang's All Here, The 119; *104*
Garbo, Greta 144, 158, 258
Garland, Judy 18, 37, 98, 100, 118, 121, 134, 137, 148, 180, 185, 187, 188–89, 201, 234; *37, 117, 118, 130–31, 133*
Garrett, Betty 208; *207*
Garrett, Sam 261
Gay Divorce 89, 90
Gay Divorcee, The 33, 90; *89*
Gaynor, Charlie 220
Gaynor, Mitzi 59, 193, 248, 249; *59, 244, 245*
Gennaro, Peter 47
Gentlemen Prefer Blondes 14
George White's Music Hall Varieties 255
George White's Scandals of 1931 132
George White's Scandals of 1932 132
George White's Scandals of 1934 255
George White's Scandals of 1935 255–56; *254*
George White's Scandals of 1939 203–4
Gershwin, George 51, 84, 85, 88–89, 90, 93, 98, 102, 118, 165, 177–78, 189, 260
Gershwin, Ira 93, 98, 181, 189
Get Hep to Love 233
Gibbons, Cedric 118
Gibson, Virginia 222; *221*
Gielgud, Sir John 100–102
Gilbert, Paul 224
Girl Crazy 90, 118–19; *118*
"Girl Hunt Ballet, The" 154; *152*

"Girl I Love to Leave Behind, The" 137
Give a Girl a Break 47; *47*
Give Out Sisters 233
Glad to See You 119
Gleason, James *230–31*
Glen Gray and the Casa Loma Orchestra 202
Goddard, Paulette 96, 210
Go into Your Dance 168; *167, 168, 169*
Gold Diggers in Paris 116
Gold Diggers of Broadway 222
Gold Diggers of 1933 107, 114, 166, 222; *109, 119*
Gold Diggers of 1935 107, 116; *112–13, 115*
Gold Diggers of 1937 107, 116
Golden Girl 59
Goldwyn, Samuel 43, 110, 111, 114
Goldwyn Follies of 1937, The 16, 43
"Good Morning" 244; *236*
Good News 45; *45*
"Gotta Feeling for You" 24; *24*
Gould, Dave 14, 90, 116, 257
Go West, Young Lady 204; *202*
Grable, Betty 15, 32, 33, 35, 51, 219, 220; *17, 32, 33, 34, 35*
Granger, Steve 214
Granlund, Nils Thor 164
Grant, Cary 4
Grayson, Kathryn 208, 209
Great American Broadcast, The 31; *31*
Great American Pastime, The 210
Great Ziegfeld, The 14, 132; *126–27*
"Greeks Never Mentioned It, The" 206
Green, Adolph 98, 100, 154, 155, 187, 191, 107, 244
Green, John 192, 207
Greenwood, Charlotte 7
Guest, Helen 164
Guys and Dolls 14

Haley, Dinny 129
Haley, Jack 32, 135; *130–31*
Haley, Jr., Jack 18–21, 44, 124–25
"Hallelujah!" 210; *211*
Hamilton, Margaret 133
Hammerstein II, Oscar 225
Hand of Death 226
"Handy with Your Feet" 169
Haney, Carol 59, 150, 153, 209, 247; *59, 208*
Hanson, Ted 214
Happy Go Lovely 44
Happy Road, The 191, 193
Hart, Lorenz 16, 45, 84, 107, 109, 132, 136, 137, 148, 179, 187, 204
Harum Scarum 226
Harvey Girls, The 137, 147–48; *138*
"Hasta Luego" 147
Haver, June 138, 219, 220; *137, 139, 214–15*
Hayworth, Rita 40, 96, 181, 201, 204; *8, 40, 40–41, 92, 178*
"Heather on the Hill, The" 154; *184–85*
"Heat Wave" 98
"Heigh, Ho, the Gang's All Here" 90; *84*
Heindorf, Ray 220
Hello, Dolly! 14, 68, 70, 195; *69–71*
Henie, Sonja 216–17
Hepburn, Audrey 102
Herbert, Hugh 168
Herbert, Victor 134, 140
Her Majesty Love 22
Herman, Jerry 211
"He Took Her for a Sleighride in the Good Old Summertime" 236
Hey, Rookie 201, 206
Hilliard, Bob 223
"History of the Beat" 85; *82*
Hit Parade of 1941 204
Hit the Deck 66, 210; *210, 211*
"Hoe Down" 118
Hold Your Hats 179

Holiday Inn 96
Holka-Polka 109
Hollywood Hotel 116
Hollywood Revue of 1929 24; *24*
"Honeysuckle Rose" 248
Honolulu 258–59, 261; *257*
"Hooray for Hollywood" 116
Hope, Bob 165
Hornblow, Jr., Arthur 225
Horne, Lena 28; *29*
Hot Cha! 255
Hunter, Tab 59; *58*
Hutton, Betty 45, 100
"Hymn to the Sun" 258

"I Am the Captain" 259
Ibert, Jacques 192
"I Can't Give You Anything but Love" 28; *29*
"I Concentrate on You" 95, 259
"I Could Love a Million Girls" 228
I Dood It 260–61; *263*
"I'd Rather Listen to Your Eyes" *170*
"I Got Rhythm" 118; *118*
"I Gotta Give My Feet a Break" 236
"I Know That You Know" 220
"I Left My Hat in Haiti" 100
"I Like Myself" 192; *193*
I Live for Love 116
"I'll Be Hard to Handle" 92, 208; *207*
"I'll Capture Your Heart" 96
"I'll See You Later Blues" 226
"I'll Take Tallulah" 260; *262*
"I'll Take You as You Are" 223
"I Love a Mystery" 240
I Love Melvin 46, 247–48; *46, 240, 246–47*
"I Love to Go Swimmin' with Wimmen" 191; *192*
"I'm a Brass Band" 53; *53*
"I May Be Wrong, but I Think You're Wonderful" 223
"I'm Feeling Like a Million" 256
"I'm Gonna Ring the Bell Tonight" 140; *140*
"I'm in Good Shape for the Shape I'm In" 136
"I'm Old-Fashioned" 96
"I'm Putting All My Eggs in One Basket" 85
"I'm Still Here" 226
Indiscreet 4
"In My Merry Oldsmobile" 236
Invitation to the Dance 192–93; *196*
"I Only Have Eyes for You" 166; *106–7, 164*
"Isn't This a Lovely Day (To Be Caught in the Rain)?" 92
"It" 210; *209*
It Comes Up Love 234
It Happens on Ice 217
"It Only Happens When I Dance with You" 207; *206*
"It's a Great Big World" 148
"It's a Lovely Day Today" 247
It's Always Fair Weather 14, 154, 155, 177, 191–92; *16, 154, 193*
"It's DeLovely" 249
"It's Dynamite" 208
"It's Magic" 222
"I've Gotta Hear That Beat" 208–9; *123*
"I Wanna Wander" 248
I Was an Adventuress 16; *20*
"I Wish I Could Be a Singing Cowboy" 204; *202*
I Wonder Who's Kissing Her Now 219; *214–15*
"I Won't Dance" 92

Jacobs, William 223
Jacobson, Arthur 233
Jam Session 206; *205*
Jean, Gloria 234; *232*
Jeanmaire, Zizi 159; *235*
Jenkins, Allen 204; *202*
Jessel, George 219

"Jimmy's Backyard" 232
Johnson, Van 263; *191, 263*
Jolson, Al 163, 165–66, 168, 170; *168*
Jolson Story, The 165, 170
Jordan, Jack 45; *45*
"Jukebox Dance, The" 259
Jumbo 122
Jupiter's Darling 50; *50*

Kalmar, Bert 100
"Kansas City" 225; *226*
Kaye, Danny 44, 248
Keaton, Buster 231, 249
Keel, Howard 50, 209
Keeler, Ruby 57, 113, 114, 122, 159, 161–73; *160, 162–65, 167–73*
"Keepin' Myself for You" 210
Kelly, Fred 74, 191; *192*
Kelly, Gene 13, 17–18, 20, 21, 37, 40, 44, 46, 98, 118, 122, 142, 148–50, 153, 154, 155, 159, 175–96, 200, 207, 210, 213, 214, 219, 220, 226, 244, 245, 247; *103, 149, 150–51, 174, 176–78, 180–97, 207, 236, 237, 238–39, 248, 249*
Kelly, Patsy 122, 164, 173
Kelly, Paula 53; *54–55*
Kendall, Kay 193; *196*
Kern, Jerome 22, 84, 85, 92, 93, 96, 136, 138, 148, 181, 208
Kerr, Walter 200
Kidd, Michael 14–15, 68, 138, 154, 191; *16*
Kid from Brooklyn, The 44
Kid from Spain, The 111
King, Charles 10; *11*
"King Who Couldn't Dance, The" 183; *183*
Kissin' Cousins 226
Kissing Bandit, The 46, 148, 208
Kiss Me Kate 57, 209–10; *208*
Kovacs, Ernie 159
Kramer, Stanley 103
Kyser, Kay 206

"La Cumparsita" 179, 183
Lady Be Good 118, 260, 262; *119, 260, 261*
Lady, Be Good! 89, 93
"Lady from the Bayou" 210; *210*
"Lady in the Tutti-Frutti Hat, The" 119
"Lady Loves, A" 46; *46*
Lahr, Bert 33, 135; *130–31*
Lamarr, Hedy 116
Lane, Burton 85
Langford, Frances 204
Larkin, Eddie 113
"Lately Song, The" 224
"La Torria" 260
Lawford, Peter 45; *45*
Lazar, Irving 219
"Lazy" 248; *244*
Leave It to Me 179
Lee, Sammy 109
Leigh, Janet 52, 64, 248; *52, 64*
Lend an Ear 220
Lennart, Isobel 155
Leonard, Jack E. 223
Lerner, Alan Jay 154, 189
Les Girls 193; *196*
Leslie, Joan 96
"Let Me Call You Sweetheart" 181
Let's Be Happy 44
"Let's Call the Whole Thing Off" 93
Let's Dance 100; *97*
"Let's Face the Music and Dance" 93
"Let's Go Bavarian" 90
"Let's K-nock K-neez" 33
Let's Make Love 195
"Let Yourself Go" 92
Levant, Oscar 100, 244
Lichine, David 147, 148
Life Begins at 8:40 132
"Life of an Elephant, The" 50; *50*
Life of the Party 202

"Life upon the Wicked Stage" 48; 48
Li'l Abner 14
Lillie, Beatrice 257
"Limehouse Blues" 98
Lippert, Robert 226
Little Colonel, The 27
Little Miss Broadway 28; 28
Littlest Rebel, The 27; 26
Living in a Big Way 183–85
"Liza" 165
Loesser, Frank 85, 100, 137, 138
Look for the Silver Lining 138, 220; 137, 139
"Looking for Someone to Love" 225; 225
Loring, Eugene 14, 102, 148, 156, 158
"Lot of Livin' to Do, A" 63; 63
Love, Bessie 10
"Love Is Here to Stay" 189; 181
Lovely to Look At 208; 207
"Lover Come Back to Me" 154
Lullaby of Broadway 220–22; 213, 221
"Lullaby of Broadway, The" 116; 115

McCleary, Albert J. 226
MacDonald, Jeanette 118, 134, 258; 129
MacLaine, Shirley 52, 53, 195; 12, 52, 53, 54–55, 56, 197
McLerie, Allyn 138
MacRae, Gordon 220, 223
"Make 'Em Laugh" 240, 244–47, 249
Make Mine Laughs 138
"Make Way for Tomorrow" 178
Male Animal, The 222
"Mambo Man" 222
Mame 210–11
Mamoulian, Rouben 102
"Man Chases a Girl, A" 248; 228
"Manhattan Downbeat" 100
Mariani, John 245
Marjorie Morningstar 195
Mark of the Renegade 148
Martin, Dean 62, 159
Martin, John 179–80
Martin, Mary 179
Martin, Steve 80; 80
Martin, Tony 148, 154, 210; 116
Mayer, Louis B. 95, 96, 155, 207, 244, 259
Mayo, Virginia 220, 222, 223; 219, 221, 222, 223
McHugh, Frank 39; 39
Meet Me in Las Vegas 155–56; 155
Meet Me in St. Louis 14, 37; 37
Melody Ranch 204
"Men Are Little Children" 242
Mercer, Johnny 85, 96, 103, 116, 169
Merman, Ethel 33, 247, 248; 245
Merry Monahans, The 236
Merry Whirl, The (The Passing Show of 1926) 132
Metro-Goldwyn-Mayer (MGM) 10, 13, 15, 18, 22, 27, 37, 45, 46, 47, 48, 50, 57, 66, 90, 95, 98, 100, 102, 118, 119, 121, 122, 124, 127, 132, 134, 137, 147, 148, 154, 155–56, 158, 180, 181, 183, 185, 187, 188, 189–90, 191, 192, 193, 195, 203, 207, 208, 209, 210, 213, 219, 220, 233, 234, 236, 242, 244, 245, 247, 248, 253, 256–57, 258, 260, 261, 263; 10–11, 15, 16, 21–24, 36, 37, 44–50, 57, 65–67, 72–74, 78–80, 84, 86, 86–87, 94–95, 96, 98, 99, 102, 103, 116–21, 123, 126–31, 133, 138, 142, 144–47, 149–58, 174, 176–77, 180–96, 206–11, 236–40, 246–50, 252–53, 255–63
"Mexiconga, The" 204
Milkman, The 244
Miller, Ann 21, 148, 188, 198–211; 123, 198, 200–211
Miller, Buzz 59; 59
Miller, Marilyn 22, 136, 138, 220, 254; 22
Million Dollar Mermaid 121; 120–21

Minnelli, Vincente 98, 154, 159, 185, 189, 191
"Minnie from Trinidad" 118
Miranda, Carmen 119
Mr. Big 234; 232
Mr. Dodds Takes the Air 223
Mr. Music 48
Mitchell, James 154; 152, 153
Moffitt, Jack 156, 210
Monroe, Marilyn 195, 248; 244, 245
Montalban, Ricardo 46, 148, 153, 208; 46, 146, 147
Montand, Yves 195, 196
Montevecci, Liliane 156; 155
"Moonlight Bay" 260
Moon over Miami 32; 32
"Mop Dance, The" 181
Moreno, Rita 61; 60
Morgan, Dennis 222
"Moses Supposes" 244; 237
Mostovoy, Leo 44; 44
Mother Carey's Chickens 169
Mother Wore Tights 35, 220; 34
Munshin, Jules 188, 191, 207; 207
Murphy, George 28, 95, 180, 257, 259; 28, 256
"Musical Extravaganza" 195; 197
Myers, Ruth 205
"My Gaucho" 208; 208
"My Heart Belongs to Daddy" 179
My Sister Eileen 52, 64; 52

"Nanette and Her Wooden Shoes" 134; 129
Neagle, Anna 128, 136; 135, 136
Nelson, Gene 213–26; 213–19, 221–27
Nelson, Ozzie 172–73
"Never Gonna Dance" 93
"Nevertheless" 98
New Faces of 1937 198, 202
Newton-John, Olivia 196
Nicholas Brothers 31, 185; 30, 31
"Night and Day" 89, 90
Night in Paris, A 132
Nijinska, Madame Bronislava 146
Ninotchka 102, 142, 158
Niven, David 103
Niven, Jr., David 18–21, 44, 124–25
"No Name Jive" 206
No, No, Nanette 57, 122, 159, 173, 211, 220
Norman, Lucille 222
"No Strings" 92

Oakie, Jack 236; 7
O'Brien, Margaret 37, 148; 37, 147
O'Brien, Virginia 148; 138
O'Connor, Donald 14, 44, 46, 228–49; 228, 230–49
O'Hara, John 179
"Oh Me, Oh My!" 220; 217
Oklahoma! 213, 225; 226
Omnibus 177
On an Island with You 46, 148; 147
"Once-a-Year-Day" 59; 59
"Once in Love with Amy" 138; 138
"One Alone" 154; 153
"One for My Baby" 96
One for the Money 179
"On Fifth Avenue" 7
"On the Atchison, Topeka and the Santa Fe" 137
On the Beach 103
On the Town 44, 155, 187–88, 190, 191, 207–8, 224; 188, 189, 207
On Your Toes 16, 43, 132, 148, 187, 233; 230–31
"On Your Toes" 148; 148
Opposite Sex, The 210
Optimists, The 254
"Orchids in the Moonlight" 90; 85
Our Dancing Daughters 22; 22–23

Over the Top 88
Ozzie Nelson and his Orchestra 172–73

Paganini 146
Page, Anita 10
Page Cavanaugh Trio 220
Painting the Clouds with Sunshine 222; 221
"Pair of New Shoes, A" 258
Pajama Game, The 10, 59; 59
Pal Joey 179–80, 181
Palmy Days 111
Pan, Hermes 15–16, 52, 90–92, 100, 102, 103, 153, 154, 158, 177, 203, 208, 210, 211, 219; 17
Panama Hattie 45
"Pan America Conga" 204
"Parade of the Wooden Soldiers, The" 27; 27
Paramount Pictures 48, 74, 96, 98, 100, 102, 204, 219, 233, 248, 249; 75, 76–77, 96, 97, 235
Party Girl 158; 158
Pas de Dieux 177–78
Passing Show of 1918, The 88
Pasternak, Joe 208–9, 263
Patrick the Great 236; 233
Pavlova, Anna 44, 145
Pennies from Heaven 79–80; 78–79, 80
Pepe 3
Perkins, Frank 223
Peters, Bernadette 79; 78–79
Petit, Roland 159; 158
"Pettin' in the Park" 114, 166
Petty Girl, The 207
"Piano Dance" 100
"Pick Yourself Up" 93
Pirate, The 185, 244
"Pirate Ballet, The" 185
Platt, Marc 8
Polito, Sol 114
"Polka Dot Polka, The" 119
Porgy and Bess 62
Porter, Cole 33, 51, 84, 85, 89, 90, 95, 96, 102, 103, 147, 158, 179, 180, 185, 193, 209, 210, 244–45, 249, 257, 258, 259
"Pottawatomie, The" 204; 201
Powell, Dick 116, 166, 168; 165, 167, 170
Powell, Eleanor 21, 27, 95, 118, 132, 200, 203, 204, 206, 207, 210, 250–64; 119, 128, 250, 252–65
Powell, Jane 46, 100, 210, 223; 46, 99, 224
Powell, William 132
"Prehistoric Man" 207–8; 207
Present Arms 109
Presley, Elvis 65, 226
"Pretty Girl Is Like a Melody, A" 98
Previn, André 155, 191, 192
Prinz, LeRoy 14, 138, 204, 220
Priorities on Parade 204
Private Buckaroo 233
Prowse, Juliet 52; 52
"Put On Your Sunday Clothes" 70; 70–71
"Puttin' On the Ritz" 98

Radio City Revels 203
Raft, George 43; 43
Ragtime 230–31
Rainger, Ralph 32
Rall, Tommy 209, 210; 209
Randolph, Roy 214
Rasch, Albertina 134
Ray, Johnny 248
Ready, Willing and Able 169; 171
Reagan, Ronald 222
Rebecca of Sunnybrook Farm 27; 27
"Red Blues, The" 158; 156–57
Reveille with Beverly 204–6; 203
Reynolds, Debbie 46–47, 210, 244, 247–48; 46, 47, 236, 246–47, 248, 249
Rich, Buddy 260; 262

Ritz Carleton Nights 132
Rigby, Harry 173, 211
Rise of Rosie O'Grady, The 164
"Ritz Rock 'n' Roll, The" 102
Rivera, Chita 53; 54–55
RKO General Pictures 15, 89, 90, 91, 93, 95, 96, 136, 138, 169, 198, 202, 203, 204, 207, 208, 256; 85, 88, 89, 91–93, 125, 135, 136, 201
Robbins, Jerome 14, 61
Roberta 92, 208
Robin and the Seven Hoods 62; 62
Robin, Leo 32, 52, 208, 210
Robinson, Bill 27, 28, 31, 93, 200, 258–59; 26, 27, 29
Rodgers, Richard 16, 45, 84, 107, 109, 132, 136, 137, 148, 179, 187, 204, 225
Rogers, Ginger 15, 90, 92–95, 96, 98–100, 114, 166, 202–3, 256, 259, 260; 86, 89, 92, 96, 109
Romance on the High Seas 119
Roman Scandals 114
Romberg, Sigmund 154, 191, 210
Romero, Alex 189
Romero, Cesar 35; 35
Room Service 203
Rooney, Mickey 37, 118, 200, 211, 234, 242, 261, 263; 36, 37, 117, 118
"Rope Dance, The" 193
Rosalie 132–34, 137, 250, 258; 128, 250
Rose Marie 122; 123
Ross, Herbert 80
Roussakoff, Senia 129
Royal Wedding 100; 99
Ruby, Harry 100
Rufus Jones for President 62
Rule, Janice 222; 222
Ryan, Peggy 234–40; 232, 233
Ryan, Robert 93
Rydell, Bobby 63; 63

Saddler, Donald 173
Salinger, Conrad 207
Sally 22; 22
Sands, Tommy 140
Sanford, Ralph 132
Saroyan, William 179
Saturday Night Fever 74, 77; 75, 76–77
"Say It with Dancing" 234
"Say It with Firecrackers" 96
Schary, Dore 155
Scheider, Roy 13, 14
Schwartz, Arthur 85, 89, 100, 154, 181, 257
Scott, Randolph 91
Second Chorus 96
Second Fiddle 216
"Second Hand Turban and a Crystal Ball, A" 249
Selznick, David O. 89, 180
Sensations of 1945 262; 264–65
Seven Brides for Seven Brothers 14, 15, 66, 191; 15
"Shadow Waltz, The" 114, 166; 119
"Shakin' the Blues Away" 207
Shall We Dance 93
"Shanghai Lil" 114, 166
Shawn, Bill 206; 205
"She's a Latin from Manhattan" 168; 169
She's Back on Broadway 223; 223
She's Working Her Way Through College 222–23; 222
Ship Ahoy 260; 262
Shipman, David 142
Shipmates Forever 168; 170
Shirley, Anne 136
"Shoes with Wings On" 98–100
"Shorty George, The" 96; 92
Show Boat 231
Show Boat (1951) 48; 48, 49
"Shriner's Ballet" 64; 64
Shubert Brothers 88, 109, 132, 256–57

268

"Shuffle Off to Buffalo" 114, 166
Sidewalks of New York, The 165
Sigman, Carl 223
Silencers, The 159; *159*
Silk Stockings 102–3, 144, 158; *102, 155, 156–57*
Silvers, Phil *178*
Sinatra, Frank 62, 148, 187, 188, 191, 208, 260, 264; *182, 207*
Singin' in the Rain 46, 142, 148–50, 155, 188, 189–91, 240, 244–47; *149, 150–51, 190, 194–95, 236, 237, 238–39, 248, 249*
"Singin' in the Rain" 190–91; *190*
Singleton, Penny 204
Sing You Sinners 233, 249
Skelton, Red 100, 208, 260, 261
Skolsky, Sidney 170
Sky's the Limit, The 96; *93*
"Slap That Bass" 93
"Slaughter on Tenth Avenue" 16, 44, 132, 187; *187*
Small Town Girl 57, 208–9; *123, 208*
Smiles 89
Smith, Queenie *230–31*
"Smoke Gets in Your Eyes" 148; *145*
"Snake Dance" 93
Sneddon, Lee *189*
Snow White 48
"So Long, Sarah Jane" 261; *263*
Sombert, Claire *193*
Sombrero 46, 153
"Somebody Loves Me" 222
Something in the Wind 240–42; *234*
"Something's Gotta Give" *101*
"Something to Dance About" 247
Something to Shout About 147
Sondheim, Stephen 61, 226
"So Near and Yet So Far" 96
Sothern, Ann 260
So This Is Paris 224–25; *224, 225*
"South Rampart Street Parade" 248
Sparks, Ned *254*
"Spic 'n' Spanish" 204
Springtime in the Rockies 35; *35*
Stage Door 202–3
Stage Door Canteen 128, 137; *137*
Stage Struck 116
Stand Up and Cheer 24; *25*
Starlift 222; *222*
State Fair (1962) 63
"Steppin' Out with My Baby" 98
Stevens, Mark 219
Stewart, James 257
Stone, Andrew 262
Stop Flirting 88
Stormy Weather 28; *29*
Story of Vernon and Irene Castle, The 93–95
"Streamlined Sheik" 201, 206
Street Singer, The 109
Streisand, Barbra 68, 70; *68–69, 70–71*
Strike Up the Band 37, 118; *37, 117*
Styne, Jule 52
Sugar Babies 200, 211
Summer Stock 188–89
Sunny (1930) 22
Sunny (1941) 128, 136; *135, 136*
Sun Valley Serenade 31; *30*
"Swan, The" 44; *44*
"Swanee River" 44
Sweet and Low 111
Sweet Charity 53, 57, 62; *12, 53–56*
Sweetheart of the Campus 170; *172–73*
Sweethearts 134; *129*
Sweet Rosie O'Grady 15; *17*
"Swingin' the Jinx Away" 257
"Swing Low, Sweet Rhythm" 204
Swing Time 93
"Swing Trot, The " 96
"Swing Your Partner Round and Round" 137, 148

" 'S Wonderful" 102

Take Me Out to the Ball Game 121, 187
Tamblyn, Russ 61, 66; *1, 66, 67*
"Tampico Tap" 165
"Tap Happy" 170; *172–73*
Tarnished Angel 203
Taylor, Joan 122; *123*
Taylor, Robert 158, 256
Tea for Two 220; *217, 218*
Temple, Shirley 24, 27, 28, 258–59; *7, 25–28*
Tension 148
Texas Carnival 208
That Funny Feeling 249
That's Dancing! 18–21, 44, 62, 124–25, 140; *21*
That's Entertainment 18, 195, 250, 253, 264
That's Entertainment, Part II 18, 195–96; *103*
"There Goes Taps" 206
"There's Gotta Be Something Better Than This" 53; *54–55*
There's No Business Like Show Business 248; *228, 244, 245*
"There's Nothing Like Love" 52; *52*
"They Can't Take That Away from Me" 93
"They've Never Figured Out a Woman" 242
"This Heart of Mine" 96–98
This Is the Army 219
This Is the Life 236, 240
Thousands Cheer 181, 261, 263
"Thou Swell" 45; *45*
"Three Bon Vivants" 225; *224*
"Three B's, The" 45; *45*
Three for the Show 51; *51*
Three Little Girls in Blue 44
Three Little Words 44, 100; *44, 98*
Three Musketeers, The 187
Three Sailors and a Girl 223–24; *224*
Three Wise Fools 148
Thrill of Brazil, The 206–7; *198*
"Thumbs Up and V for Victory" 206; *203*
Thurber, James 222
Till the Clouds Roll By 48, 148; *145*
Time of Your Life, The 179
Time Out for Rhythm 204; *202*
"Tip Toe Through the Tulips" 222
"Tom, Dick and Harry" 210
Tom Thumb 66; *66, 67*
Tonight and Every Night 40; *40, 41*
Tonight We Sing 44; *44*
"Too Darn Hot" 210
Too Many Girls 204; *201*
"Too Marvelous for Words" 169; *171*
Top Hat 92, 93; *85, 88*
Top Man 234
"Totem Tom-Tom" 122; *123*
Toumanova, Tamara 44; *44, 196*
Travolta, John 74, 77; *75, 76–77*
Trotti, Lamar 220
True to the Army 204
Tune, Tommy 70, 73; *70–71, 73*
Tunnel of Love, The 191, 195
Turnell, Dee *149*
Turner, Lana *116*
20th Century-Fox 15, 24, 27, 28, 31, 33, 35, 44, 52, 59, 63, 68, 102, 116, 119, 165, 195, 216, 217, 219, 220, 233, 236, 247, 248, 255; *7, 13, 14, 17, 18–20, 25–35, 44, 52, 59, 69–71, 82, 101, 104, 197, 214–15, 228, 241–45, 254*
Twiggy 72; *72*
Two Tickets to Broadway 208
Two Weeks with Love 46; *46*

"Under the Bamboo Tree" 37; *37*
Unfinished Dance, The 148; *147*
United Artists 18, 61; *1, 60, 61, 137, 264–65*
Universal Pictures 43, 53, 148, 158, 224, 233, 234, 236, 240, 242, 244, 248; *12, 42, 43, 53–56, 224, 225, 232–34*
Unsinkable Molly Brown, The 47; *47*

Vallee, Rudy 204
Van, Bobby 57, 209, 210; *57, 208*
Van Heusen, Jimmy 249
Van Manen, Hans 159
"Varsity Drag, The" 45; *45*
Varsity Show 116; *115*
Vera-Ellen 14, 44, 100, 187, 188, 208, 247; *44, 98, 187, 188, 241, 242–43*
Verdon, Gwen 53, 59; *58*
"Victory Polka, The" 206; *205*
Viva Las Vegas 65; *65*

"Wait and See" 148
"Wait Till Paris Sees Us" 224
Wake Up and Live 32; *32*
Walking My Baby Back Home 248
Walt Disney Productions 48, 140; *141*
Walters, Charles 14, 98, 100, 207
"Waltz in Swing Time" 93
"War Chant" 260
Warner, Jack 116, 119
Warner Brothers Inc. 22, 43, 59, 95, 113, 114, 116, 118, 119, 138, 161, '166–69, 173, 213, 219, 220, 222, 223, 224, 233; *4, 22, 38, 39, 58, 59, 62, 102, 106–13, 115, 119, 137, 139, 140, 160, 162–65, 167–71, 213, 216–19, 221–25, 230–31*
Warren, Harry 85, 98, 100, 103, 113, 114, 116, 137, 163, 166, 169, 189, 220, 223
Watch the Birdie 208
Watts, Jr., Richard 166
"Wedding of the Painted Doll, The" 13
Weldon, Joan 154
"We're in the Money" 114; *109*
West Point Story, The 220; *219*
West Side Story 14, 61, 188; *1, 60, 61*
"We Won't Be Happy Till We Get It" 140
What a Way to Go 195; *197*
"What Does an English Girl Think of a Yank?" 40; *41*
"Whatever Lola Wants" 59; *58*
What's Buzzin' Cousin 206; *204*
What's Cookin' 233
When Johnny Comes Marching Home 234
"When the Idle Poor Become the Idle Rich" 102
"When the Midnight Choo-Choo Leaves for Alabam" 248
"When You Wore a Tulip" 236
"Where Did You Learn to Dance?" 248
Where's Charley 14, 137–38; *139*
White, George 203, 255, 256
White, Onna 64, 211
White Christmas 44, 248
Whiteman, Paul 255
Whiting, Richard 116, 169
"Who?" 138
Whoopee 33, 110–11, 165
"Why Am I So Gone about That Gal" 193
Wilcox, Herbert 136
Wild North, The 148
"Wild, Wild West, The" 138
William Morris Agency 110, 203
Williams, Esther 50, 121, 122, 148, 166, 263; *120–21*
Willson, Meredith 47
Wilson, Sandy 73
Wise, Robert 61
"Wishing Waltz, The" 15; *17*
Wizard of Oz, The 13, 127, 134–36; *130–31, 133*
Women, The 210
Wonder Bar 114, 119; *111*
Wonder Man 44
Wonders of Aladdin, The 249
"Won't You Charleston with Me?" 73; *73*
Wood, Natalie 195

Woody Herman's Band *264–65*
Words and Music 44, 45, 148, 187; *45, 149, 187*
"Words Are in My Heart, The" *112–13*
Wright, George 134

Xanadu 196

"Ya Gotta Give the People Hoke" 249
"Yam, The" 93; *92*
Yankee Doodle Dandy 14, 39, 178, 220; *38, 39*
Yes Sir, That's My Baby 242
Yolanda and the Thief 98
Yorkin, Bud 103
"You Are My Lucky Star" 257
"You Can Bounce Right Back" 249
You Can't Take It with You 203; *200*
"You'd Be So Nice to Come Home To" 147
"You Excite Me" 40; *40*
"You Gotta Know How to Dance" 169
"You Gotta Pull Strings" 132
You'll Never Get Rich 40, 96
Youmans, Vincent 84, 85, 89, 122, 173, 210, 220
Young, Robert 260
Young, Terence 159
Young Girls of Rochefort, The 195
"Young Man of Manhattan" 89
Young People 7
"Your Broadway and My Broadway" 257; *258*
Your Cheatin' Heart 226
"You're All the World to Me" 100; *99*
"You're Easy to Dance With" 96
You're My Everything 35; *35*
"You're the Top" 103
Your Show of Shows 225
Youskevitch, Igor 193
"You Started Something" 32; *32*
"You Stepped Out of a Dream" 118; *116*
"You Were Meant for Me" 13
You Were Never Lovelier 40, 96; *92*
"You, Wonderful You" 189
"You Worry Me" 85

Zanuck, Darryl F. 27, 33, 113, 166
Ziegfeld, Florenz 22, 96, 132, 165, 255
Ziegfeld Follies 96–98, 147, 153, 183; *94–95, 144–45, 186*
Ziegfeld Follies of 1927, The 207
Ziegfeld Girl 118; *116*
"Zing Went the Strings of My Heart" 220; *213*
Zorina, Vera 43; *20, 43*

Project Director:
MARGARET L. KAPLAN

Editor:
LORY FRANKEL

Designer:
RAYMOND P. HOOPER

Photo Editor:
BARBARA LYONS

Jacket front: Fred Astaire, from *Top Hat,* 1935   Courtesy RKO General Pictures. Jacket back, left to right: Gene Kelly, from *It's Always Fair Weather,* 1955   © 1955 Loew's Inc.; Shirley Temple, from *Young People,* 1940   © 1940 Twentieth Century-Fox Film Corporation; Ray Bolger, from *Sweethearts,* 1938   © 1938 Loew's Incorporated. Renewed 1965 Metro-Goldwyn-Mayer Inc.; Ruby Keeler, from *Go into Your Dance,* 1935   © 1935 First National Pictures, Inc. Renewed 1962 United Artists Associated, Inc. All rights reserved; James Cagney, from *Footlight Parade,* 1933   Copyright © 1933 Warner Bros. Pictures, Inc. Renewed 1961 United Artists Associated, Inc. All rights reserved; Donald O'Connor, from *There's No Business Like Show Business,* 1954   © 1954 Twentieth Century-Fox Film Corporation; Cyd Charisse, from *Singin' in the Rain,* 1952   © 1952 Loew's Inc. Renewed 1979 Metro-Goldwyn-Mayer Inc.

Endpapers: *The Boy Friend* (MGM, 1971).
Half-title page: *West Side Story* (United Artists, 1961). Carole D'Andrea and Russ Tamblyn explode with youthful vitality in "The Dance in the Gym."
Title page: *Pepe* (Columbia, 1960). The final dance on film for two consummate hoofers, Dan Dailey and Maurice Chevalier.
Page 4: *Indiscreet* (Warners, 1958). Cary Grant reveals—to Ingrid Bergman (left) and his movie fans—a gift for nifty footwork.
Page 7: *Young People* (Fox, 1940). A veteran at twelve, Shirley Temple performs "On Fifth Avenue" with Jack Oakie and Charlotte Greenwood.

Library of Congress Cataloging in Publication Data
Thomas, Tony, 1927-
That's dancing!
    1. Dancing in moving-pictures, television, etc.—
    United States—History. I. Title.
GV1779.T48   1984   791.43'72   84—9237
ISBN 0—8109—1682—7

Published in 1984 by Harry N. Abrams, Incorporated, New York
All rights reserved. No part of the contents of this book may be reproduced without the written permission of the publishers

Printed and bound in Japan

SONG CREDITS

FILM COPYRIGHTS

Goldwyn-Mayer Inc. 85 above: *Top Hat*, Courtesy RKO General Pictures 85 below: *Flying Down to Rio*, Courtesy RKO General Pictures 86: *The Barkleys of Broadway*, © 1949 Loew's Incorporated. Renewed 1976 Metro-Goldwyn-Mayer Inc. 86–87: *The Band Wagon*, © 1953 Loew's Incorporated. Renewed 1981 Metro-Goldwyn-Mayer Inc. 88: *Top Hat*, Courtesy RKO General Pictures 89: *The Gay Divorcee*, Courtesy RKO General Pictures 91: *Follow the Fleet*, Courtesy RKO General Pictures 92 above: *Carefree*, Courtesy RKO General Pictures 92 below: *You Were Never Lovelier*, © 1970 Columbia Pictures Corp. 93: *The Sky's the Limit*, Courtesy RKO General Pictures 94–95: *The Ziegfeld Follies*, © 1947 Loew's Incorporated. Renewed 1973 Metro-Goldwyn-Mayer Inc. 96 above: *Blue Skies*, Copyright © 1946 by Universal Pictures, a Division of Universal City Studios, Inc. Courtesy of MCA Publishing, a Division of MCA, Inc. 96 below: *The Barkleys of Broadway*, © 1949 Loew's Incorporated. Renewed 1976 Metro-Goldwyn-Mayer Inc. 97: *Let's Dance*, © 1949 Paramount Pictures Corporation 98: *Three Little Words*, © 1950 Loew's Incorporated. Renewed 1977 Metro-Goldwyn-Mayer Inc. 99: *Royal Wedding*, © 1951 Loew's Incorporated 101: *Daddy Long Legs*, © 1955 Twentieth Century Fox Film Corporation 102 above: *Silk Stockings*, © 1957 Loew's Incorporated and Arthur Freed Productions, Inc. 102 below: *Finian's Rainbow*, Warner Bros. Inc. © 1968 103: *That's Entertainment, Part II*, © 1976 Metro-Goldwyn-Mayer Inc. 104: *The Gang's All Here*, © 1943 Twentieth Century Fox Film Corporation 106–7: *Dames*, © 1934 Warner Bros. Pictures, Inc. Renewed 1961 United Artists Associated, Inc. 108: *42nd Street*, © 1934 Warner Bros. Pictures, Inc. Renewed 1960 United Artists Associated, Inc. 109: *Gold Diggers of 1933*, © 1933 Warner Bros. Pictures, Inc. Renewed 1960 United Artists Associated, Inc. 110: *Footlight Parade*, © 1933 Warner Bros. Pictures, Inc. Renewed 1961 United Artists Associated, Inc. 111: *Wonder Bar*, © 1934 First National Pictures, Inc. Renewed 1961 United Artists Associated, Inc. 112 – 113, 113, 115 above: *Gold Diggers of 1935*, © 1935 First National Pictures, Inc. Renewed 1962 United Artists Associated, Inc. 115 below: *Varsity Show*, © 1937 Warner Bros. Pictures, Inc. Renewed 1964 United Artists Television, Inc. 116: *Ziegfeld Girl*, © 1941 Loew's Incorporated. Renewed 1968 Metro-Goldwyn-Mayer Inc. 117: *Strike Up the Band*, © 1940 Loew's Incorporated. Renewed 1967 Metro-Goldwyn-Mayer Inc. 118 above: *Babes on Broadway*, © 1941 Loew's Incorporated. Renewed 1968 Metro-Goldwyn-Mayer Inc. 118 below: *Girl Crazy*, © 1943 Loew's Incorporated. Renewed 1970 Metro-Goldwyn-Mayer Inc. 119 above: *Gold Diggers of 1933*, © 1933 Warner Bros. Pictures, Inc. Renewed 1960 United Artists Associated, Inc. 119 below: *Lady Be Good*, © 1941 Loew's Incorporated. Renewed 1968 Metro-Goldwyn-Mayer Inc. 120–21: *Million Dollar Mermaid*, © 1952 Loew's Incorporated. Renewed 1980 Metro-Goldwyn-Mayer Inc. 123 above: *Small Town Girl*, © 1953 Loew's Incorporated. Renewed 1980 Metro-Goldwyn-Mayer Inc. 123 below: *Rose Marie*, © 1954 Loew's Incorporated. Renewed 1982 Metro-Goldwyn-Mayer Film Co. 125: *Four Jacks and a Jill*, Courtesy RKO General Pictures 126–27: *The Great Ziegfeld*, © 1936 Metro-Goldwyn-Mayer Corporation. Renewed 1963 Metro-Goldwyn-Mayer Inc. 128: *Rosalie*, © 1937 Metro-Goldwyn-Mayer Corporation. Renewed 1964 Metro-Goldwyn-Mayer 129: *Sweethearts*, © 1938 Loew's Incorporated. Renewed 1965 Metro-Goldwyn-Mayer Inc. 130–31, 133: *The Wizard of Oz*, © 1939 Loew's Incorporated. Renewed 1966 Metro-Goldwyn-Mayer Inc. 135, 136: *Sunny*, 1941 137 left: *Stage Door Canteen*, © 1943 United Artists Corp. 137 right: *Look for the Silver Lining*, © 1948 Warner Bros. Pictures, Inc. Renewed 1976 United Artists Associated, Inc. 138: *The Harvey Girls*, © 1945 Loew's Incorporated. Renewed 1973 Metro-Goldwyn-Mayer Inc. 139 above: *Look for the Silver Lining*, © 1948 Warner Bros. Pictures, Inc. Renewed 1976 United Artists Associated, Inc. 139 below: *Where's Charley?*, Warner Bros. Inc. © 1952 140: *April in Paris*, Warner Bros. Inc. © 1952 141: *Babes in Toyland*, © 1961 Walt Disney Productions 142: *Brigadoon*, © 1954 Loew's Incorporated. Renewed 1982 Metro-Goldwyn-Mayer Film Co. 144–45: *Ziegfeld Follies*, © 1947 Loew's Incorporated. Renewed 1973 Metro-Goldwyn-Mayer Inc. 145: *Till the Clouds Roll By*, © 1946 Loew's Incorporated 146: *Fiesta*, © 1947 Loew's Incorporated. Renewed 1974 Metro-Goldwyn-Mayer Inc. 147 above: *The Unfinished Dance*, © 1947 Loew's Incorporated. Renewed 1974 Metro-Goldwyn-Mayer Inc. 147 below: *On an Island with You*, © 1948 Loew's Incorporated. Renewed 1975 Metro-Goldwyn-Mayer Inc. 149 above left, right: *Words and Music*, © 1948 Loew's Incorporated. Renewed 1975 Metro-Goldwyn-Mayer Inc. 149 below: *Singin' in the Rain*, © 1952 Loew's Incorporated. Renewed 1979 Metro-Goldwyn-Mayer Inc. 150: *The Band Wagon*, © 1953 Loew's Incorporated. Renewed 1981 Metro-Goldwyn-Mayer Inc. 150–51: *Singin' in the Rain*, © 1952 Loew's Incorporated. Renewed 1979 Metro-Goldwyn-Mayer Inc. 152: *The Band Wagon*, © 1953 Loew's Incorporated. Renewed 1981 Metro-Goldwyn-Mayer Inc. 153: *Deep in My Heart*, © 1954 Loew's Incorporated. Renewed 1982 Metro-Goldwyn-Mayer Film Co. 154: *It's Always Fair Weather*, © 1955 Loew's Incorporated. Renewed 1983 MGM/UA Entertainment Co. 155, 156–57: *Silk Stockings*, © 1957 Loew's Incorporated and Arthur Freed Productions, Inc. 158 above: *Party Girl*, © 1958 Loew's Incorporated and Euterpe Inc. 158 below: *Black Tights*, © 1961 Eagle Lion 159: *The Silencers*, © 1966 Meadway-Claude Productions Co. 160: *42nd Street*, © 1934 Warner Bros. Pictures, Inc. Renewed 1960 United Artists Associated, Inc. 162–63: *Footlight Parade*, © 1933 Warner Bros. Pictures, Inc. Renewed 1961 United Artists Associated, Inc. 164: *Dames*, © 1934 Warner Bros. Pictures, Inc. Renewed 1961 United Artists Associated, Inc. 165: *Footlight Parade*, © 1933 Warner Bros. Pictures, Inc. Renewed 1961 United Artists Associated, Inc. 167 above: *Flirtation Walk*, © 1934 First National Pictures, Inc. Renewed 1961 United Artists Associated, Inc. 167 below, 168, 169: *Go into Your Dance*, © 1935 First National Pictures, Inc. Renewed 1962 United Artists Associated, Inc. 170: *Shipmates Forever*, © 1935 Warner Bros. Pictures, Inc. Renewed 1962 United Artists Associated, Inc. 171 above: *Colleen*, © 1936 Warner Bros. Pictures, Inc. 171 below: *Ready, Willing and Able*, © 1937 Warner Bros. Pictures, Inc. Renewed 1964 United Artists Associated, Inc. 172–73: *Sweetheart of the Campus*, © 1969 Columbia Pictures Corporation 174: *Brigadoon*, © 1954 Loew's Incorporated. Renewed 1982 Metro-Goldwyn-Mayer Film Co. 176–77: *Dubarry Was a Lady*, © 1943 Loew's Incorporated. Renewed 1970 Metro-Goldwyn-Mayer Inc. 178: *Cover Girl*, © 1972 Columbia Pictures Corp. 180, 181: *An American in Paris*, © 1951 Loew's Incorporated. Renewed 1979 Metro-Goldwyn-Mayer Inc. 182, 183: *Anchors Aweigh*, © 1945 Loew's Incorporated. Renewed 1972 Metro-Goldwyn-Mayer Inc. 184–85, 185: *Brigadoon*, © 1954 Loew's Incorporated. Renewed 1982 Metro-Goldwyn-Mayer Film Co. 186: *Ziegfeld Follies*, © 1947 Loew's Incorporated. Renewed 1973 Metro-Goldwyn-Mayer Inc. 187: *Words and Music*, © 1948 Loew's Incorporated. Renewed 1975 Metro-Goldwyn-Mayer Inc. 188, 189: *On the Town*, © 1949 Loew's Incorporated. Renewed 1976 Metro-Goldwyn-Mayer Inc. 190 above: *Singin' in the Rain*, © 1952 Loew's Incorporated. Renewed 1979 Metro-Goldwyn-Mayer Inc. 190 below: *An American in Paris*, © 1951 Loew's Incorporated. Renewed 1979 Metro-Goldwyn-Mayer Inc. 191: *Brigadoon*, © 1954 Loew's Incorporated. Renewed 1982 Metro-Goldwyn-Mayer Film Co. 192: *Deep in My Heart*, © 1954 Loew's Incorporated. Renewed 1982 Metro-Goldwyn-Mayer Film Co. 193: *It's Always Fair Weather*, © 1955 Loew's Incorporated. Renewed 1983 MGM/UA Entertainment Co. 194–95: *Singin' in the Rain*, © 1952 Loew's Incorporated. Renewed 1979 Metro-Goldwyn-Mayer Inc. 196 above: *Invitation to the Dance*, © 1954 Loew's Incorporated. Renewed 1982 Metro-Goldwyn-Mayer Film Co. 196 below: *Les Girls*, © 1957 Loew's Incorporated and Sol C. Siegel Productions, Inc. 197: *What a Way to Go*, © 1964 Apjac-Orchard Productions, Inc. and Twentieth Century Fox Film Corporation 198: *The Thrill of Brazil*, © 1973 Columbia Pictures Corporation 200: *You Can't Take It with You*, © 1966 Columbia Pictures Corporation of California, Ltd. 201: *Too Many Girls*, Courtesy RKO Pictures, Inc. 202 above: *Time Out for Rhythm*, © 1969 Columbia Pictures Corporation 202 below: *Go West, Young Lady*, © 1969 Columbia Pictures Corporation 203: *Reveille with Beverly*, © 1971 Columbia Pictures Corp. 204: *What's Buzzin' Cousin*, © 1971 Columbia Pictures Corp. 205 above: *The Thrill of Brazil*, © 1973 Columbia Pictures Corporation 205 below: *Jam Session*, © 1972 Columbia Pictures Corp. 206: *Easter Parade*, © 1948 Loew's Incorporated. Renewed 1975 Metro-Goldwyn-Mayer Inc. 207 above: *On the Town*, © 1949 Loew's Incorporated. Renewed 1976 Metro-Goldwyn-Mayer Inc. 207 below: *Lovely to Look At*, © 1952 Loew's Incorporated. Renewed 1980 Metro-Goldwyn-Mayer Inc. 208 above: *Small Town Girl*, © 1953 Loew's Incorporated. Renewed 1980 Metro-Goldwyn-Mayer Inc. 208 below: *Kiss Me Kate*, © 1953 Loew's Incorporated. Renewed 1981 Metro-Goldwyn-Mayer Film Co. 209: *Deep in My Heart*, © 1954 Loew's Incorporated. Renewed 1982 Metro-Goldwyn-Mayer Film Co. 210, 211: *Hit the Deck*, © 1955 Loew's Incorporated. Renewed 1982 Metro-Goldwyn-Mayer Film Co. 213: *Lullaby of Broadway*, Warner Bros. Inc. © 1951 214–15: *I Wonder Who's Kissing Her Now*, © 1947 Twentieth Century Fox Film Corporation 216: *The Daughter of Rosie O'Grady*, Warner Bros. Inc. © 1950 217, 218: *Tea for Two*, Warner Bros. Inc. © 1950 219: *The West Point Story*, Warner Bros. Inc. © 1950 221 above: *Lullaby of Broadway*, Warner Bros. Inc. © 1951 221 below: *Painting the Clouds with Sunshine*, Warner Bros. Inc. © 1951 222 above: *Starlift*, Warner Bros. Inc. © 1951 222 below: *She's Working Her Way through College*, Warner Bros. Inc, © 1952 223: *She's Back on Broadway*, Warner Bros. Inc. © 1953 224 above: *Three Sailors and a Girl*, Warner Bros. Inc. © 1953 224 below, 225: *So This Is Paris*, Copyright © 1955 by Universal Pictures, a Division of Universal City Studios, Inc. Courtesy MCA Publishing, a Division of MCA, Inc. 226: *Oklahoma!*, Photographs of Gene Nelson in "Kansas City" courtesy Rodgers and Hammerstein 228: *There's No Business Like Show Business*, © 1954 Twentieth Century Fox Film Corporation 230–31: *On Your Toes*, © 1949 Loew's Incorporated. Renewed 1976 Metro-Goldwyn-Mayer Inc. 232: *Mr. Big*, Copyright © 1943 by Universal Pictures, a Division of Universal City Studios, Inc. Courtesy of MCA Publishing, a Division of MCA, Inc. 233: *Patrick the Great*, Copyright © 1945 by Universal Pictures, a Division of Universal City Studios, Inc. Courtesy of MCA Publishing, a Division of MCA, Inc. 234: *Something in the Wind*, Copyright © 1947 by Universal Pictures, a Division of Universal City Studios, Inc. Courtesy of MCA Publishing, a Division of MCA, Inc. 235: *Anything Goes*, © 1955 Paramount Pictures Corporation 236, 237, 238–39: *Singin' in the Rain*, © 1952 Loew's Incorporated. Renewed 1979 Metro-Goldwyn-Mayer Inc. 240: *I Love Melvin*, © 1953 Loew's Incorporated. Renewed 1980 Metro-Goldwyn-Mayer Inc. 241, 242–43: *Call Me Madam*, © 1953 Twentieth Century Fox Film Corporation 244, 245: *There's No Business Like Show Business*, © 1954 Twentieth Century Fox Film Corporation 246–47: *I Love Melvin*, © 1953 Loew's Incorporated. Renewed 1980 Metro-Goldwyn-Mayer Inc. 248, 249: *Singin' in the Rain*, © 1952 Loew's Incorporated. Renewed 1979 Metro-Goldwyn-Mayer Inc. 250: *Rosalie*, © 1937 Metro-Goldwyn-Mayer Corporation. Renewed 1964 Metro-Goldwyn-Mayer Inc. 252–53: *Broadway Melody of 1936*, © 1935 Metro-Goldwyn-Mayer Corporation. Renewed 1962 Metro-Goldwyn-Mayer Inc. 254: *George White's Scandals of 1935*, © 1934 Fox Film Corporation 255: *Born to Dance*, © 1936 Metro-Goldwyn-Mayer Corporation. Renewed 1963 Metro-Goldwyn-Mayer Inc. 256: *Broadway Melody of 1938*, © 1937 Metro-Goldwyn-Mayer Corporation. Renewed 1964 Metro-Goldwyn-Mayer Inc. 257: *Honolulu*, © 1939 Loew's Incorporated. Renewed 1966 Metro-Goldwyn-Mayer Inc. 258: *Broadway Melody of 1938*, © 1937 Metro-Goldwyn-Mayer Corporation. Renewed 1964 Metro-Goldwyn-Mayer Inc. 259: *Broadway Melody of 1940*, © 1940 Loew's Incorporated. Renewed 1967 Metro-Goldwyn-Mayer Inc. 260, 261: *Lady Be Good*, © 1941 Loew's Incorporated. Renewed 1968 Metro-Goldwyn-Mayer Inc. 262: *Ship Ahoy*, © 1942 Loew's Incorporated. Renewed 1969 Metro-Goldwyn-Mayer Inc. 263 above: *The Duchess of Idaho*, © 1950 Loew's Incorporated. Renewed 1977 Metro-Goldwyn-Mayer Inc. 263 below: *I Dood It*, © 1943 Loew's Incorporated. Renewed 1970 Metro-Goldwyn-Mayer Inc. 264–65: *Sensations of 1945*, © 1944 Andrew Stone Pictures Corp. 269: *Top Hat*, Courtesy RKO General Pictures